U0367282

民航服务专业新形态系列教材

空乘实用英语教程

主　编　孙庆芳　高锋

副主编　晏岚

清华大学出版社

北京

内 容 简 介

本书是空中乘务专业英语教材，内容包括空乘面试、客舱广播、客舱情景、职业演讲及技能测评，旨在培养空乘人员的英语核心素养与职业综合能力。技能测评模块可用来评估空乘专业学生或空乘学员的语言应用能力和对职业的综合认知。本书可作为民航相关专业院校和培训机构的教材使用，也可作为广大对空乘工作岗位感兴趣的社会人士面试备考图书使用。

图书在版编目（CIP）数据

空乘实用英语教程/孙庆芳，高锋主编. —北京：清华大学出版社，2022.4（2024.3重印）
民航服务专业新形态系列教材
ISBN 978-7-302-60452-5

Ⅰ. ①空…　Ⅱ. ①孙…　②高…　Ⅲ. ①民用航空－乘务人员－英语－高等学校－教材　Ⅳ. ①F560.9

中国版本图书馆 CIP 数据核字（2022）第 052823 号

责任编辑：聂军来
封面设计：常雪影
责任校对：刘　静
责任印制：宋　林

出版发行：清华大学出版社
　　　　　网　　　址：https://www.tup.com.cn，https://www.wqxuetang.com
　　　　　地　　　址：北京清华大学学研大厦A座　　　　邮　　编：100084
　　　　　社 总 机：010-83470000　　　　　　　　　　邮　　购：010-62786544
　　　　　投稿与读者服务：010-62776969，c-service@tup.tsinghua.edu.cn
　　　　　质量反馈：010-62772015，zhiliang@tup.tsinghua.edu.cn
　　　　　课件下载：https://www.tup.com.cn，010-83470410
印　装　者：三河市龙大印装有限公司
经　　　销：全国新华书店
开　　　本：185mm×260mm　　　印　　张：16　　　字　　数：317千字
版　　　次：2022年6月第1版　　　　　　　　　　印　　次：2024年3月第2次印刷
定　　　价：49.00元

产品编号：092052-02

随着中国民航业的蓬勃发展，民航业的国际化程度日益提高，作为民航业窗口的空乘服务更需要展现出一流的国际化特色。因此，各航空公司对空乘人员的英语水平和职业素养提出了较高的需求。目前，市场上的空乘英语书籍大多以英语学科细化分类的方式呈现，如关于乘务英语阅读、客舱情景会话等方面的教材，没有重点突出在"当代民航精神"和"三个敬畏"的指引下，当代乘务员应具备的语言素养与职业技能的有效融合。因此，编写一本能够聚焦空乘人员的语言应用核心能力，兼顾思想性和实用性的教材已经迫在眉睫。本书契合了上述要求，同时引入了课程思政教学理念，考虑了融媒体背景下数字化教材的特点，进行了有益的探索和尝试。

本书旨在培养空乘或民航相关专业学生对专业英语的职业应用能力。从实用角度出发，本书以提升空乘英语应用能力为主线，内容涉及空乘面试、客舱广播、客舱情景、职业演讲、技能测评等核心职业能力版块。本书以能力为本位，侧重实践与技能，兼顾考核与评价，以期提升民航空乘相关专业学生的英语应用能力和核心职业素养。

全书分为六大版块，其主要内容如下。①空乘面试，包括各大航空公司的招聘广告、申请表格、简历撰写、面试中的常见问题，能够帮助学生了解求职面试的相关注意事项、掌握简历撰写方法、提升面试技巧。②客舱广播，包括客舱广播的相关知识、技巧以及航班流程中服务类广播词和安全类广播词的系统学习范例与练习。该部分对广播词中的难点进行了注释，并对相关内容进行引申归纳和背景知识的拓展，如世界三大航空公司联盟、各航空公司常旅客计划、广播词中的数字表达、各种节日欢迎词、航班延误的原因汇总等。③客舱情景，基于乘务员职业素养编写相应客舱情景对话，从职业忠诚、团队合作、安全指导、服务意识、应急意识、沟通技巧、劝说技巧、医疗急救、旅游引导、出入境常识等维度出发，引入课程思政，在职业精神和相关职业能力的指导下，练习客舱对话，拓展服务意识，掌握客舱文化，提升跨文化交际能力和沟通技巧。④职业演讲，阐明英语演讲的相关技巧和要点，并提供了空乘职业相关话题的数篇演讲范文，内容涵盖空乘面试技巧介绍、空乘职业素养、客舱安全、服务意识、团队合作等方面。职业主题演讲可塑造学生的职业认识，培养学生的职业认同感；适当的演讲练习也可进一步巩固学生的基本功，拓展学生的思维。⑤技能测评，根据《民航乘务员国家职业技能标准》及空乘职业规范的知识技能要求，将英语技能与职业岗位能力相结合，编写相应题库，分为笔试和口试。笔试题库包括客舱情景用语、客舱服务和安全的基本常识、医疗急救用语、世界地理常识、民航知识等；口试题库包括客舱专业术语的英文表达、客舱广播词的编播朗读、机上服务场景的即兴回答、机上特情处理表达等，突出训练及考核学生的岗位技能，提高学生专业英语的综合应用能力。⑥附录，包括涵盖整个航行流程的客舱常用语句、乘务英语术语汇总、国外航空公司安全演示广播词范例、乘务英语词汇（英－美）一览表、机场常用标识、机上应急设备图标、世界货币一览表、世界主要航空公司代码及图标，内容丰富实用、工具性极强，方便学生查询使用。

本书由上海民航职业技术学院民航乘务学院孙庆芳、高锋担任主编，晏岚担任副主编。孙庆芳老师具有十多年的空乘专业英语教学经验，持有中航协客舱乘务服务技能教员证书、1+X民航空中服务教员证书；高锋老师作为学科带头人，长期从事空乘专业英语教学，入选民航局国际化人才库基础库；晏岚老师承担空乘专业英语多门课程教学，经过航司乘务员岗位培训，并取得相关证书。在本书编写过程中，得到了民航乘务学院孙军和吴欣两位领导的大力支持，在此表示衷心的感谢。同时，也感谢乘务教研室王维、刘珏、肖建云、吴江华等老师的关心和鼓励。

本书在编写过程中参考了近年来民航乘务方面的相关书籍及文献资料，在此对相关人员表示诚挚的谢意。由于编者水平有限，书中难免有疏漏或不妥之处，恳请专家及读者不吝指正。

编　者

2022 年 3 月

目　录

⊠ 第1章　空乘面试 ·· 1

第一节　英文面试应对策略 ·· 2

第二节　外航招聘要求解读 ·· 6

第三节　外航申请表格填写 ·· 7

第四节　个人英文简历制作 ·· 12

第五节　英文自我介绍 ·· 14

第六节　面试常见问题汇总 ·· 17

⊠ 第2章　客舱广播 ·· 26

第一节　客舱广播概述 ·· 27

第二节　客舱广播技巧要素 ·· 27

第三节　客舱广播的分类 ·· 28

第四节　客舱英语广播的重要性 ···································· 28

第五节　客舱广播学习实例 ·· 29

第六节　客舱广播练习 ·· 83

⊠ 第3章　客舱情景 ·· 94

第一节　职业忠诚 ·· 95

第二节　团队合作 ·· 99

第三节　安全指导 ·· 104

第四节　服务意识 ·· 108

第五节　应急意识 ·· 114

第六节　沟通技巧 ·· 117

第七节　劝说技巧 ·· 121

第八节　医疗急救 ·· 123

第九节　旅游引导 ·· 129

第十节　出入境常识 ·· 133

◈ 第4章　职业演讲 ……………………………………………… 136

　　第一节　英语演讲本质 …………………………………… 137

　　第二节　演讲前的准备 …………………………………… 139

　　第三节　撰写演讲稿 ……………………………………… 142

　　第四节　演讲技巧 ………………………………………… 143

　　第五节　演讲话题汇总 …………………………………… 147

◈ 第5章　技能测评 …………………………………………… 158

　　第一节　测试大纲 ………………………………………… 159

　　第二节　书面测试 ………………………………………… 162

　　第三节　口语测试题库 …………………………………… 181

◈ 附录 ………………………………………………………… 196

　　附录1　客舱常用语句 …………………………………… 196

　　附录2　乘务英语术语汇总 ……………………………… 214

　　附录3　国外航空公司安全演示广播词范例 …………… 227

　　附录4　乘务英语词汇（英-美）一览表 ……………… 232

　　附录5　机场常用标识 …………………………………… 235

　　附录6　机上应急设备图标 ……………………………… 237

　　附录7　世界货币一览表 ………………………………… 239

　　附录8　世界主要航空公司代码及图标 ………………… 244

◈ 参考文献 …………………………………………………… 247

第1章
空乘面试

章前导读

本章主要针对空乘英文面试的环节设计。首先，我们针对航空公司招乘中的英文面试提出了应对策略和方案，以便让大家有一个总体性的把握。考虑到国外航空公司与国内航空公司的差异，本章列举并剖析了如何解读外航招聘广告，并就如何做好必要的准备进行了说明，包括如何正确填写外航申请表。其次，我们通过列举英文简历的样张，指导大家如何设计具有特色的简历。面试中的常见问题包括通识类、客舱情景意识类、企业文化拓展类，以及部分航空公司典型广播词的朗读等相关问题。

本章旨在提高学生对面试英语的综合把握，包括内容、技巧和应对策略等，同时，提升学生的自信心和对英文简历的设计美感；并通过对航空公司企业文化的了解，逐步提高职业认知水平和认清职业定位。

思政园地

青年的价值取向决定了整个社会未来的价值取向。对于青年，扣好人生第一粒扣子至关重要。作为一名民航人，乘务员要爱岗敬业，筑梦蓝天。青年学生需通过积累学识，提升能力，明确目标，为就业面试打下坚实的基础。教师可引导学生在简历制作中展现自身优点，强化学生对企业的文化认知，从而培养其积极进取、乐观向上的人生观和价值观。

　　乘务员是航空公司的一道靓丽风景线。他们在向世人展示自己风貌的同时，也为航空公司赢得了旅客的赞誉。一名合格的乘务员，在工作中除了态度热情、保持微笑和娴熟的服务技能外，还应该具备与工作岗位相关的英语知识，并在实际工作中，用流利的英语为国际旅客服务。因此，航空公司在招聘乘务员过程中，英文面试已成了必不可少的一个环节。求职者只有熟悉应聘流程，掌握必要的英语口语能力，将语言能力、思辨能力、沟通技巧、面试技巧、职业素质、情景意识和团队协作融会贯通，才能以良好的第一印象和优异的综合素质成为航空公司的首选对象。

　　例如，新加坡航空公司 2019 年在我国的招聘，其对语言的招聘条件设定为"fluent in written and spoken English and Mandarin"（即流利的中英文书面语和口语）。除了外航之外，国内的航空公司如国航也设定了"具有良好的英语口语水平"的要求。对此，除了一些速成的短期强化班之外，部分针对性较强的教材如《未来空姐面试指南》《新编航空乘务人员面试英语》等也应运而生。就一般民航类院校来说，对于空乘专业的学生也会开设通识阶段的《英语听说》和专业用途英语阶段的《乘务英语听说》和《客舱广播词朗读》这样的课程。但是即便如此，部分学生在面对国内外航空公司的英文环境时，还是表现不足。因此，我们认为有必要进行相关航空公司英文面试对策的梳理。一方面，使面试者能有的放矢；另一方面也为准备面试的人员提供有益的参考和借鉴。

一、英文自我介绍的组成及提升策略

　　英文自我介绍一般设定 1 分钟左右的时间，面试者简单介绍自身的基本情况，包括兴趣爱好、家庭成员、面试动机等，通常以 10 ～ 15 句话为宜。考官侧重于考察面试者的基本词汇量、语音语调，同时兼顾连读、失爆等技巧。对于自我介绍，很多面试者由于缺乏自信，会呈现出一种在背诵的感觉，一旦紧张，就会卡壳。其实，在这一环节，面试者可以对自我介绍文稿提前熟悉，并请专业老师或专业人士修改润色，但切忌一背到底。有些面试者，往往会上气不接下气，仿佛一定要在 1 分钟内把所有的内容都说完。这样不但缺失了英文朗读必要的重音、节奏、升降调等基本因素，也会让面试官觉得面试者说的英语过于生硬、不自然。

　　面试者可以将自身的内容按模块设定，并以一定的逻辑条理进行串联。如第一模块讲基本信息，第二模块讲兴趣爱好，第三模块讲应聘动机。层层递进，环环相扣。表达类似于演讲，亚里士多德的逻辑三角中修辞人格（ethos）、修辞情感（pathos）以及修辞论证

（logos）同样具有适用性。在这个过程中，表达者将自身的内容，以一定的修辞进行组织，从而引起听者的认同和共鸣。面试者可以有效融合平时礼仪课程提及的微笑、眼神交流等非语言因素，与考官思想同步。一旦面试官对你的自我介绍产生兴趣了，面试官也会结合你的内容进行提问。如有的学生提到了自己喜欢瑜伽，那面试官常常会设问"How long have you been in love with yoga?""Do you think Yoga is beneficial to your body?"等开放性问题，如果考生能够应对自如，就能给面试官留下良好的第一印象。

对于基础相对薄弱的考生，想要避免口音影响，增加语言的纯正感，就需要平时的操练。目前手机端有许多值得推广的 App，这些 App 能将生活、诗歌、电影等各类题材的英语以碎片化的方式进行解构，让学习者身临其境。部分高校推送的公众号，如复旦大学的"池馆燕语"中的"雪梨读诗"、清华大学的"THU 生活英语慕课"都是比较成熟的平台；还有民航英语类的公众号，如"客舱博视""航空英语"、Cabin Crew Academy 上的素材都是可以模仿学习的。在实际教学中，除了关注这些平台以提高学生的基础语言水平，为了强化中上等水平学生的能力，也可选用在线平台按照学时开设课程，同时辅助以 TED 演讲、专家的广播词录音等语言素材和测试工具来对学生进行多维度的提升训练。

二、 客舱英文广播词的考核点及应对策略

由于广播词朗读本身能较好地考核面试者对语音语调、情感因素、专业词汇的融通，部分航空公司也会选用客舱广播词的部分内容要求面试者进行朗读。国内外航空公司的广播词手册一般包含了常用广播词、特殊情况广播词、景点介绍等版块。以国内某航空公司为例，考官会让面试者朗读一段类似以下难度的广播词。

"Welcome aboard. For your safety and comfort, please take your assigned seat according to the numbers displayed under the overhead compartments. Please place your bags carefully in the overhead compartments or under the seats in front of you. Do not place them in the aisles or obstruct the emergency exits. In order to allow other passengers to access their seats, please do not block the aisles as you are putting your luggage in the overhead compartments. Thank you."

在这个例子中，面试官会发现，对于考生而言，displayed、obstruct、access 都是难度较高的词汇，需要特别注意；同时对于部分词组 welcome aboard、overhead compartments、emergency exits、in front of you 需要连读失爆，个别经常读错的词汇如 aisle、allow 需要注意。同时，对意群停顿、重读音节、流利程度等方面的考察也能达到较好的效果。

客舱英文广播作为客舱广播的重要组成部分，是最能体现乘务员英语能力的重要指标。在国内航空公司的岗前培训中，除了客舱情景对话，就是广播词的双语编播。作为语音系统的一部分，如何正确地将其量化，也是校企双方都会考虑的问题。在教育部和国家语言文字工作委员会 2018 年发布的《中国英语能力等级量表》中，对于语音系统五级（共

九级）的界定如下：能在日常交流中恰当使用重读、连读、弱化和失去爆破；能利用音调和音高表达诧异、愤怒和惊喜等情绪；能使用重音、调型、音高、音量等方法吸引和保持听者的注意力；能使用升调、降调表明开始说话或者结束说话。而在航空公司的考核中，语音语调、流利熟练、情感饱满等都是其考评的一个指标。例如，东航内部的 CAET 考评系统中，英文广播词的考核也是乘务员飞国际航线的必备环节。其实，无论何种标准，乘务员只要掌握了语音、语调、语气、语速、技巧和情感等因素，就能达到理想的编播效果。

除了具备一些基本的播音技巧和呼吸控制法，情感的融入也显得尤为必要。常常有旅客反映很多航班上乘务员对客舱广播的敷衍了事，既没有节奏感，也没有共鸣感。其实，对于客舱中常见的服务广播和应急广播，学生在平时训练中应注意整体把握两者的特点：服务广播的温柔、亲切和舒缓，应急广播的简短、有力和精准。在客舱广播词的教学上，教师可以将标准音放在学习平台让学生反复听读，也可定期进行在线语音作业的录制提交，单独纠错，各个击破。同时，加入阶段性班级小组互评考核和同课程老师共同考核、广播词大赛考核，最后融入校企合作的服务大赛和技能大赛的项目考核点。通过从点到面，由小到大，构建从短期到长期的时长效应。真正让学生注重积累，反复强化，有错必纠，融会贯通。同时，也让学生在实操比赛中明确把握广播词在工作中的有效定位。在很多客舱服务技能大赛中，项目组会突出考核 Safety Demonstration（客舱安全演示）这一难点；而在客舱应急大赛中，项目组会突出考核 Emergency Evacuation（紧急撤离，包括陆地撤离及水上撤离）中 15 秒开舱门指令。语言技能和客舱服务及应急技能的融通使得人才的培养更加立体，满足了行业对高素质人才的需求。同时，通过对比，发现差异，并将表现优异和不足的视频进行对比分析，以期通过优秀的比赛案例引导更多的学生，使之从中受益，并推广至下一级学生，使得受众面不断拓展。

三、 即兴提问的内容和应对方案

相比较前面两者，即兴问答要相对难得多。它能考验应试者的临场组织能力、应变能力、沟通能力、思辨能力、创新能力；涉及外籍人员的考官，还有跨文化交际能力；涉及外航面试的小组考核，还有团队协作能力。以国内某航空公司为例，由于该航空公司目前的招聘主要是英语口试，而无笔试，故口语考核就成了很多应试者的一道门槛。在即兴提问的问题中，也基本分成两大类：生活通识类和专业知识类，如 What do you think of your college life？ 和 Why smoking is not allowed？ 前者要结合自身谈谈大学生活的收获；后者要结合专业知识说明航班禁烟的原因。如果面试的时间设定为每人 5 分钟，除去 1 分钟自我介绍，那即兴问题就是 4 ～ 5 个问题。与书面考核强调语法的准确性不同，口语考核强调内容的整体感。这就需要应试者有充实的内容和正确的语言表达，部分应试者仅仅回答"Yes"或"No"就突显了知识的不足，淘汰率就会增大。多数航空公司在口语考核上会从语音和语调、语法和词汇、流利和熟练度、反应速度、叙述内容、逻辑和表达方面进行评价。考虑到节约时间和个别应试者基础薄弱的问题，部分航空公司也会采用中英互译的方式进行考核，如翻译"请将您的电子设备关闭，手机调制到飞行模式"。这就涉及专业英语教学方面了。部分外航也会以小组合作的形式，进行团体面试。通过角色分工，任务部署来考验团队协作能力和语言能力。以某外航公司为例：航空业是个竞争行业，假如你是市场营销人员，你如何劝服更多的旅客乘坐你们航空公司的航班？（形式：单独介绍 3 ~ 5 分钟，小组 8 ~ 10 人，包括姓名介绍和演讲，可涉及优势服务、特色服务、旅客心理、航线介绍等。）这就涉及除了专业英语之外，更广阔的旅客心理学、服务理念等范畴。

民航类院校空乘专业一般均设有乘务英语听说课程。该课程除了包含一般的客舱情景对话，还往往加以功能性英语的操练。如何将两者有效融合，是很多教师会考虑的一个问题。对于客舱情景对话，有条件的学校会结合教室和模拟客舱进行演练；一般无模拟客舱的学校也可以在多媒体教室进行模拟仿真表演。表演固然将语言活用了起来，但也会给部分基础弱的学生带来思维的单一化，即只会回答特定问题的特定答案。所以，需要用功能性英语的多样化来进行补充，既要考虑一般性，也要注重多样化。这就需要教师在平时的教学中除了教授标准版，还要适当增加拓展版。除了教授指定教材上的表达之外，教师也可适当补充一些句型，设定多样化的场景，发挥学生的主观能动性，利用头脑风暴法或者思维导图的模式，进行延伸式的发散性思维塑造。PSL（problem-solving learning）或者 TBL（task-based learning）是目前职业院校行之有效的一种方法，学生既有参与感，也有成就感。尝试将教材中内容或情景以任务工单的形式进行下发，然后进行实时评价也是一种有益的做法。

在校企合作的前提下，教师也可借鉴各大航空公司在岗前培训中用到的客舱英语进行适当补充。由于存在飞机机型的差异，部分用语也要注意微调。教师要善于总结好共性的内容，也应注重航空公司个体的差异。目前，很多学校均有来自企业的专家或者双师型教师，对于英语专业出身的教师，需要加强和他们的合作。有条件的教师也可去企业实习积累，在实践中弥补专业短板。在课堂或者客舱教学受限的情况下，教师可借助线上课堂或者精品课程的平台，有效合理地安置教学内容，构建互联网环境下的 EOP（English for occupational purposes）教学。有益的翻转课堂是良好的补充，对于不同难度的专业术语和交际任务也要进行梯度设计。对于相对容易的部分，进行线上知识教学，让学生提前完成接受型知识的输入；对于相对困难的重点和难点，进行线下实践教学，让学生通过语言和任务的融合，进行产出型任务的输出。

随着民航国际化进程的加速，英文面试是航空公司面试中极其重要的一环。不管是国内航空公司还是国外航空公司招聘，两者都对应试者提出了很高的语言要求。从自我介绍到专业的广播词朗读和即兴问答环节，乃至演讲或者团队协作能力的考核，都需要应试者在有限的时间内，克服紧张焦虑，增强自信表达，将通识英语、专业用途英语、行业知识和技能以口语技能辅助以适当的肢体语言进行有效表达，顺利完成交际任务。作为专业英语教师，既要注重差异化教学，也要有线上和线下的相互补充，结合阶段考核、学期考核、竞赛和技能大赛等形式，形成点线面、立体化的评价模式。最终，课程目标和空乘专业的人才培养目标形成衔接：学生掌握全面扎实的知识技能，具备高效灵活的沟通能力，切实提升外语能力。

第二节　外航招聘要求解读

一、外航简介

与国内航空公司相比，外航的乘务员首先需要有过硬的英文和母语的表达能力，这是进入外航的第一步。这就需要面试者通过国内的大学英语四级考试或更高水平的英语测试，也可参加国际认证的托业考试（TOEIC）、雅思（IELTS）、托福（TOEFL），达到一定的级别即可。

中国籍的乘务员想要进入外航工作，一般都需要经过外航统一的社会招聘，通过初试、复试等环节，最后与中介FASCO（如北京外航服务公司）签订合同后正式入职。在初试的环节中，外航一般与国内航空公司相似，包括体检、语言、心理测试等环节。复试阶段，有些外航注重英语口语表达和小组团队协作，如需要面试者对某一问题发表自己的看法等。

加入外航的优势是可以接触其他国籍的乘务员，飞越不同的国际航线，拓展自己的视野，提升自己的跨文化交际能力。但也有些问题需要考虑，由于部分外航的基地一般都是在国外，需要乘务员远离家人，并适应当地的饮食和居住条件。同时，外航的薪资待遇也存在差异，较好的航空公司与一般的航空公司可能会有一两倍的落差。另外，在航班的安排上，乘务员飞行航班的频率相对也不会那么密集。

二、外航空乘应聘条件

（1）学历：大专或以上学历。

（2）年龄：通常21周岁及以上。具体要求以外航广告上的要求为准。

（3）身体条件：五官端正，仪态大方；身体健康，体检合格，视力良好；身高160厘米以上。外航对于空乘身高的要求是应这项工作实际操作的需要来定的，一般常会提到"摸高"的概念，因为空乘人员需要能够摸到头部上方的行李架，摸高需达到206～212厘米（可踮脚，摸高视各航空公司服务的机型而定）。具体要求以外航招聘时的具体规定为准。

（4）外语能力：流利的中、英文口语表达及书写能力。熟练的英文运用能力是外航空乘能胜任其工作的基本及必备的条件之一。另外，一些航空公司会将掌握其相关的小语种或者方言作为加分项。招聘过程也通常全部以英文方式进行。

（5）政审：个人及直系亲属无犯罪记录，个人档案正规完整。

（6）职业素养：性格开朗，具有团队精神，能够在压力下工作；具有良好的客户服务意识、灵活的应变能力及良好的沟通能力。部分航空公司也会要求游泳能力。当然，在后续培训过程中，游泳救生也是空乘必须掌握的紧急救援课程，有的会进行水试，要求应聘者穿上救生衣在深水区可以游一定距离。

（7）工作经历：没有特殊要求，如果有服务业等相关行业经验的当然更好。但最重要的是有服务意识和亲和力。

第三节　外航申请表格填写

下面，我们先来熟悉一份来自新西兰航空的英文招聘广告。

Air New Zealand Recruiting — Shanghai Based
Airline Crew Chinese Flight Attendants

Air New Zealand is currently operating direct flights from Shanghai and Beijing to Auckland New Zealand. We are looking to recruit additional Chinese Flight Attendants who will operate out of Shanghai's Pudong Airport and Beijing's Capital Airport. Successful applicants will be based in Shanghai.

We need talented, responsible and service oriented crew who can provide outstanding customer service. Capable of enduring physical work as some lifting required. You must be a competent swimmer.

Flying is a robust and dynamic job and involves much time away from home as such will appeal to people who like a varied lifestyle as well as who like the challenge of shift work.

Air New Zealand was last year voted as having the best passenger service in the world—something we are very proud of. Our crew is part of the success to this award and as such we recruit to a very high standard. If you think you have what it takes to be an Air New Zealander please read on.

Successful candidates will be trained in New Zealand and will then join a team of talented colleagues based in Shanghai working in a friendly "New Zealand" environment.

Requirements:

- College Diploma and above.

- Age: 22 and above.

- Height: Female,160cm and above; Male,170cm and above.

- Adhere to rules and regulations.

- Be physically fit and able to pass a medical assessment.

- Be fluent in spoken and written English language.

- Be able to swim at least 50 meters—unaided.

- Previous experience in a customer-facing environment preferred.

Please click here to download and complete an application form—in Chinese and English and post to the following address before November 3rd 2019 with a full-size color photo and A4-size copies of ID certificate, education diploma, and swimming certificate attached to: Beijing Foreign Airlines Service Corporation, 12—13 Diplomatic Apartments Jianguomenwai, Beijing, Second Dept of Foreign Affairs

Postcode: 100600

（Noted on envelope: Application for Air NZ flight attendant）

（No phone or visit will be received for this recruitment）

Interview will be held in Shanghai. Please pay attention to the time and venue notice on FASCO website.

（资料来源：北京外航服务公司）

参考译文：

新西兰航空上海基地招聘
中国籍乘务员

新西兰航空目前从上海、北京直飞新西兰的奥克兰。我们正招募在上海浦东机场和北京首都机场出港的乘务员。成功的求职者将会以上海为驻地。

我们需要的是秉承天赋、敢于担当，能以服务为导向的乘务员。他们既能提供出色的客舱服务，也能忍受艰苦的体力劳动，如提行李。你必须要会游泳。

飞行是一项充满活力、动感十足的工作。它需要你长期远离家乡。喜欢尝试多变的生活，乐于挑战倒班的节奏的有意者，可来一试。

去年，新西兰航空获得了全球最佳服务奖，这是我们引以为豪的地方。成功该归因于机组成员的努力，所以我们对招聘提出了高标准、严要求。如果你觉得自己天生属于我们团队，请继续阅读。

成功的应聘者将在新西兰接受培训，然后加入上海的团队，他们同样也是一批具有才华的人士，在友好的"新西兰式"氛围中敬业工作。

空乘实用英语教程

基本要求：

- 大专学历及以上。

- 年龄：22 岁及以上。

- 身高：女性，160 厘米及以上；男性，170 厘米及以上。

- 遵规守纪。

- 身体健康，能通过医疗体检。

- 流利的英语口语和书面语。

- 能游泳至少 50 米（无辅助）。

- 有面向客服服务经验的工作者优先考虑。

请您点击这里下载中英文格式简历，填写完毕并打印后，于 2019 年 11 月 3 日前，连同一张全身彩色照片，A4 纸大小的身份证复印件，学历复印件和会游泳证明一起寄至：北京市建国门外外交公寓 12 号楼 13 号，北京外航服务公司 外事二部

邮编：100600

（请在信封上注明：应聘新西兰航空空乘）

（本次招聘恕不接待来电来访）

面试将在上海进行。具体面试时间和地址会在北京外航服务公司网站上通知，请密切留意。

在该广告招聘中，第一段是新西兰航空招聘中国籍乘务员的基本要求。出于其航线考虑，该公司主要是为上海基地招聘从上海浦东机场和北京首都机场出港的乘务员。

第二段中，对于乘务员的职业要求，首先用到了三个关键词：talented（天资聪颖）、responsible（敢于承担）、service oriented（服务导向）。其次是考虑到岗位服务和应急能力的两个角色：customer service servant（客户服务人员）和 competent swimmer（游泳胜任者）。尤其对能够胜任体力活（physical work）做了强调。

第三段中，从工作特点 robust and dynamic（强健和动感）出发，呼吁敢于尝试多变生活（a varied lifestyle）和勇于挑战换班工作（the challenge of shift work）的人加入团队。

第四段中，新西兰航空给出了引以为豪的最佳服务奖（the best passenger service）和较高的招聘标准（a very high standard）。并在最后一段告知：成功的候选人会在新西兰进行培训，然后分配至上海基地，在友善的（friendly）企业氛围中工作。

在具体的招聘细节中，对学历、年龄、身高，以及遵守规章制度，通过医疗急救测试，掌握流利的英文口语与书面表达，具备 50 米独立游泳能力，拥有客服经验等方面进行了重点规定。

由于中国籍乘务员去外航工作都需要通过 FASCO（北京外航服务公司），下面我们可以通过对新西兰航空申请表的中英文填写，来掌握填写该申请表的基本组成版块：基本信息、教育背景、工作经历、声明确认等。特别要注意申请表填写说明。

（1）申请表须用中、英文分别填写。

（2）可以下载后手工填写或直接在计算机上录入后打印出来。

（3）如手工填写务必要字迹清晰。

（4）请认真填写，内容务必要完整，不得有空项。

（5）个人声明部分的签字须由本人亲笔签名。

（6）请随申请表提供一张本人近期站立全身正装照。

（7）未按要求填写和提供照片的视为无效申请。

　　FASCO（北京外航服务公司）的中、英文申请表如下所示。

Please attach a recent passport-size photograph of yourself here.

EMPLOYMENT APPLICATION
POSITION APPLIED : FLIGHT ATTENDANT

BASIC PERSONAL INFORMATION	FIRST NAME:		LAST NAME:		DATE OF BIRTH:		
	PLACE OF BIRTH:		HUKOU:		GENDER:		
	ID NUMBER:				CEL PHONE NO.:		
	EMAIL:				HOME TEL.:		
	RESIDENTIAL ADDRESS:				MARITAL STATUS:		
					NATIONALITY:		
	POSTAL ADDRESS (if different from above):				HEIGHT (in meters):		
					WEIGHT (kg):		

EDUCATION BACKGROUND	NAME OF SCHOOL	PERIOD WITH SCHOOL		Other Qualification(s) Obtained and Date(s)	
		FROM Mth/Yr	TO Mth/Yr		
				Highest Education Certificate	
				Foreign Languages（G: Good; F: Fair; L: Little）	
				Written:	
				Spoken:	

DETAILS OF PRESENT & PREVIOUS EMPLOYERS	NAME OF PRESENT COMPANY	Length of time being employed		POSITION	SALARY
		FROM Mth/Yr	FROM Mth/Yr		
	NAME OF PREVIOUS COMPANY	Length of time being employed		POSITION	SALARY
		FROM Mth/Yr	FROM Mth/Yr		

续表

Name of the personal profile location and contact number		
Are you able to swim at least 50 meters—unaided	Yes ( )	No ( )
DECLARATION		

I declare that the information given by me in this application for employment is true to the best of my knowledge and that I have not withheld any relevant particulars. I have disclosed all the information required to be given in this application. This declaration shall, if I am employed by the Company, be part of my contract of service. I accept that if any of the information given by me in this application for employment is in any way false, or incorrect, the Company shall have the right to dismiss me without notice and without assigning any reason.

Signature:　　　　　　　　　Date:

（资料来源：北京外航服务公司）

参考译文：

此处请附上
2 寸近期
个人照片

空中乘务员职位申请表格

基本信息	名：		姓：		出生日期：		
	出生地：		户口所在地：		性别：		
	身份证号码：			手机：			
	电子邮箱：			家庭电话：			
	现居住地址：			婚姻状况：			
				国籍：			
	现邮寄地址（如果和上面不同）：			身高（米）：			
				体重（千克）：			

教育背景	学校名称	在校时间		其他证书与获得时间
		自 年 月	到 年 月	
				最高学历
				外语水平（良好、一般、差）
				写作：
				口语：

工作背景	目前公司名称	工作时间		职位	薪水
		自 年 月	自 年 月		
	曾工作过公司名称	工作时间		职位	薪水
		自 年 月	自 年 月		

档案存放地名称及联系电话			
能否在没有辅助的条件下游泳 50 米？	是 ( )	否 ( )	

本人声明，以上内容全部真实有效。如果虚假，本人将承担一切后果。

申请人签名：　　　　　　　　　填表时间：

简历是求职者的名片，也是航空公司认识求职者的有效途径。简历制作的好坏直接表明了求职者的态度、信息化能力以及营销自己的策略。有些求职者还会在简历后面附上单独的申请信（a letter of application）或推荐信（a letter of recommendation）来突出自己的优点和特长。

英文简历一词可以用来自法语的 résumé 或者来自拉丁语的 CV(curriculum vitae)表示。在美国，CV 主要是用于申请学术、教育、科研职位，或者申请奖学金等；而在欧洲、中东、非洲和亚洲等地，CV 则更常用于应聘工作。CV 的长度由其内容确定，有时可长达10 页，年轻专业人士的履历一般长度都在 2～4 页，而资深专业人士的通常在 6～8 页。具体应包括：姓名、地址、电话号码及电子邮件地址；文化程度；受何奖励和大学奖学金等级；教学经历；论著发表；语言或其他技能，课外活动及个人爱好等。

résumé 比 CV 稍微简单，大多只需 1 页。有 2 页的求职者一般具有广泛的工作经验。具体应包括：姓名、地址、电子信箱和电话号码；工作岗位（可选）；教育经历；荣誉奖励；有关功课（可选）；经历（列出组织、地址、日期、工作名称、成绩和职责简述）。

有时候，过多的描述并不利于录取官提取有力的信息。通常申请的简历不宜过长，1～2 页比较适宜。一份简洁明了、突出优势的简历绝对会给求职者加分。下面我们来看两种比较具备代表性的英文简历。一种为表格式；另一种为块状式。

以下两份简历都包括了个人基本信息、联系方式、工作经历和特长技能。其中第一份通过所学课程突出了行业的专业性；另一份通过自我评价突出了性格特点。在个人资料里，一般都会有姓名、性别、联系方式、身高、体重等内容；在教育背景和所获荣誉中会有学习经历、获奖与荣誉；工作经历中会有兼职、实习和相关服务岗位的实践经历。同时，可加入个人爱好、职业技能和应聘岗位等。

Name	Grace Yang	Gender	Female	Date of Birth	Oct. 8th, 1994	
Nationality	Chinese	Residence	Shanghai	Political Status	The Communist Youth League Member	PROFILE
E-mail	abc@163.com	Graduaiton Institution	Shanghai Civil Aviation College	Major	Cabin Service	
Highest Degree	Associate Degree	Cell phone		123456789		
Permanent Address	No. 1 West Longhua Road, Xuhui District			Zip Code	200232	

12

续表

Educational Background	2009—2012 Shanghai Civil Aviation College (College) 2006—2009 YuYing School (High School)
Previous Experience	Chairperson of Students Union; Sales agent for Customer service
Language Skills	Mandarin Test (Level-2); College English Test (Band4)
Courses Taken	A Psychological Study of Civil Aviation Service; An Introduction to Civil Aviation; Medical First Aid; Make-up Course; A Body-fitting Training Course; Etiquette for Civil Aviation Service; English for Flight Attendants; Transportation of Civil Aviation Passengers; Laws for Civil Aviation; Japanese for Cabin Attendants; Cabin Service; Cabin Emergency-handling Skills.
Merits	Fluent oral English, good at swimming

Résumé

Name: Jenifer Lin   **Gender:** Female

Nationality: Chinese   **Date of Birth:** 1998.2.1

Weight: 50kg   **Height:** 167cm

Degree: College Degree   **Code:** 200232

Cell-phone: 12345648900

Home Address: No. 1 West Longhua Road, Xuhui District, Shanghai

Email-Address: 22222222222@163.com

PROFILE

Education Background:

2017.9—2020.6 Shanghai Civil Aviation College (College)

2014.9—2017.6 Yucai Middle school (Middle School)

2010.9—2014.6 Shanghai Experimental School (Primary School)

Honors & Awards:

Top a Student in the first semester; 1st Price of Etiquette Competition in 2018

Language Ability:

Certificate of Mandarin Test: Level 2

Public English Test System (PETS): Band 3

Self-Evaluation:

I am organized, ambitiousness and hard-working.

I am willing to create more value for your company with my gorgeousness.

Thank you for reading my résumé and hopefully.

I can win a chance to meet with you.

英文自我介绍通常会有 1 分钟的或 3 分钟两类。以常见的 1 分钟左右的自我介绍为例，一般可以包括个人的基本情况、家庭成员、兴趣爱好、学习成绩、自我评价等方面，也可以归纳为四个方面："我是谁""我做过什么""我做成过什么""我想做什么"。在做自我介绍时，应根据时间，适当选择内容。

（1）我是谁：包括姓名以及取名的出处。例如取名苏慧的同学会用 Sophia 来作英文名，该词有表示"智慧、聪明"的含义；取名辛娅茹的同学会用 Cynthia 来作英文名，该词有表示"月亮女神"的含义；还有叫朱迪的同学会用 Judith，或者林依洁则可能用 Jessica，前者表示"受赞美的"，后者引申为幸福、吉祥的意思。可以通过对中文名和英文名的注解，拓展背后的文化。例如：My name is Sophia Su, and I come from Shanghai. My English teacher suggests this English name for me, because it means clever and elegant.

（2）我做过什么：包括了学习经历和工作经历。可以是求学，也可以是一件值得骄傲的事情。如通过了大学英语四级、六级考试或者取得芭蕾舞等级证书等。通过一个点，突出自己的性格。这些性格词汇也能与行业需要进行对接。例如：With my great efforts, I have passed the College English Test Band-4, which is beneficial to my future job.

（3）我做成过什么：可以包括参加校内外的比赛，从事志愿者或社会公益活动。通过一个事迹，从中获得成就感，并有效对接自己的人生观和价值观，也可以通过在大学阶段完成的一件事来说明自己的成长和成才。例如：During my college life, I have joined the Students' Union to be a volunteer for school and social works. I have learned how to help others, which makes me feel so happy.

（4）我想做什么：可以谈谈自己的职业理想、生涯规划或者对乘务员这个岗位的理解和体会，从而坚定自己的目标与信仰。Since I was a child, I was looking forward to working in the blue sky. To be a flight attendant is not only my dream, but also my family's hope. I believe I am competent for the job, and I can do it well.

下面通过三个自我介绍来分析一下三位同学的思路和了解各自的优点。

Sample 1:

My name is Joyce. My major is In-flight Service. I'm lively, cheerful and ambitious. I like to treat everything around me with a smile. A friendly smile can make people feel happy and relaxed. At school, I acquire the basic knowledge and professional skills very hard. And with my tireless efforts, I have passed the College English Test Band-4 when I was a sophomore.

In my spare time, I also like watching English TV programs. During the process of watching, I try my best to understand the programs without the help of subtitle translation, so as to enlarge my English vocabulary and improve my pronunciation.

When I face some difficult problems, I'll never give up, and I'll keep going and find my way out to solve the problems. I feel that my strongest point is my ability to stick to things to get them done. I feel a real sense of accomplishment when I finish a job and it turns out just as I'd planned.

Sample 2:

Ladies and gentlemen,

Good morning. My name is Jessie. I am 20 years old, and my hometown is Tianjin. I will graduate from my College this year. My major is In-flight Service. I am optimistic and confident. I own the ability to work independently with a mature and resourceful mind.

I like to treat everything around me with a smile. A friendly smile can convey a good intention to people. When facing difficulties, I never shrink from them, I always smile to confront them and have the courage to move forward. I have full confidence in a bright future.

From childhood, I already had a dream that I could fly in the blue sky like a swallow. I like travelling very much. That is why I'm standing here for this interview, and I hope that I will have the opportunity to make the dream come true.

Sample 3:

Ladies and gentlemen,

Good afternoon. My name is Christina. Now I will introduce myself briefly.

I am 20 years old, and I am currently a senior student in a college, which is one of the most professional colleges in our country with 40 years' history.

Soaring in the sky as a flight attendant has been a dream for me since childhood. In the past 2 years, I spent most of my time on study. Therefore, I passed CET-4 with ease and I also studied Japanese as my second foreign language.

I think the most important qualifications about being a flight attendant are smile, team work, and psychological quality. I have full confidence in a bright future and I believe I can do it well.

I am energetic, co-operative and independent. Being a flight attendant is hard; it needs the ability to work efficiently and effectively, and also willingness to work under pressure with leadership and strong determination. In a word, I believe I am qualified for the job.

Thank you!

为了突出新意，有些同学也会融入星座知识。如 I'm an Aries. It is said that people of this zodiac sign are intended to be courageous leaders. To some extent, I agree with that. 通过一

定的文化注解，让自己的表达与众不同。还有些同学会加入谚语，来增加语言的生动性和趣味性。如用 Time and tide wait for no man.（时不我待。），说明时间的宝贵。其他类似的例子如下：

（1）Adversity makes a man wise, not rich.

（2）Honesty is the best policy.

（3）A rolling stone gathers no moss.

（4）Every man is the architect of his own fortune.

（5）Beauty without virtue is a rose without fragrance.

提升英语口语的关键在于掌握以下几点：思辨能力（critical thinking）、沟通技巧（communication strategies）、表达技巧（expression skills）、职业素质（professionalism）、情景意识（situational awareness）、团队协作（team work spirit）、第一印象（first impression）。

对于基础相对薄弱的同学，也可以参考下面的模板。

（1）Hello. My name is...

（2）I live in... (city/ municipality).

（3）I'm... years old.

（4）My birthday is...

（5）I'm a senior student / sophomore of...

（6）My favorite subject is... (English for Cabin crew)

（7）My favorite sport is...

（8）There are... people in my family. They are...

（9）My father is... and my mother is...

（10）I would like to be a... because...

（11）My hobby is... In my free time, I like...

（12）My favorite food is... and my favorite drink is...

（13）My favorite day of the week is... because...

（14）My favorite month is... because...

（15）My favorite singer is... just because...

（16）I like... (movie), which is amazing.

（17）My favorite place... I like it because...

（18）The most beautiful place in my country is...

（19）The most impressive place I have been to is... because...

（20）I study English because...

（21）I am intended to become a flight attendant because...

（22）I am a... person and I'm always ready to help others.

当然，在自我介绍过程中，也有些禁忌需要注意。例如避免将个人爱好说得过长、头重脚轻、空洞和毫无逻辑感、过多或过于显摆自己的成绩、说谎和胡编乱造、举止言谈非职业化等。

英文自我介绍是个人语音水平、个人家庭背景、职业认知和社会责任体现的一个重要载体。在陈述过程中，面试者除了自信、微笑，还应具有正能量导向。在传递知识和技能的同时，表达对中西方文化的理解，肯定自我的价值观，并对职业精神提出自己的理解和行业认同感。

第六节　面试常见问题汇总

一、 通识类英语问题

通识类英语问题主要包括面试者的特长和缺点、社会经历、责任感等。当然也可以包括求职者对企业和乘务员职业认知的一些看法。例如：

（1）Could you list your main advantages compared with other candidates?

I am a communicative and optimistic person. I love to be with a diversity of people. To be a cabin attendant can improve my personal experience in dealing with different kinds of people. And of course, I could travel a lot to expand my horizons.

（2）Do you know the basic qualifications for a good cabin attendant? / How do you become a qualified flight attendant?

To be a qualified flight attendant, I have to meet both physical requirements as well as mental requirements, such as height and vision, team work spirit and endurance.

（3）What is the biggest difficulty you have faced until now?

Several years ago, I failed in college entrance examination and I could not enter the college I liked. I became so depressed. Then my father told me, "all roads lead to Rome." And after that I came to this college and it turned out to be a sunshine to me.

（4）What are your weaknesses and merits?

I am good at helping others and I like to work with my colleges. I take the team work spirit seriously. Occasionally I am a little sensitive and emotional. But I'm trying to improve it.

（5）What do you think are your responsibilities?

Safety is the first and most important matter for every airline. Therefore, as a cabin attendant, I should always have the safety awareness in my mind. Meanwhile, to provide a satisfying service for each passenger is also my duty. All in all, both safety and service are important for each airline.

（6）How do you handle the feeling of boredom out of the daily repetition?

Cabin service consists of repetitive work sometimes, so I could take part in some leisure activities to release my pressure.

（7）Do you have another future plan in the next five years?

In the following years, I would work hard to become an excellent purser, who can manage the cabin affairs efficiently. After that, I want to be a trainer in the training department.

（8）What attracts you to be a flight attendant?

I hope I could have the chance to meet people from all kinds of cultures and backgrounds. I also want to impress everyone I meet as I offer the best possible service while flying.

（9）Tell me something about your personality, which is good for work.

I am a capable candidate, very patient and responsible. I can make quick decisions in emergency and I am enthusiastic about my work.

（10）Could you say something about your neighbor/roommate/classmate(s)?

My neighbor is such a friendly person. She always likes to share her DIY cake with me. And I have really learnt a lot of cooking skills from her.

（11）What essential certificates for work do you have?

I have obtained the following certificates: Computer operator's qualification certificate; Red Cross first aid certificate; driving license; practical English test for college students; CET (College English Test, Band-4/6); Cabin Attendants' Professional Skills Test.

（12）Why do you choose our airline / How do you know about our airlines?

Your company is one of the most famous airlines in the world. It has won an excellent reputation for its customer service. Employees of your company would enjoy lots of opportunities to develop themselves and make more contribution to the company.

（13）Why is English so important in international flight?

Passengers from all over the world would use English as a means of communication. And some menus and instructions are printed in English. We need to use English as an instrument for understanding.

（14）What do you do in your spare time?

Music and dancing are two favorite interests in my life. Now I am a member of the School

Dancing Club. We often take part in different kinds of after-school activities (extracurricular activities).

（15）What do you think of your college life?

I think my college life is the most unforgettable period in my life. I lived a colorful life and made some good friends. My teachers, especially my English teacher helped me a lot.

（16）Did you join any clubs at college?

Yes, I joined the Volunteer Club. During our spare time, we often did some charity work which gave me a sense of achievement (enjoyment).

（17）Could you say something about your hometown?

My hometown is... which is located in the East/South/West/ North part of China. It is a historical /dynamic city. There are many places of interest. If you are interested in history, I recommend you to visit...

（18）Which season do you prefer? List the reasons.

My hometown is in North China, and I am fond of winter. Snow is so amazing that everyone would play on the ground. Many parents build snowmen with their children. That's wonderful.

（19）What are some of the taboo topics?

Western people take the concept of personal privacy seriously. Taboo topics include salary, age, religion and so on. In cabin communication, we should avoid such topics.

（20）What's your definition of success?

Most people consider that wealth means success. However, from my point of view, success means how do you achieve your goal no matter how difficult it is. Success is satisfaction from work, and happiness from life.

二、 客舱情景意识类英语问题

客舱情景意识类英语问题主要突出对求职者应变能力的考核。它包括对客舱突发情况的处理和应对策略。这一块内容需要面试者有一定的专业背景，也会在航空公司复试中得以呈现。

（1）What would you say if you spill a cup of water onto the passenger's computer?

I'm terribly sorry. Let me turn the computer over and remove the battery now. Let's wait a few minutes and I will go and get a towel for you.

（2）What would you say to passengers if the flight is delayed?

① We have been informed that due to the air traffic control, our flight will be delayed for several minutes. I understand your feeling. May I offer you some water? We will keep you informed.

② Are you connecting any flight? Would you mind telling me the information of your next flight?

（3）What would you say if a passenger asks you "Why should seat belt be fastened during the flight?"

For the safety of passengers, it is advised to fasten the seatbelt during the flight. The sudden turbulence and emergency situation would also cause some kind of unexpected things.

（4）What would you do if you stain the PAX's clothes during the service?

① I'm terribly sorry. May I wipe it off first?

② May I help you to clean the satin in the restroom? Please follow me.

③ I'll report it to the purser right now, please wait a minute, and would you like a cup of tea or something else?

（5）What would you do when a passenger asks for tablets for air sickness?

① Have you ever experienced this kind of symptom before?

② Have you ever taken our tablets on-board before? Would you please read our waiver and put your signature on? Please read and sign this waiver before you take the pills.

③ Here are the tablets and water. You should feel better in about 30 minutes. If you need further assistance, please let me know.

（6）What will you do when a passenger requests a seat change?

① I understand your feeling. It will be very inconvenient when a family sit separated. Please wait a moment and let me check if there is any vacant seat.

② Excuse me, Mr. ××, would you mind switching seats with this lady so that she can take care of her kids?

③ Thank you for your help. Would you like me to move your baggage over?

（7）What will you do to help an unaccompanied minor to embark?

① Hello. Welcome aboard! You are so brave to travel alone.

② I'll keep these papers from now on, and I will give it to our ground staff when we land. Now let me take you to your seat.

③ Is this your first time to travel by airplane? Let me show you how to use the seat belt. Slip the belt into the buckles and pull it tightly. Please try it by yourself.

④ Very good, you are so good at this.

（8）What would you do to help an unaccompanied minor using the lavatory?

① This is the lavatory. You can open the door like this and leave the door unlocked, and I will be waiting for you outside.

② This is the lavatory, open the door like this. You can slip the bar here to lock the door, and be careful when you open it.

③ This is the call button, if you need any help, just press the button, and I will be right with you.

（9）If a passenger has a heart attack on board, what do you do?

I will use the basic first aid or call for assistance immediately. Then I'll ask if there are doctors or nurses traveling on this flight and ask them for help.

（10）What will you do when a wheel chair passenger embarks?

① Hello! Welcome aboard! May I help you?

② I've already put your luggage in the overhead locker, don't worry. Please contact us if you'd like to take something out.

③ There is a lavatory in/at the back/front of cabin. Here is the call button. Just press the button if you need any assistance.

（11）What will you do for a wheel chair passenger during the flight?

① The lavatory is at ××, I will take you there, be careful!

② This is the call button, if you need any help, please press the button.

③ We will have the wheelchair ready for you when we land. Please remain seated, we will come and assist you once the aisle is clear.

（12）What will you do when a wheel chair passenger disembarks?

The wheel chair is ready for you at the door. I'll take your luggage and help you to disembark.

（13）What will you do when a passenger with a baby embarks?

① Hello, welcome aboard! May I help you with your luggage ?

② What's your seat number? OK, follow me, please!

③ If you need to change the diaper for baby, there is a lavatory with diaper panel in the mid-cabin.

④ For your baby's safety, I will set the cradle after take-off.

（14）How would you inform a passenger that the cradle has been set-up?

The cradle has been already installed, let me put a blanket and pillow in it, it will make your baby feel more comfortable. If you need any further assistance, please contact me at any time.

（15）Before landing, how would you help passengers who used cradle on flight?

① The cabin pressure changed during landing, which will make the baby uncomfortable. So it's better to wake him/her up.

② Our plane will be landing in about 30 minutes. May I help you to fasten the belt for your baby?

③ I will come to you if you need any assistance after landing.

（16）How would you greet our CIP (Commercial Import Person)?

You are our golden card holder (platinum card holder), and welcome aboard ×××. My name is ×××, it's my pleasure to be at your service. Here is the newspaper for you. We also prepared two choices of entrée, A and B, which one do you prefer? If there is anything I can do for you, please let me know. We hope you will enjoy the flight.

（17）How would you confirm with the passenger who ordered special meal before the flight?

Excuse me! Are your Mr/Mrs ×××? Is your seat number ×××? Did you order ××× meal before the flight? We will take it to you before the meal service.

（18）How would you serve senior passengers in flight?

① Hello, welcome aboard! May I help you with your luggage?

② What's your seat number? OK, follow me please!

③ I've already put your luggage in the overhead locker, don't worry. Please contact us if you'd like to take something out.

④ This is the call button, if you need any help, please press the button.

⑤ I'll stow your cane in the cloakroom. If you need it, please let me know.

（19）How would you serve blind passengers?

① Hello, welcome aboard! May I help you with your luggage?

② Your seat number is ×××. I'll take you there.

③ I've already put your drink at 2 o'clock position, entrée at 6 o'clock position, fruits at 11 o'clock position... Here is your fork. Here is your knife...

④ The lavatory is behind you. If you need to use it, contact me please. I'll be right here.

（20）What would you do if a passenger finds out some foreign matter in his/her meal?

① I'm terribly sorry. I understand your feeling. May I get another one for you?

② I'll report it to the purser right now, please wait a minute, and would you like a cup of tea or something else?

三、 企业文化拓展类问题

企业文化拓展类问题主要考查面试者对所面试航空公司概况的了解程度。如果面试者对这一部分比较熟悉，且能用英文向面试官流利地陈述，这是可以加分的项目。

1. Air China

Air China is one of the major airlines in our nation, with its headquarters in Beijing. It was established and commenced (began to) operations on July 1st 1988. As a Star Alliance member, Air China is the only national flag carrier in our country, operating flights to most of the leading international and domestic cities. Its service philosophy is "credibility, convenience, comfort and choice."

2. China Eastern Airlines

China Eastern Airlines is one of the three largest airlines in China, with its headquarters in Shanghai. It has established an air transport network around the globe. Many awards on service and safety have been obtained during the past 10 years. With the concept of "world-class hospitality with eastern charm", it will create more value for our nation.

3. China Southern Airlines

China Southern Airlines is one of the largest airlines in our nation, with its headquarters in Guangzhou. Currently, it operates more than 350 routes around the world. Its service philosophy is "customers, staff, advantage, innovation and return."

4. Juneyao Airlines

It is one of the largest privately-owned airlines in our nation. The group headquarters is located in the most dynamic and developed city—Shanghai. Many of the travelers are business travelers. It holds a big flying fleet throughout China, Japan and Thailand. The concept of customer service is safety, punctuality and delicacy.

5. Spring Airlines

It is one of the largest privately-owned airlines in our nation, which is famous for its low-cost operation. The group headquarters is located in Shanghai. Many of the airplanes are designed mostly for travelers. It holds a big flying fleet throughout Southeast Asia. The concept of customer service is safety, smile and sincerity.

四、 航空公司广播词朗读问题

航空公司广播词朗读问题通过让求职者朗读广播词，既考查了求职者对语音、语感、意群的整体把握，也考核了其对专业词汇的掌握程度。部分航空公司也会通过随机抽查来进行考查。

1. Boarding（Juneyao Airlines）

Welcome aboard. For your safety and comfort, please take your assigned seat according to the numbers displayed under the overhead compartments. Please place your bags carefully in the overhead compartments or under the seats in front of you. Do not place them in the aisles or obstruct the emergency exits. In order to allow other passengers to access their seats, please do not block the aisles as you are putting your luggage in the overhead compartments. Thank you.

2. PED Restriction（Without Video）

Ladies and gentlemen,

Cabin doors have been closed. According to CAAC regulations, lithium power bank should be turned off. You may use your small portable electronic devices, such as mobile phones, after setting to airplane mode. Mobile phones without airplane mode, interphones and remote control equipment are prohibited during the entire flight. Headsets and oversized laptop of tablet PC are prohibited in critical flight phases, such as taxi, takeoff, decent and landing. In order to ensure flight safety, cigarette and equivalent smoking are prohibited in this flight. Thank you.

3. Duty-free Sale

Ladies and gentlemen,

For passengers who are interested in purchasing duty-free items, we will begin our in-flight sales service very soon.

Our Duty-free Goods Catalog, with product information, can be found in the seat pocket in front of you.

For passengers with connecting flight, please note that liquid items purchased onboard are subject to safety regulations on Prohibiting Liquid Items onboard. Please feel free to contact any of our cabin attendants for detail information. Thank you.

4. Boarding（Air China）

Ladies and gentlemen,

Good morning. Welcome aboard Air China, a proud Star Alliance member. All your hand luggage should be securely stowed in the overhead compartment or under the seat in front of you. Please take your assigned seats as soon as possible and leave the aisle clear for others to be seated. Thank you.

5. Safety Demonstration

Ladies and gentleman,

We will now demonstrate the use of the life vest, oxygen mask and seatbelt, and show you the location of the emergency exits.

Your life vest is located under your seat. Slip the life vest over your head.

Bring the waist strap around our waist. Fasten the buckles and tighten it by pulling it outwards.

To inflate your life-vest, pull the red tabs firmly downwards. But do not inflate it in the cabin.

To inflate further, blow into these mouthpieces.

Your oxygen mask is located in a compartment above your head. It will drop automatically in case of decompression.

Pull a mask down sharply to activate the flow of oxygen.

Place the mask over your nose and mouth. Pull the elastic strap over your head and tighten it by pulling the end of the strap. In a few seconds, the oxygen will begin to flow.

There are emergency exits on this aircraft. They are located in the front, the rear, the middle and the upper deck.

In the event of an evacuation, emergency floor-lights will illuminate a darkened cabin, leading to these exits.

The safety instruction is in the seat pocket in front of you, please read it carefully as soon as possible.

Thank you.

6. Boarding (China Southern Airlines)

Ladies and gentlemen,

Welcome aboard China Southern Airlines!

Your seat numbers are indicated on the edge of the overhead bin. Please take your assigned seats.

Your carry-on baggage can be placed in the overhead bin or under the seat in front of you. For the convenience of other passengers, please keep the aisle clear. (We hereby remind you that the ××× device is banned for transport either in carry-on baggage or checked baggage.)

Thank you for your cooperation.

7. Boarding (China Eastern Airlines)

Ladies and gentlemen,

Please place your hand-carried items in the overhead compartment or under the seat in front of you. Please keep the aisle clear, and we will assist you if you need any help. Thank you.

8. Emergency Descending

Ladies and gentlemen,

There is an emergency decent. Please remain seated with your seat-belt securely fastened, stow your tray table and return your seat back to the upright position, and put your carry-on baggage under the seat in front of you.

Thank you for your cooperation.

第2章
客舱广播

章前导读

　　本章为客舱广播的分析篇。首先对客舱广播进行了概述，简析了客舱广播的重要性、特性以及技巧要素。然后根据客舱广播的内容及播报目的，将其分为客舱服务类广播和客舱安全类广播两大类，并分别介绍了其播报特点。同时，强调了客舱英语广播的播报质量在民航国际化大背景下的重要性。通过分类梳理各类典型的客舱广播词作为学习实例，帮助学生系统地认知各航段的广播并方便后期查阅；并且，每篇广播后均做了详细解释，包括相应的知识背景的拓展归纳，以帮助学生加深理解。最后是客舱广播词中常见篇章的练习汇总，通过对学习范例的进一步拓展，训练学生各情景下的客舱英语广播表达能力。

　　本章中对客舱广播重要性、分类及特点的理论介绍，旨在帮助学生理清知识结构，拓展知识脉络；通过对客舱英语广播实例的系统梳理、知识归纳与各情景下的拓展练习，旨在提高学生对客舱英语广播的系统认知和综合应用能力。

思政园地

　　青年学生肩负时代使命，既要高扬理想风帆，又要静下心来刻苦学习，努力练好人生和事业的基本功。客舱广播是乘务员的必备基本技能，教师应当引导学生励志勤学、刻苦磨炼，不断进行理论知识的学习和广播实例的操练，做到知行合一、育训结合。在客舱广播的教学中，既融入相关专业知识，又渗透爱国情怀，培养学生职业责任感、练就扎实的外语专业技能，传达出客舱服务广播的亲切热情和客舱安全广播的坚定沉稳。

第一节 客舱广播概述

　　客舱广播是乘务员在客舱服务工作中通过声音向乘客传达信息的一种方式。它作为乘务员客舱服务内容中的重要组成部分，也是客舱服务的重要窗口。优质的客舱广播可以给旅客带来舒适、安心的乘机体验，架起乘客和航空公司之间的沟通桥梁。客舱播音是信息服务的主要内容之一，是提高服务效率和服务质量、确保飞行安全的重要手段。

　　客舱广播不仅是对广播词的直接播送，更是一门情景再现的艺术，乘务人员通过语气、声调、节奏的运用来向乘客传达信息，并引起听众的共鸣。客舱广播员应在正确理解、准确把握广播词稿件的基础上，全身心地投入感情。一般来说，客舱播音要使用普通话、英语两种或两种以上语言，要求语音标准，内容准确，吐字清晰、流利。朗读广播词时，需做到语调生动，抓住播音内容的特点，节奏流畅和谐；用心感受乘客所需和环境特点，根据不同的内容传达不同的思想感情；声音亲切、自然，语速适中。通过播音，旅客可以明确而深切地感受到航空公司的服务精神、安全意识、工作效率和服务态度。

第二节 客舱广播技巧要素

　　客舱播音伴随整个航程，亲和温情、专业化的客舱广播可以给乘客带来良好的感受，也是航空公司对外展示服务形象的一张名片。良好的客舱播音主要有以下几个要素。

　　（1）标准的中英文发音。标准的发音是广播的基础，平时要注重发音技巧训练，准确流利的发音是完成优质广播的前提。

　　（2）适当的语气语调。朗读客舱广播词的语气、语调不是一成不变的，对不同类型、不同时间段的广播语气应适当调整。例如，欢迎词广播应亲切热情，安全类广播应坚定有力，夜航广播应适当降低音量，下降致意时应欢快并且适当升高音量等。

　　（3）适中的语速。客舱广播应运用适当均匀的语速来表达信息和传递感情，让乘客在乘机时有舒适的听觉体验。

通常，客舱广播根据其内容和播报目的可以分为服务类广播和安全类广播两大类。服务类广播按照飞行流程又包括起飞前、起飞后、平飞中、落地前、落地后、特殊情况等阶段广播，主要通过广播让乘客了解航班的航程、时间以及机上的服务项目。服务类广播的朗读要求语气亲切自然、舒缓热情。

安全类广播主要是对飞机上安全设备和安全措施以及注意事项进行介绍，包括起飞前的电子设备使用规范广播、安全示范广播、滑行提示广播，航行中的颠簸广播，落地前的安全检查、应急广播等。安全类广播的朗读要求语言庄重、规范、清晰、流畅，语气坚定沉稳。

服务类广播和安全类广播中又各自包含一些特殊情况处理和特情广播。前者包括专包机航班广播，它需要根据不同的乘客受众调整广播用语，使用恰当的表达。后者包括航班上遇到的各类应急和突发情况，它需要乘务员做到反应及时、应变到位，适时准确地做出判断，并对乘客做好解释安抚，播音要及时、有效，沉稳自若。

第四节　客舱英语广播的重要性

随着我国民航强国建设的推进和国际化进程的进一步深化，客舱英语广播也成了国际旅客服务的重要窗口。各航空公司对乘务员的英语广播资质也有相应考核，航司招聘也将英语广播作为常考项目。因而，各民航院校都将客舱英语广播作为必修的教学内容。广播的教学内容涵盖从登机到航班降落的整个航行过程，客舱英语广播的朗读技巧涉及爆破音、重音、连读、意群与停顿、节奏、语调、韵律等。教学中应注重对学生朗读的准确性和技巧性的训练与检测，引导学生准确深刻的理解广播内容，从而更好地展现朗读的情感表达技巧，实现学生语言基本技能训练与职业标准、岗位语言需求相对接，提升学生职场环境下广播词朗读的标准化、规范化水平，进一步帮助学生认识到民航客舱工作的重要性，从而培养其职业责任感和对职业的热爱，使其将来能够更好地展示航空企业文化形象。

第五节 客舱广播学习实例

一、客舱服务类广播（Cabin Service Announcement）

准确、流畅、亲和、温馨的客舱服务广播可以给乘客带来舒适的乘机体验，也能为航空公司赢得公众美誉。

（一）起飞前

飞机起飞前（prior to take-off）的服务广播主要包括登机广播、登机牌确认广播、欢迎词等。

1. 登机广播（Boarding）

Ladies and gentlemen,

Welcome aboard _____, a member of Star Alliance/Sky Team Associates/One World Affiliates. Your seat numbers are shown on the edge of the rack. Kindly stow all your carry-on baggage securely in the overhead bins or under the seats in front of you. Do not place them in the aisles or obstruct the emergency exits. Please take your assigned seats as quickly as possible and keep the aisles clear.

Thank you for your cooperation!

女士们，先生们：

欢迎搭乘星空联盟成员 / 天合联盟成员 / 寰宇一家成员 _____ 航空公司班机。您的座位号码位于行李架边缘。请将您所有的手提行李存放在行李架上或您前面座椅下方。请不要在紧急出口旁、过道上放置行李。找到座位的旅客请您尽快入座，保持过道通畅。

谢谢合作！

Notes

［1］登机广播的目的主要是问候乘客，并就乘客登机时有关对号入座和行李摆放等问题进行提示。广播时注意语气亲切自然，给乘客带来温馨的登机感受。

［2］登机广播开头通常使用 Welcome aboard 或者在 Welcome aboard 后面加上具体航空公司名称开头，如 Air China、China Eastern Airlines、China Southern Airlines、Juneyao Airlines、Spring Airlines 等，问候及欢迎乘客。

［3］Star Alliance/Sky Team/One World: 目前国际上的三大航空公司联盟——星空联盟、天合联盟、寰宇一家。

① Star Alliance（星空联盟）包括 Air China（中国国际航空）、Air Canada（加拿大航空）、All Nippon Airways（全日空航空）、Singapore Airlines（新加坡航空）、United Air（USA）（美国联合航空）、Lufthansa（德国汉莎航空）等航空公司。

② Sky Team（天合联盟）包括 Air France（法国航空）、Delta Air Lines（达美航空）、Korean Air（大韩航空）等航空公司。

③ One World（寰宇一家）包括 Cathay Pacific（国泰航空）、American Airlines（美国航空）、British Airways（英国航空）、Qantas（澳大利亚航空）、Qatar Airways（卡塔尔航空）等航空公司。

[4]"座位号显示在……"中的"显示"一词可以用 show、display、indicate 表示。

[5] 摆放行李可以使用 stow、store、put、place 等动词。

[6] carry-on baggage 指随身携带行李、手提行李，类似的表达还有 hand baggage、cabin baggage。

[7] 乘客登机后行李一般摆放在头顶上方行李架或是座椅下方。头顶上方行李架的表达有：overhead bin/locker/compartment/rack。

[8] assign:（v.）指定；assigned:（adj.）指定的。

[9] take one's seat 就座；take one's assigned seat 在指定的座位就座

[10] aisle:（n.）过道（本词的发音是难点，注意字母 s 不发音）。靠过道的座位：aisle seat；靠窗座位：window seat。

[11] obstruct:（v.）阻塞；近义词 block（v.）。

2. 登机牌确认广播（Boarding Pass Recheck）

Ladies and gentlemen,

This is _____ Airlines flight _____ (code-shared with _____ Airlines) from _____ to _____, (via _____). We will land at _____ Airport Terminal _____. And the aircraft is an Airbus 320 (Boeing 747/...). Please confirm your flight number on your boarding pass.

Thanks for your cooperation!

女士们，先生们：

您乘坐的是_____航空_____航班，由_____飞往_____（中途经停_____）。（本次航班与_____航空公司_____航班实施代码共享）。本次航班将停靠_____机场_____号航站楼。本架飞机机型为空客 320（波音 747/……）。请您再次核对一下您的登机牌。

感谢您的合作！

Notes

[1] 登机牌确认广播主要目的是防止乘客错乘。播音时应当注意航班号、起始地和目的地等信息应当清晰明确。

[2] code share: 代码共享或称联营航班，是现代航空业一种相当普遍的经营模式，有多家航空公司共同经营某一航线。目前国际上三大航空公司联盟——星空联盟、天合联盟及寰宇一家，最初都是由原本就有班号共同合作的航空公司组成联盟的核心集团，再逐渐吸收新伙伴而扩大至今日的规模。

[3] via: (*prep.*) 通过，经由。例如: The news reached me via my assistant. 那消息是通过我的助理转告我的。

[4] terminal: (*n.*) 候机楼，航站楼，或称 terminal building。通常机场里的 T1、T2、T3，指的就是 1 号航站楼、2 号航站楼、3 号航站楼。

[5] Airbus 320, Boeing 747，这些都是机型 (the type of the aircraft) 的表达。Airbus 320 读作 Airbus three twenty, Boeing 747 读作 Boeing seven four seven。

[6] confirm: (*v.*) 确认核对，同样也可以用 verify 表示此含义。

➡ 小知识 ⬅

这里对广播词中经常出现的几种数字类型的读法做出以下说明。

（1）机型（Type of Aircraft）读法如表 2-1 所示。

表 2-1　机型读法

机　　型	英语表述
A321	Airbus three twenty-one
A380	Airbus three eighty
A330-200	Airbus three thirty, two hundred
B737	Boeing seven three seven
B747-8	Boeing seven four seven dash eight
B777-200	Boeing triple seven, two hundred

（2）航班号（Flight Number）读法如表 2-2 所示。

表 2-2　航班号读法

航班号	英语表述
CA1315	CA one three one five
MU5085	MU five zero eight five / MU five o eight five
CZ327	CZ three two seven / CZ three twenty seven
CZ610	CZ six ten

（3）飞行距离（Flight Distance）读法如表 2-3 所示。

表 2-3　飞行距离读法

飞行距离	英语表述
1176km	one thousand one hundred and seventy-six kilometers
9030km	nine thousand and thirty kilometers
1508km	one thousand five hundred and eight kilometers

（4）时间（Time）读法如表 2-4 所示。

表 2-4　时间读法

时　　间	英语表述
00：00	twelve midnight/ at midnight
00：15	zero fifteen in the morning
07：10	seven ten a.m. /seven ten in the morning
10：00	ten a.m. /ten o'clock in the morning
12：00	twelve o'clock noon
12：15	twelve fifteen p.m. /fifteen past twelve at noon
15：30	three thirty p.m. /three thirty in the afternoon
15：55	five to four p.m. /five to four in the afternoon/three fifty-five p.m./ three fifty-five in the afternoon

对于 morning / afternoon / evening 一般按照如表 2-5 所示时间点进行定义。

表 2-5　时间点定义

时　　间	英语表述
00：00—12：00	morning
12：00—18：00	afternoon
18：00—24：00	evening

（5）日期（Date）读法如表 2-6 所示。

表 2-6　日期读法

日　　期	英语表述
1 月 1 日	January (the) first
2 月 2 日	February (the) second
3 月 3 日	March (the) third
4 月 15 日	April (the) fifteenth
5 月 28 日	May (the) twenty-eighth

（6）年份（Year）读法如表2-7所示。

表2-7　年份表示

年　　份	英语表述
2008 年	two thousand and eight
2010 年	two thousand and ten
2015 年	two thousand and fifteen
2020 年	two thousand and twenty

（7）温度（Temperature）读法如表2-8所示。

表2-8　温度读法

温　　度	英语表述
15℃	fifteen degrees Celsius
0℃	zero degrees Celsius
−8℃	minus eight degrees Celsius

3. 欢迎词（Welcome）

Announcement 1

Ladies and gentlemen,

Good morning (afternoon/evening).This is your chief purser/purser on this flight. We are honored to welcome you aboard Air China, a proud member of the Star Alliance. To all our Phoenix Miles members, it is a pleasure to see you again and we are looking forward to inviting more passengers to join our frequent flyer program. We wish you an enjoyable and comfortable experience on board. Our service will be provided 20 minutes after take-off and concluded 30 minutes before landing. For your safety, we recommend that you keep your seatbelt fastened in case of a sudden turbulence, even if the seatbelt sign goes off. Cabin Crew will stop all the cabin service 30 minutes before landing. In the meanwhile, the lavatories will be closed. Please feel free to contact us if you need any assistance during the flight.

Thank you.

女士们、先生们：

早上（下午／晚上）好！我是本次航班的乘务长，再次感谢您选乘星空联盟成员中国国际航空公司的航班。我们非常高兴和所有凤凰知音贵宾再次相见，并欢迎更多旅客加入国航常旅客计划。祝愿您有一段愉快而舒适的旅程。我们将在起飞后20分钟至着陆前30分钟，为您提供客舱服务。在飞行途中，会遇到不稳定气流，为了您的安全，即使安全带灯熄灭，也建议您全程系好安全带。飞机着陆前30分钟，我们将结束客舱服务，卫生间也将停止使用，如果您在航班中需要任何帮助，请与我们的乘务员联系。

谢谢！

Announcement 2

Ladies and gentlemen, members of "Eastern Miles",

Good morning (afternoon/evening/happy new year/...).Welcome aboard this flight of China Eastern Airlines, a member of Sky Team Alliance. This is your cabin manager/purser speaking.

Today is the first day of traditional Chinese Lunar New Year. With the arrival of this happy and peaceful festival, we the crew members give you our best regards. We wish everyone success, happiness and good health in the year of the Ox (Tiger/rabbit/long, etc.) . We believe that our blessing may bring you good luck in the New Year.

Meanwhile, I'd like to address thanks to the elite members of Eastern Miles. Your persistent support given to us is highly appreciated.

Our flight distance (from _____ to _____) is _____ KM, and the flying time is _____ hours and _____ minutes. We wish you a pleasant flight.

Thank you.

女士们、先生们、东方万里行会员们：

早上好(下午好 / 晚上好 / 新年好……)。欢迎您乘坐天合联盟成员中国东方航空班机。我是本次航班的客舱经理乘务长。

今天是大年初一，是中国传统的新春佳节。在这个喜庆祥和的节日里，我们全体机组成员向您致以最诚挚的问候！祝您牛年（虎年 / 兔年 / 龙年……）吉祥，万事如意，身体健康！愿我们的祝福，在新的一年里能给您带来好运！

同时，也感谢我们尊敬的"东方万里行"白金卡、金卡等常旅客会员们一直以来对东航的支持。

从_____到_____的飞行距离为_____，飞行时间大约需要_____。祝您旅途愉快！

谢谢！

Notes

[1]欢迎词广播一般是向乘客表示欢迎，节日时需加上节日问候。欢迎词中一般还会向乘客说明目的地、飞行时间、飞行距离等。

[2] purser：(*n.*) 乘务长，chief purser 主任乘务长，cabin manager 客舱经理

通常，乘务员的职业晋升路径（career path）为 cabin attendant-senior cabin attendant-purser-chief purser/cabin manager。

［3］Phoenix Miles: 国航的"凤凰知音"常旅客计划，为会员提供多种里程累积途径和可供兑换的奖品。

［4］Eastern Miles: 东航的"东方万里行"常旅客计划。

［5］frequent flyer program: 简称 FFP，常旅客计划，是指航空公司、酒店等行业向经常使用其产品的客户推出的以里程累积或积分累积奖励为主的促销手段，以吸引旅客持续选择其服务。几乎每家航空公司都有自己的常旅客计划，如前面提到国航的凤凰知音（Phoenix Miles），东航的东方万里行（Eastern Milestone），还有南航的明珠俱乐部（Sky Pearl Club），厦航的白鹭俱乐部（Egret Miles），美联航的前程万里（Mileage Plus）等。

［6］conclude:（v.）结束。例如: The program was concluded with a song. 节目在一首歌曲中结束。

［7］recommend:（v.）推荐，建议。例如: The committee has recommended that the training program (should) be improved. 委员会建议培训计划应当改进。

［8］assistance:（n.）协助。例如: I'm just glad to be of assistance. 我很乐意帮助你。

［9］Chinese Lunar New Year: 中国农历新年 / 春节，也可作 Spring Festival。

此处欢迎词中加入了节日祝福，一般来说一些重要节日需要广播节日祝福，如元旦（New Year's Day）、除夕（the New Year's Eve）、春节（正月初一至初五）（Spring Festival/Chinese New Year）、元宵节（Lantern Festival）、五一劳动节（Labor Day）、端午节（Dragon Boat Festival）、中秋节（Mid-Autumn Day）、国庆节（National Day）等。

［10］the year of the Ox: 牛年，中国十二生肖（Chinese Zodiac）的表达依次为: Rat、Ox、Tiger、Rabbit、Loong、Snake、Horse、Sheep、Monkey、Rooster、Dog、Pig。

［11］address:（v.）向……致辞，演说。例如: He addressed the audience in an eloquent speech. 他对听众讲起话来滔滔不绝。

［12］persistent:（adj.）持续的，不断的；也可作 continuous。例如: A persistent wind frustrated my attempt to rake the lawn. 持续不停的风阻碍了我整理草坪的打算。

➡ 小知识 ⬅

一、欢迎词广播中的节日贺词（Festival Greetings）

1. 元旦（New Year's Day）

It is New Year's Day today and we have entered the year of the _____. Our crew members wish to give you all our new years regards. Thank you for your confidence in and support for _____. We wish you and your family good health and happiness in the New Year.

今天是元旦佳节，崭新的一年已经到来。我们全体机组成员向您致以新年的问候。感谢您在过去一年中，对_____的信赖和支持！衷心祝福您和家人，在新的一年里身体健康、阖家幸福！

2. 春节（Chinese Lunar New Year / Spring Festival）

Today is the first day of traditional Chinese Lunar New Year or the Spring Festival. With the arrival of this happy and peaceful festival, we the crew members give you our best regards. We wish everyone success, happiness and good health in the year of _____. We trust our blessing may bring you good luck in the New Year.

今天是大年初一，是中国传统的新春佳节。在这个喜庆祥和的节日里，我们全体机组成员向您致以最诚挚的问候！祝您_____年吉祥，万事如意，身体健康！愿我们的祝福，在新的一年里能给您带来好运！

3. 元宵节（Lantern Festival）

Today is January 15th in the Chinese lunar calendar. It is the Chinese traditional Lantern Festival. On behalf of the entire crew here extends our sincere greetings to you. We wish you a good holiday!

今天是农历正月十五，是我国传统的佳节"元宵节"。元宵代表着团圆、美满；在此，我谨代表机组全体人员为您送上真诚的祝福，祝您假期愉快！

4. 三八妇女节（International Women's Day）

Today is the International Women's Day, a festival for all women. We, the crew members give our sincere regards to all female passengers. We wish you good health and happiness.

今天是三八国际妇女节，是属于广大女性的节日。我们全体机组成员特别向今天航班中的女性朋友们致以衷心的问候！祝您健康、美丽、快乐！

5. 五一国际劳动节（International Workers' Day）

Today is the International Workers' Day, a festival for all workers. We, the crew members, give our highest respects and festive greetings to all of you. We wish you and your families a pleasant and enjoyable holiday.

今天是五一国际劳动节，是所有劳动者的节日。我们全体机组成员向大家致以崇高的敬意和节日的问候！祝您和家人，度过一个轻松、愉快的假期！

6. 五四青年节（Youth Day）

Today is May 4th, Youth Day in China. Youth is the most exciting and wonderful chapter in our lives. We would like to extend our festive greetings to the young friends onboard, and wish all our passengers' everlasting youth. We hope that you will enjoy our service during the flight!

今天是五四青年节。青春，是人生乐章里最动人的华彩，是人生书卷里最美妙的篇章。在此，我们特别向航班上的各位青年朋友致以节日的问候，并祝愿所有的旅客朋友们青春永驻，梦想成真。愿我们的服务温暖您的旅途！

7. 母亲节（Mother's Day）（5月的第二个星期日）

Today is Mother's Day, a common and yet great holiday. As an ancient Chinese poem goes, "who says mine heart like a blade of grass, could repay her love's gentle beams of spring sun." We would like to extend our festive greetings to all the mothers onboard our flight today and wish all mothers in the world good health and happiness!

今天是母亲节，一个平凡而又伟大的节日。"谁言寸草心，报得三春晖"。在此，我们特别向今天航班上的妈妈们致以节日的问候，愿天下所有的母亲健康快乐，永远幸福！

8. 六一儿童节（International Children's Day）

Today is the International Children's Day, a festival for all children. We give our best regards to all children on this aircraft. We wish you health and happiness every day.

今天是六一国际儿童节，是所有小朋友们的节日。我们祝今天航班上的各位小朋友节日快乐！希望各位小朋友健康、快乐地成长！

9. 端午节（Dragon Boat Festival）

In Chinese lunar calendar, today is May 5th. It is the Chinese traditional festival, the Dragon Boat festival. On behalf of the entire crew here extends our sincere greetings to you.

今天是农历五月初五端午节，是中国的传统节日，又名龙舟节。在此，我谨代表机组全体人员祝大家节日快乐。

10. 父亲节（Father's Day）（6月的第三个星期日）

Today is Father's Day. As a Chinese saying goes, "Father's love is as great as a mountain." We would like to extend our festive greetings to all fathers onboard our flight today, and wish all fathers in the world good health and all the best!

今天是父亲节。人们常说"父爱如山"。在此，我们特别向今天航班上的父亲们致以节日的问候，并祝愿天下所有的父亲身体健康，顺心顺意。

11. 八一建军节（Army Day）

Today is August 1st, Army Day. We the crew members are sending our greatest respect and highest regards to all active army and retired veterans on this aircraft.

今天是八一建军节，我们全体机组成员向今天航班上所有的现役军人和退役老兵致以崇高的敬意和节日的问候！

12. 教师节（Teachers' Day）

Today is Teacher's Day. We the crew members are sending our greatest respect and highest regards to all educators. We wish you all the best with your work and good health.

今天是教师节。我们全体机组成员向今天航班上所有的教育工作者致以深深的敬意和节日的问候！祝老师们工作顺利、身体健康！

13. 中秋节（Mid-Autumn Day）

Today is the traditional Mid-Autumn Day. We the crew members are giving you our best regards on this family reunion day. We wish you and your family happiness and prosperity!

今天是中华民族的传统佳节——中秋节。在这个阖家团圆的日子里，我们全体机组成员向您致以节日的问候！祝您和家人阖家欢乐、幸福平安！

14. 国庆节（National Day）

Today is the ×× anniversary of the founding of our great motherland. On this day, when the whole country is celebrating this festival, let's show our best wishes to our country. We hope our country will continue to be peaceful and prosperous. We also wish you and your family an enjoyable and memorable vacation.

今天是我们伟大祖国成立××周年的纪念日。在这举国欢庆的日子里，让我们一起衷心祝愿祖国——国泰民安、繁荣富强！祝您和家人度过一个轻松愉快，难以忘怀的假期！

15. 重阳节（Double Ninth festival）（农历九月九日）

Today is the traditional Chinese Chongyang Festival, or Double Ninth Festival, a holiday for all senior citizens. In this golden autumn season, we sincerely wish all the senior citizens onboard good health and longevity, and wish all the passengers well-being and happiness.

We hope that our service will give you a pleasant journey!

今天是中华民族的传统佳节——重阳节，一个属于老年人的节日。在这秋高气爽的季节里，我们衷心祝福航班上的各位爷爷奶奶健康长寿，并祝愿所有的旅客朋友们幸福平安。

愿我们的服务温暖您的旅途！

二、起飞前的特殊情况（Special Situations Prior to Take-off）

（一）航班延误（Delay）

Ladies and gentlemen,

We are sorry to inform you, (①~⑬), our departure will be delayed. A / B, On behalf of _____ Airlines, we apologize for any inconvenience and thank you for your patience.

① due to air traffic control at ××× Airport;

② due to congestion on the runway;

③ due to unfavorable weather conditions at ××× Airport (heavy fog/thunderstorm/heavy rain/typhoon/heavy snow/ice storm);

④ due to bad weather on our route;

⑤ due to late arrival some (transit) passengers;

⑥ due to additional meal loading;

⑦ due to mechanical trouble /technical reasons;

⑧ due to baggage loading /overweight cargo;

⑨ due to loading documents haven't been sent to the aircraft;

⑩ due to deicing of the aircraft / the runway;

⑪ due to completion of refueling;

⑫ due to an oil leak;

⑬ as some passengers have not boarded the aircraft, the ground staff must now remove their luggage from the hold.

A. Please remain seated. We will keep you informed;

B. You are kindly requested to disembark with all your hand baggage./Your hand baggage may be left onboard, but please take valuables with you. Please follow our ground staff to the waiting lounge where re-boarding information will be announced.

女士们、先生们：

非常抱歉地通知您，由于（①~⑬），飞机暂时不能起飞。A/B，对于本次航班延误给您带来的不便，我们_____航空向您深表歉意。感谢您的耐心等待。

① 交通管制；

② 跑道拥挤；

③（大雾／雷雨／暴雨／台风／大雪／冰雹）×××机场天气条件不合适；

④航路天气；

⑤部分（中转）旅客尚未登机；

⑥临时加餐；

⑦机械故障；

⑧行李装载（等待装货）；

⑨机载文件未到；

⑩飞机／跑道需要除冰；

⑪飞机加油；

⑫飞机漏油；

⑬有旅客未登机，地面人员正在卸下他们的托运行李。

A. 请您在座位上休息等候，有消息我们将立刻通知您；

B. 请您带好所有手提行李／您的手提行李可以放在飞机上，但贵重物品请您随身携带好，跟随我们的地面工作人员到候机室休息等候，再次登机信息将会广播通知。

Notes:

［1］inform:（v.）告知。

［2］apologize for: 为……感到抱歉，也可以用 be sorry for。

［3］air traffic control: 航空交通管制。等待航空管制的起飞指令可以用 wait for the take off clearance。

［4］inconvenience:（n.）不便 convenience 的反义词。

［5］en route: 在途中。

［6］transit passengers: 中转旅客。

［7］deicing:（n.）除冰。

［8］ground staff: 地勤人员。

［9］disembark:（v.）下机。也可以用 deplane、get off the plane。

［10］waiting lounge: 候机室，也可以用 airport lounge、waiting room、departure lounge。

一般来说，飞机延误可以分为航空公司原因和非航空公司原因两大类。

1. 航空公司原因

（1）机械故障（舱门、空调、APU 故障）。

Due to technical problem (aircraft door malfunction /air conditioner malfunction / APU malfunction).

（2）工作人员正在排除飞机故障，请您在机上耐心等候。

Because our engineers are solving/dealing with the technical problem now. / Passengers are required to stay on board.

（3）货物（行李）装载。

Due to cargo（luggage）loading.

（4）临时增加食品/等候食品装载。

Due to (additional) meal loading.

（5）飞机调配（临时更换飞机）。

Due to relocation (change) of the aircraft.

（6）飞机晚到。

Due to late arrival of the incoming aircraft.

2. 非航空公司原因

（1）天气原因包括以下4类。

① 航路天气状况不佳。

Due to bad weather conditions on our scheduled route.

② 机场上空天气状况不佳（浓雾/雷雨/暴风雨/暴风雪/沙尘暴）。

Due to a dense fog/thunderstorm/heavy rainstorm/snowstorm/sandstorm in the surrounding area of the airport.

③ 机身（跑道上）有冰雪需清除。

Due to de-icing the aircraft (runway).

④ 等待除冰车。

Due to waiting for a de-icer.

（2）机场原因包括以下3类。

① 罢工。

Due to a strike at ＿＿＿＿＿ (airport).

② 因排队的飞机较多，我们正在等待起飞的命令。

Due to lining up for take-off clearance.

③ 跑道需清除杂物或零件。

Due to waiting for the runway to be cleared of barrier (or stray part).

（3）边防原因包括以下3类。

① 由于边防（移民局）人员未到，无法开门下客。

Due to waiting for inspection of immigration officer.

② 由于几位旅客的护照问题。

Due to some passengers' disembarkation for passport reason.

③ 由于飞机离港文件不全。

Due to waiting for take-off document.

（4）旅客原因包括以下 5 类。

① 旅客临时取消行程，基于安全原因，必须卸下托运行李。

Because a passenger cancelled journey, we need to off-load the checked baggage for security reasons.

② 等待旅客。Due to the late arrival of connected passengers.

③ 旅客人数与舱单不符。Due to confirming the number of passengers on board.

④ 机场繁忙，部分旅客还未能通过安全检查 / 边防检查。

Due to congestion in the (security/ immigration) area, some passengers have not passed the security check / border inspection.

⑤ 行李架空间有限，需为旅客办理机上行李托运手续。

Because some of passengers' luggage is required to be checked-in on board as the overhead compartment space is very limited.

（二）航班取消（Cancel）

Ladies and gentlemen,

We are sorry to inform you that our flight is cancelled due to _____. Please take all your hand luggage with you including boarding pass, valuables and travel documents. Make sure you have nothing left onboard.

If you need any assistance, please contact our ground staff after disembarkation. We apologize for the inconvenience caused and thank you for your understanding.

女士们、先生们：

非常抱歉地通知您，由于 _____，本次航班被迫取消。请所有旅客携带全部手提行李下机，包括您的登机牌、贵重物品、旅行证件。请确认（您的座位上、椅袋中、头顶上方的行李架里）没有遗留任何个人物品（后再下机）。

如果您需要任何帮助，请联系我们的地勤人员。

由此带来的不便，我们深表歉意，感谢您对我们工作的理解。

Notes:

[1] We regret to inform you that... 很抱歉地通知您……

同样也可以用 We are sorry to inform you that... 来表达类似的含义。

［2］cancel:（*v.*）取消。

［3］disembarkation:（*n.*）下机。

（二）起飞后

在飞机起飞后的平飞阶段,乘务员要使用广播向乘客介绍航线信息以及飞行途中的相关注意事项与提供的餐饮、娱乐、免税品销售等各项服务。此部分广播词的朗读注意态度亲切、热情。

1. 航线及服务介绍（Route and Service Introduction）

Announcement 1

Ladies and gentlemen,

Welcome aboard _____.

Our plane has departed from _____ to _____. The distance between _____ and _____ is _____ kilometers and the estimated flight time is _____ hour(s) and _____ minutes.

A. DOMESTIC

We expect to arrive at our destination at approximately _____ (a.m./p.m.).

B. INTERNATIONAL

There is a _____ hour time difference between _____ and _____. We are expected to arrive at our destination at approximately _____ (a.m./p.m.) on _____ (date) local time.

This is a non-smoking flight. Smoking or using e-cigarettes anywhere in the aircraft is against the law. For your safety, please always keep your seatbelt fastened while seated in case of turbulence.

(In a few moments, our cabin crew will be offering you mineral water/mineral water and hot drinks/hot and cold drinks, as well as breakfast/ lunch/dinner/light meal/ snack/ refreshment.)

We wish you a pleasant journey.

Thank you!

女士们、先生们:

欢迎您选乘_____。

我们的飞机已经离开_____前往_____,由_____到_____的飞行距离是_____千米,预计空中飞行时间_____小时_____分钟。

A. 国内

预计到达的时间为_____点_____分（上午/下午）。

B. 国际

与_____的时差为_____小时，我们预计在当地时间星期_____（上午／下午）

_____点到达。

我们的航班全程禁止吸烟，包括电子香烟。在飞行途中，会遇到不稳定气流，为了您的安全，请在座位上休息时，系好安全带。

（稍后，我们的乘务员将会为您提供矿泉水／矿泉水和热饮／多种冷热饮料和早餐／午餐／晚餐／轻正餐／小吃／点心。）

我们愿您度过一段愉快的旅程。

谢谢！

Announcement 2

Ladies and gentlemen,

We have left _____ for _____. Along this route, we will be flying over the provinces of _____, passing the cities of _____, and crossing over the _____. Breakfast (lunch, supper) has been prepared for you. We will inform you before we serve it.

Now we are going to introduce the use of the cabin installations. This is a ×× aircraft. The back of your seat can be adjusted by pressing the button on the arm of your chair. The call button and reading light are above your head. Press the call button to summon a flight attendant. The ventilator is also above your head. By adjusting the airflow knob, fresh air will flow in or be cut off. Lavatories are located in the front of the cabin and in the rear. Please do not smoke in the lavatories.

女士们、先生们：

我们的飞机已经离开_____前往_____，沿这条航线，我们飞经的省份有_____，经过的主要城市有_____，我们还将飞越_____。我们为您准备了××餐。供餐时我们将广播通知您。

下面将向您介绍客舱设备的使用方法：今天您乘坐的是××型飞机。您的座椅靠背可以调节，调节时请按座椅扶手上的按钮。在您座椅的上方备有阅读灯开关和呼叫按钮。如果你有需要乘务员的帮助，请按呼唤铃。在您座位上方还有空气调节设备，你如果需要新鲜空气，请转动通风口。洗手间在飞机的前部和后部。在洗手间内请不要吸烟。

Notes

[1] depart:（v.）出发，离开；departure:（n.）离开，出发。与之相对应的表示"到达"的表达 arrive（v.）和 arrival（n.）。

〔2〕the estimated flight time: 预计飞行时间。EDT（=Estimated Departure Time）预计起飞时间；EAT（=Estimated Arrival Time）预计到达时间。

〔3〕approximately:（*adv.*）大约。

〔4〕time difference: 时差。

〔5〕local time: 当地时间。

〔6〕e-cigarettes: 电子香烟。

〔7〕be against the law：违规，违法。也可以用 violate the law 来表达。

〔8〕turbulence:（*n.*）颠簸；turbulent:（*adj.*）颠簸的。

〔9〕mineral water：矿泉水。

〔10〕餐饮表达：早餐—breakfast，午餐—lunch，晚餐—dinner，夜宵、快餐、点心—refreshment，轻正餐—light meal，小吃—snack。

〔11〕leave... for...: 离开……去……（for 后面加目的地）。

〔12〕route:（*n.*）路线，航线。

〔13〕cabin installations: 客舱设备，也可以用 cabin facilities 表达。

〔14〕adjust:（*v.*）调节，调整；类似表达 regulate（*v.*）。

〔15〕call button: 呼唤铃。

〔16〕reading light: 阅读灯。

〔17〕summon:（*v.*）召唤，也可以用 call 表达。

〔18〕ventilator:（*n.*）通风口。

〔19〕knob:（*n.*）旋钮。注意词组的搭配: turn the knob 旋转旋钮，press the button 按压按钮。

〔20〕rear:（*n.*）尾部。

2. 餐前广播（Announcement Before Meal Service）

Ladies and gentlemen,

We will be serving breakfast lunch/dinner/light meal/snack/refreshment...）soon. Today, we offer choices of _____ and _____.

Meanwhile, we will offer you cold and hot drinks and wine. For your convenience, please put down your tray table and adjust your seat back to the upright position during the meal service.

Thank you.

女士们、先生们:

我们将为您提供早餐（午餐/晚餐/夜宵/轻正餐/小吃/快餐/点心），主菜种类有_____和_____。

同时还将为您提供冷热饮料及葡萄酒。为了方便您和他人用餐，请放下小桌板，调直座椅靠背。

谢谢。

Notes

adjust your seat back to the upright position 将座椅靠背调直，同样含义的表达还有 straighten your seat back，return your seat back to the upright position。相反，休息时将座椅靠背倾斜放倒的表达为 recline the seat back。

3. 机上娱乐（In-flight Entertainment）

Ladies and gentlemen,

Now we will be showing programs such as film, music and others. We hope you will enjoy them.

Please use the headsets in the seat pocket in front of you. Choose the channel that corresponds with the programs that you wish to watch. You may ask your cabin attendants for assistance.

Thank you!

女士们、先生们：

现在我们将为您提供电影、音乐及其他机上娱乐节目，希望您能喜欢。

您可以使用前方座位口袋里面的耳机，并选择您想要收看节目的相应频道。若需要帮助，您可以咨询乘务员。

谢谢！

4. 免税品销售（国际航班）（Duty-free Sale (International Flights)）

Ladies and gentlemen,

We will soon be offering the in-flight duty-free items, which include cigarettes, wines and spirits, cosmetics, gifts and other items. For more details, please refer to the Duty-Free Shopping Guide in the seat pocket in front of you.

All items are priced in US dollars. Please check with the flight attendants for prices in other currencies. Most major currencies and US dollar, traveler's checks are accepted for your purchases. The major credit cards are also accepted.

Thank you!

女士们、先生们：

现在将进行免税品销售，有香烟、葡萄酒、烈酒、化妆品、礼品及其他物品。更多详情可在您前方座椅口袋中的免税品购物指南中查阅。

所有产品均以美元标价，若您想了解其他货币标价，请咨询乘务员。大多数主要货币和美元，旅行支票都可以用在您的购买中。主要的信用卡也可以接受。

谢谢！

Notes

［1］duty free items: 免税品。例如：Generally speaking, duty free items on board include tobacco and liquor, luxurious items, make-up/cosmetics, jewelry, souvenir. 一般机上免税品包括烟酒、奢侈品、化妆品、珠宝、纪念品这几大类。

［2］Duty Free Shopping Guide: 免税品购物指南。类似含义的表达还有 catalog/inventory/brochures of duty free items 等。

［3］Usually the following currencies in cash can be used to buy duty-free commodities: USD, Euro, Korean Won, Japanese Yen, Australian Dollar, British Pound, Canadian Dollar, CNY, Hong Kong Dollar, Swiss Franc as well as Singapore Dollar. 大多数情况下，机上免税品销售可接受的货币主要有：美元、欧元、韩元、日元、澳元、英镑、加元、人民币、港币、瑞士法郎、新加坡元等。汇率的英文表达为：exchange rate。

［4］traveler's check: 旅行支票。

［5］credit card: 信用卡。

［6］不同支付方式的表达方式：pay in cash（现金支付）、pay by credit card（信用卡支付）、pay by WeChat/Alipay（微信 / 支付宝支付）。

5. 入境及海关规定（Entry Documents）

Ladies and gentlemen,

For your convenience, we'll be showing you a video to help to complete the immigration form. After the video, we will distribute immigration and customs forms. Both forms need to be completed prior to arrival and submitted when going through Customs and Immigrations.

All Chinese citizens include mainland citizens, Hong Kong, Macao and Taiwan residents and Overseas Chinese need not complete entry forms.

But all passengers need to declare the flight number and show the officials the tickets or boarding pass when going through immigrations.

Thank you.

女士们、先生们：

为了方便您办理入境手续，现在播放"入境指南"录像节目。请您注意收看后，在飞机落地前填好入境卡和申报单，落地后交给移民局和海关检查站。

所有中国公民（包括内地居民、香港居民、澳门居民、台湾居民及华侨）入境免填入境登记卡。

但所有旅客在办理入境手续时，需主动说明所乘航班班号，并请保留机票或登机牌，以便核准。

谢谢。

Notes

[1] immigration form: 入境表。同样含义的表达还有 entry form。

[2] distribute: (*v.*) 分发。

[3] customs form: 申报表。同样含义的表达还有 declaration form。

➡ 小知识 ⬅

Special Situations After Take-off 起飞后特殊情况

1. 寻找医生（Request for Medical Assistance/Call for a Doctor）

Ladies and gentlemen,

We have a passenger for urgent medical assistance. If you are medical personnel, please kindly contact our flight attendant. Thank you.

女士们、先生们：

现在飞机上有一位乘客需要紧急医疗救护。如果您是医务人员，请您与乘务员联系。谢谢。

Notes:

[1] urgent: (*adj.*) 紧急的；副词形式为 urgently。

[2] medical assistance: 医疗救护。

[3] medical personnel: 医务人员。

2. 失物招领（Lost and Found）

Ladies and gentlemen,

May I have your attention, please? If any passenger has lost a _____ (in the terminal/at the security check point/in the cabin/in the lavatory), please contact the cabin crew immediately. Thank you.

女士们、先生们：

请注意：哪位旅客在_____（候机厅、安检口、客舱内、前／中／后舱洗手间）遗失了_____，请与客舱乘务员联系。谢谢。

Notes:

security check point: 安检口。

3. 系统故障（System Malfunction）

Ladies and gentlemen,

As our entertainment system is unstable, we are going to reboot the system. It will take about ××× minutes. We sincerely apologize for the inconvenience and thank you for your understanding.

As our entertainment system is out of service, we are unable to provide you with movie programs. sincerely apologize for the inconvenience and thank you for your understanding.

Due to malfunction of the water system, we are unable to provide you with hot beverage, as well as water supply in lavatories. sincerely apologize for the inconvenience and thank you for your understanding.

女士们、先生们：

由于娱乐系统不稳定，我们需要重新启动系统，大约需要等待×××分钟。非常抱歉带给您不便，也谢谢您的谅解。

由于娱乐系统故障，我们无法为您（继续）播放影片。非常抱歉带给您不便，也谢谢您的谅解。

由于机上供水系统出现故障，我们无法为您提供热饮及洗手间用水。非常抱歉带给您不便，也谢谢您的谅解。

Notes:

［1］unstable:（*adj.*）不稳定的。

［2］reboot:（*v.*）重新启动。

［3］out of service: 故障，失效。

［4］malfunction:（*n.*）故障，例如: Results have been delayed owing to a malfunction in the computer. 由于计算机发生故障，计算结果推迟了。

（三）着陆前

飞机着陆前（before landing）的广播主要介绍目的地机场的到达时间、天气、温度等。同时提醒乘客准备着陆时的安全事项以及下机后根据天气增减衣物。广播时注意语气亲切温和，一些重要信息播报务必做到清晰明确。

1. 着陆前预报时间和下降致谢（Time & Descending）

Ladies and gentlemen,

We will be arriving at _____ airport in 20/30 minutes. Our flight will be parking at Terminal _____. There is _____ hour time difference between _____ and _____. The local time in _____ is _____ a.m./p.m. on _____ (date). The ground temperature is _____ degrees Celsius, or _____ degrees Fahrenheit. Before disembarkation, you may change your clothes according to the outside temperature.

We will start to descend shortly. Thank you for your support and cooperation during the flight. Please fasten your seat belt, open the window shade, put the tray table in place, bring your seatback upright and unplug your headphones and electronic devices. Please make sure the large portable electronic devices are stowed properly. The lavatories will be closing soon.

(night flight) We will now dim the cabin light. If you would like to read, we suggest you using your reading light.

On behalf of the entire crew, we would like to thank you for your support and cooperation during the flight.

Thank you.

女士们、先生们：

飞机大约在20/30分钟后到达_____机场，并停靠在____号候机楼。_____与_____的时差为_____小时，当地时间是星期_____上午（下午）_____点。地面温度为_____℃，_____℉。（下机前，您可根据室外温度适当调整衣物。）

飞机即将开始下降。感谢各位旅客在这段旅途中给予我们的支持和配合。现在，请您系好安全带，打开遮光板，收起小桌板，调直椅背，取下耳机以及连接在座椅电源上的数据连接线，妥善存放笔记本电脑等大型便携式电子设备。机上洗手间将停止使用。

（夜航）：稍后我们将调暗客舱灯光，需要阅读的旅客，建议您打开阅读灯。我们全体机组成员对您在旅途中给予的支持和配合，表示最诚挚的谢意。

谢谢！

> ### Notes
>
> ［1］park:（v.）停靠。
>
> ［2］ground temperature: 地面温度。
>
> ［3］Celsius:（n.）摄氏度，同 Centigrade，符号 ℃。

Fahrenheit: 华氏度，符号为℉。

温度转换计算公式：

$$℉ =（℃×9/5）+32 \ 或 \ ℃=（℉ -32）×5/9$$

［4］descend:（v.）下降，反义词为 ascend（v.）上升。

［5］unplug:（v.）拔出，反义词为 plug（v.）接上插头。

［6］stow properly: 妥善存放。

［7］dim:（v.）调暗。

2. 着陆前的景点介绍（Introduction of scenic spots before landing）

Ladies and gentlemen,

May I have your attention, please? After 2 hours and 30 minutes' flight, we will be arriving at Shanghai, one of the largest cities in China. Now please allow me to give you a brief introduction to Shanghai.

Shanghai is located on the eastern coastline of the East China Sea and at the south mouth of the Yangzi River. Tourist attractions include the unique classical garden Yu Garden, Longhua Scenic Spot known for its beautiful peach blossom and the Bund along Huangpu River.

Thank you!

女士们、先生们：

请注意，经过 2 小时 30 分钟的飞行，我们将抵达中国最大的城市之一上海。现在请允许我简单介绍一下上海。

上海位于东海东部海岸线上，位于长江南口。旅游景点包括独具特色的古典园林豫园、以美丽桃花著称的龙华风景区和黄浦江外滩。

谢谢！

➡ 小知识 ⬅

Special Situations Before Landing 着陆前的特殊情况

1. 返航 / 备降（Return/ Alternate Flight）

1）备降（降落站天气不好）（Diversion (bad weather at destination)）

Ladies and gentlemen,

We are sorry to inform you that due to unfavorable weather conditions over ____ airport, our final destination, we cannot land there for the time being. Therefore, the Captain has decided to divert to ____ airport and remain there until weather conditions improve. We will keep you informed of anything related to landing at this alternate airport. We expect to arrive there at ____.

We appreciate your understanding and cooperation.

女士们、先生们：

非常抱歉地通知您，由于降落站____机场天气不符合飞行标准，目前飞机无法降落，机长决定降落在____机场，待天气好转后再继续飞行。备降后的有关事宜，我们会随时通知您，飞机预计在____点____分到达____机场。

感谢您的理解与配合！

Notes:

[1] divert:(*v.*) 转移，备降。

[2] updated:(*adj.*) 更新的，得到最新信息的。

[3] alternate airport: 备降机场。

2）返航（Return to the Original Airport）

Ladies and gentlemen,

The captain has just informed us that due to ____ (mechanical problems/bad weather on the route/shutdown of the destination airport), we must return to ____ airport. We expect to land there at ____. Further information will be given to you as soon as possible. We apologize for any inconveniences caused and appreciate your understanding.

Thank you!

女士们、先生们：

我们刚刚接到机长的通知，由于____（飞机出现了一些机械故障/航路天气不符合飞行标准/降落站机场关闭），我们现在必须返回____机场，飞机预计将在____点____分到达。返航后的有关事宜，我们会随时通知您。由此给您带来的不便，我们深表歉意，请您予以谅解。

谢谢！

返航、备降的原因主要有以下几种。

（1）due to extreme weather condition/dense fog/thunderstorm/heavy rainstorm/snowstorm in the surrounding area of the airport /on route 由于天气状况不佳 / 浓雾 / 雷雨 / 暴风雨 / 暴风雪 / 航路天气状况不好

（2）due to technical problem 机械故障。

（3）due to strike in the ××× airport ××× 机场罢工。

（4）as a passenger on board needs an urgent medical assistance/as a lady on board is going into childbirth 由于机上有一位重病旅客 / 由于一位即孕妇将分娩

2. 空中盘旋（Holding/Circling）

Ladies and gentlemen,

This is your (chief) purser speaking. The Captain has just informed us that due to ____ (unfavorable weather conditions/low visibility/heavy traffic) at ____ airport, we have been ordered by Air Traffic Control to hold over ____ (city) until we receive clearance to continue. Further information will be provided as soon as available.

Thank you for your understanding and cooperation!

女士们、先生们：

现在是（主任）乘务长广播，我们刚刚接到机长的通知：由于____机场____（天气不好 / 能见度较低 / 空中交通繁忙），我们将按照空中交通管制要求在____上空盘旋，直到获得放行许可。进一步的消息，我们将随时通知您。

感谢您的理解与配合！

Notes:

［1］hold over...：在……上空盘旋，也可使用 circle over。

［2］receive clearance：获得放行许可。

3. 延误着陆（Delay in Arrival）

Ladies and gentlemen,

The captain has advised us that due to ____, our arrival time will be delayed about ____ (hours/minutes). We will keep you informed of our schedule.

Thank you.

女士们、先生们：

我们刚刚收到机长通知，由于____，本次航班将推迟落地时间，进一步的消息，我们将及时通知您 / 预计在____（小时 / 分钟）后到达。

谢谢。

Notes:

延误着陆的原因主要有空中管制（air traffic control）、航路有强顶风（strong head wind）等。

（四）着陆后

飞机着陆后（after landing）的广播主要介绍目的地情况（停靠的航站楼、天气温度等），中转航班还需告知乘客相关注意事项，国际航班需要提醒旅客办理出入境手续，要求广播时语气亲切；在着陆后的滑行阶段提醒乘客相关安全事项，语气要平和坚定；飞行完全停稳后提醒乘客不要遗忘行李、有序下机，语气要温和。

1. 国内终点着陆（Domestic Landing）

Ladies and gentlemen,

We have just landed at _____ airport, Terminal _____. The outside temperature is _____ degrees Celsius or _____ degrees Fahrenheit.

Kindly remain seated with your seatbelt fastened and make sure that your hand baggage is stowed properly until the seatbelt sign goes off, and please be careful when opening the overhead compartments, as items inside may fall out.

（HOLDING BOARDING PASS FOR CONNECTING FLIGHTS: For passengers transferring to international flights, please clear Immigration at this airport. In compliance with Chinese Customs regulations, you are subject to Customs Inspection with all your personal belongings. Please take all your belongings with you as any items left behind will be removed.）

Thank you for flying _____. It has been a pleasure looking after you. We hope to see you again soon.

Have a nice day/evening in _____. Good-Bye!

女士们、先生们：

我们刚着陆在_____机场。我们将在_____号候机楼进港。机舱外的温度_____℃，_____℉。

请继续留在座位上并系好安全带，确保您的手提行李妥善安放，直到安全带指示灯熄灭。当您提拿行李时，小心打开行李架，以免行李滑落。

（通程登机航班国内着陆：继续转乘国际航班的旅客，请您在本站办理出境手续。根据中国海关规定，请将您的手提行李带下飞机，接受海关检查。请将您的随身物品全部带走，否则将会被工作人员移走。）

全体机组成员再次感谢您选乘_____航空公司的航班。我们很荣幸与您共同度过了一段愉快的旅程，期待与您再次相会。

祝您在_____愉快，再见！

Notes

［1］domestic:（*adj.*）国内的。与 international 相对应。

［2］connecting flight: 转机航班。

［3］transfer to: 转机到……

[4] clear Immigration: 完成出入境检查。

[5] in compliance with: 按照, 遵照。

[6] be subject to: 受支配, 例如: These arrangements are subject to periodic reviews. 这几项安排须定期检查。

[7] personal belongings: 个人物品。

2. 国内中途着陆（Domestic Transit）

Ladies and gentlemen,

We have just landed at _____ airport, Terminal _____. The outside temperature is _____ degrees Celsius or _____ degrees Fahrenheit.

Kindly remain seated with your seatbelt fastened and make sure that your hand baggage is stowed properly until the seatbelt sign goes off, and please be careful when opening the overhead compartments, as items inside may fall out.

For passengers continuing on to _____, please disembark with all your hand luggage and take note of the boarding announcement in the departure hall. Please take all your belongings with you as any items left behind will be removed.

(We apologize for the delay of this flight and any inconvenience, and highly appreciate your patience and understanding.)

Thank you for flying _____, code shared with _____. It has been a pleasure being with you. We hope to see you again soon.

Have a nice day/evening in _____. Good-Bye!

女士们、先生们：

欢迎您来到_____机场。我们将在_____号候机楼进港。机舱外的温度_____℃,_____℉。

飞机还将滑行一段距离,为了您和他人的安全,请继续留在座位上并系好安全带,确保您的手提行李妥善安放,直到安全带指示灯熄灭。当您提拿行李时,小心打开行李架,以免行李滑落。

继续前往_____的旅客,请携带全部手提行李下机,等候广播通知再次登机,遗留在飞机上的物品,将被卸下飞机。

（由于航班延误,影响了您的行程,我们深表歉意,感谢您的耐心与谅解。）

全体机组成员再次感谢您选乘_____航空公司与_____航空公司代码共享的航班。我们很荣幸与您共同度过了一段愉快的旅程,期待与您再次相会。

祝您在_____愉快，再见！

3. 国际终点着陆（International Landing）

Ladies and gentlemen,

We have just landed at _____ airport, Terminal _____. There is a hour time difference between _____ and _____. The local time in _____ is _____ a.m./p.m. on _____（date）. The outside temperature is _____ degrees Celsius or _____ degrees Fahrenheit.

Kindly remain seated with your seatbelt fastened and make sure that your hand baggage is stowed properly until the seatbelt sign goes off, and please be careful when opening the overhead compartments, as items inside may fall out.

A. If your destination is _____, please claim your checked baggage and clear Immigration at this airport. All transit passengers should proceed to the transit lounge.

B. For passengers arriving from _____（a foreign city）, please proceed to the International Lounge to complete Customs procedures. For passengers arriving from _____（a domestic city）, please proceed to the Domestic Lounge.

（We apologize for the delay of this flight and any inconvenience, and highly appreciate your patience and understanding.）

Thank you for flying _____, code shared with _____. It has been a pleasure looking after you. We hope to see you again soon.

Have a nice day/evening in _____. Good-Bye!

女士们、先生们：

欢迎您来到_____机场。我们将在_____号候机楼进港。_____与_____的时差为_____小时，现在是_____（到达站）时间星期_____上午（下午）_____点_____分。机舱外的温度_____℃，_____℉。

请继续留在座位上并系好安全带，确保您的手提行李妥善安放，直到安全带指示灯熄灭。当您提拿行李时，小心打开行李架，以免行李滑落。

A.（直飞或出境终点站）到达_____的旅客，请在本站办理检疫、入境及海关手续。转乘其他航班的乘客，请到中转柜台办理中转手续。

B.（入境经停后到达终点站）由_____（海外城市）到达本站的旅客，请走国际厅，办理海关手续；由_____（国内城市）到达本站的旅客，请走国内厅。

（由于航班延误，影响了您的行程，我们深表歉意。）

全体机组成员再次感谢您选乘_____航空公司与_____航空公司代码共享的航班。我们很荣幸与您共同度过了一段愉快的旅程，期待与您再次相会。

祝您在＿＿＿＿愉快，再见！

4. 国内转国际经停 / 国际转国内经停（Domestic—International/International—Domestic）

Ladies and gentlemen,

We have just landed at airport, Terminal ＿＿＿＿＿. There is an hour time difference between ＿＿＿ and ＿＿＿. The local time in ＿＿＿ is ＿＿＿ a.m./p.m. on ＿＿＿ (date). The outside temperature is ＿＿＿ degrees Celsius or ＿＿＿ degrees Fahrenheit.

Kindly remain seated with your seatbelt fastened and make sure that your hand baggage is stowed properly until the seatbelt sign goes off, and please be careful when opening the overhead compartments, as items inside may fall out.

A. (Outbound flight): If your destination is ＿＿＿, please claim your checked baggage. For passengers continuing on to ＿＿＿, please disembark with all your hand luggage and proceed to clear Immigration. There will be boarding announcement in the departure hall. Please take all your belongings with you as any items left behind will be removed. If you are continuing your journey on another flight, please proceed to the transit lounge.

B. (Inbound flight): If your destination is ＿＿＿, please clear your Quarantine, Immigration, and Customs at this airport. For passengers continuing on to ＿＿＿, please disembark with all your hand luggage and proceed to clear Immigration and Quarantine. Please take all your belongings with you as any items left behind will be removed. There will be boarding announcement in the departure hall. You will clear Customs at our final destination. If you are continuing your journey on another flight, please proceed to the transit lounge.

（We apologize for the delay of this flight and any inconvenience, and highly appreciate your patience and understanding.）

★ For passengers continuing on to ＿＿＿ (city), there will be a crew change on arrival in ＿＿＿. On behalf of Captain and my team, I wish you a pleasant journey.

For passengers leaving us in ＿＿＿, it's been a pleasure looking after you on this flight. Thank you for flying ＿＿＿, code shared with ＿＿＿. We hope to see you again soon.

Have a nice day/evening in ＿＿＿. Good-Bye!

女士们、先生们：

欢迎您来到＿＿＿机场。我们将在＿＿＿号候机楼进港。＿＿＿与＿＿＿的时差为＿＿＿小时，现在是＿＿＿（到达站）时间星期＿＿＿上午（下午）＿＿＿点＿＿＿分。机舱外的温度＿＿＿℃，＿＿＿℉。

飞机还将滑行一段距离，为了您和他人的安全，请继续留在座位上并系好安全带，确保您的手提行李妥善安放，直到安全带指示灯熄灭。当您提拿行李时，小心打开行李架，以免行李滑落。

A. 去程：到达_____的旅客，请在本站领取交运行李。继续前往_____的旅客，请携带全部手提行李下机，在本站办理出境手续，等候广播通知再次登机。遗留在飞机上的物品，将被卸下飞机。如果您需转乘其他航班，请到中转柜台办理中转手续。

B. 回程：到达_____的旅客，请在本站办理检疫、入境及海关手续。继续前往_____的旅客，请携带全部手提行李下机，遗留在飞机上的物品，将被卸下飞机。请在本站办理入境及检疫手续，等候广播通知再次登机。海关手续将在_____（终点站）办理。如果您需转乘其他航班，请到中转柜台办理中转手续。

（由于航班延误，影响了您的行程，我们深表歉意，感谢您的耐心与理解。）

★继续前往_____的旅客，感谢您一路与我们同行，新的乘务组即将加入您的后续航程，祝您下一段旅途愉快。

在_____下机的旅客，全体机组成员再次感谢您选乘_____航空公司与_____航空公司代码共享的航班。我们很荣幸与您共同度过了一段愉快的旅程，期待与您再次相会。

祝您在_____愉快，再见！

Notes

[1] outbound flight: 离港航班，去程航班。inbound flight 为回程航班。

[2] claim: (v.) 认领，baggage claim area 行李认领区。

[3] checked baggage: 托运行李。

[4] proceed to: 继续。

[5] transit lounge: 过境休息室。

[6] clear your Quarantine, Immigration, and Customs: 办理检疫、入境及海关手续。

[7] crew change: 机组变更。

5. 国际转国际经停（International—International）

Ladies and gentlemen,

We have just landed at _____ airport, Terminal _____. There is a _____ hour time difference between _____ and _____. The local time in _____ is _____ a.m./p.m. on _____ (date). The outside temperature is degrees Celsius or _____ degrees Fahrenheit.

Kindly remain seated with your seatbelt fastened and make sure that your hand baggage is stowed properly until the seatbelt sign goes off, and please be careful when opening the overhead compartments, as items inside may fall out.

A. If your destination is _____, please clear Quarantine, Immigration, and Customs and claim your checked baggage at this airport. For passengers continuing your journey on another flight, please proceed to the transit lounge.

B. If you are continuing on to _____, please disembark with all your hand luggage and there will be boarding announcement in the departure hall. Please take all your belongings with you as any items left behind will be removed. There is no need to clear Immigration here.

(*Transit Passengers Remain On Board.*)

For passengers continuing on to _____ (city), please remain in your original assigned seats, our Cabin Crew will be conducting the cabin preparations. This flight is a non-smoking flight. When the aircraft being refueled, please do not use mobile phones or any other portable electronic devices, laptops must be switched off and stowed in the overhead compartments. Thank you for your cooperation.

Thank you for flying with us, there will be a crew change on arrival in _____ (port), and on behalf of Captain and my team, I wish you a pleasant onward journey.

For passengers leaving us in _____, it has been a pleasure looking after you. Thank you for flying _____, code shared with _____. We hope to see you again soon.

Have a nice day/evening in _____. Good-Bye!

女士们、先生们：

欢迎您来到_____（机场）。我们将在_____号候机楼进港。_____与_____的时差为_____小时，现在是_____（到达站）时间星期_____上午（下午）_____点_____分。机舱外的温度_____℃，_____℉。

飞机还将滑行一段距离，为了您和他人的安全，请继续留在座位上并系好安全带，确保您的手提行李妥善安放，直到安全带指示灯熄灭。当您提拿行李时，小心打开行李架，以免行李滑落。

A. 到达_____的旅客，请在本站办理检疫、入境及海关手续，并到国际到达大厅领取您的托运行李。如果您需转乘其他航班，请到中转柜台办理中转手续。

B. 继续前往_____的旅客，请携带全部手提行李下机，等候广播通知再次登机。遗留在飞机上的物品，将被卸下飞机。您无须在本站办理入境手续。

（*转乘旅客请在机上等候。*）

继续前往_____的旅客，请您在原位休息等候，我们将进行客舱准备工作，本次航班为禁烟航班。如果飞机进行地面加油程序，请您不要使用手机或任何其他便携电子设备，

手提电脑必须关机并放置在头顶上方的行李架内，请您予以配合。

感谢您一路与我们同行，新的乘务组即将加入您的后续航程，祝您下一段旅途愉快。

在_____下机的旅客，全体机组成员再次感谢您选乘_____航空公司与_____航空公司代码共享的航班。我们很荣幸与您共同度过了一段愉快的旅程，期待与您再次相会。

祝您在_____愉快，再见！

Notes

original assigned seats: 原来分配的座位，原座位。

6. 着陆后滑行时（Taxiing After Landing）

Ladies and gentlemen,

Our aircraft is still taxiing. For your safety and that of others, please remain seated with your seat belts securely fastened until the "Fasten Seat Belt" sign has been turned off. Please do not stand up or open the overhead bins.

Thank you for your cooperation!

女士们、先生们：

我们的飞机还将继续滑行一段时间，为了您和他人的安全，在"系好安全带"指示灯关闭之前，请您在座位上坐好并保持安全带系好的状态，不要站起身或打开头顶上方的行李架。

谢谢您的配合！

Notes

taxi:（v.）滑行。

7. 下机（Disembarkation）

Ladies and gentlemen,

The aircraft has come to a complete stop，please take all your personal belongings when you leave the aircraft. Please double check your seat, seat pocket and the overhead bins. We'll open the front (back/front and back) door(s). Please mind your steps when you disembark. We hope to see you again soon and thank you for flying with _____. Have a nice day!

Thank you！

女士们、先生们：

飞机已经停稳，请小心打开行李架，带好您的全部手提物品下机。请再次确认您的座椅上、座椅口袋中及头顶上方的行李架内没有遗留任何个人物品。稍后，我们将开启（前 / 后 / 前和后）登机门，请您下机时注意脚下台阶。再次感谢您乘坐_____航空公司的班机，我们下次旅途再会。祝您愉快！

　　谢谢！

Notes

mind one's step: 注意脚下台阶。

→ 小知识 ←

Special Situations After Landing 着陆后特殊情况

1. 等待停机位（未到位）（Delay (Parking Area)）

Ladies and gentlemen,

　　Due to the congestion of the airport, we will be making a brief stop while we wait for the parking area. Please remain in your seat and fasten your seat belt until further directed.

　　Thank you!

女士们、先生们：

　　由于机场繁忙，我们的飞机需在此等待停机位，稍后还将继续滑行。请您坐在座位上，不要解开安全带，等待进一步的指示。

　　谢谢！

Notes:

［1］congestion:（n.）拥堵。

［2］parking area: 停机位。

2. 等待摆渡车 / 客梯车 / 廊桥（Waiting for shuttle bus/ramp/boarding bridge）

Ladies and gentlemen,

　　As we are waiting for shuttle bus (ramp/boarding bridge) at the airport, you may take your seat and have a rest.

　　Thank you for your cooperation!

女士们、先生们：

　　由于_____机场的摆渡车（客梯车 / 廊桥）还没有到位，我们暂时还不能下机，请您在座位上休息等候。

　　感谢您的配合！

（五）特殊航班广播

在民用航空中，通常还有以下两种特殊航班（inaugural flight）。特殊航班上有独特的航班广播。

1. 首航（Inaugural Flight）

Ladies and gentlemen,

Welcome aboard the inaugural flight of _____, from _____ to _____.

Our flight distance is _____ km, and the flying time is _____ hours _____ minutes.

On this auspicious first flight we look forward to providing you a memorable and pleasurable experience onboard.

女士们、先生们：

欢迎您搭乘吉祥航空公司的航班，踏上_____至_____的首航之旅。

从_____至_____的飞行距离为_____千米，飞行时间大约需要_____时_____分。

在此吉祥首飞航班上，我们全体机组成员将竭诚为您提供服务，为您留下值得纪念的愉快航行。

Notes

［1］inaugural flight: 首航。例如：The A380 embarked on its inaugural flight in April 2005 to great fanfare. A380 于 2005 年 4 月开始了声势浩大的首航。

［2］auspicious:（*adj.*）吉祥的。例如：Fish should always be the last dish on the menu and it is particularly auspicious to have a little left over at the end. 鱼应该作为菜单上的最后一道菜并且最后剩下一些表示有余，会特别吉利。

2. 专机（Chartered Flight）

Your Excellency Chairman/President/Premier/Prime Minister _____, Ambassador _____, and all other members of the delegation,

Captain _____ and the entire crew are pleased to welcome you aboard _____ Airlines' special flight to _____, and we are honored to be at your service.

We wish you a pleasant journey! Thank you!

尊敬的_____主席 / 总统 / 总理 / 首相阁下、尊敬的_____大使、尊敬的代表团贵宾们：

您（们）好！本次航班的机长＿＿＿＿及机组全体人员热烈欢迎您乘坐＿＿＿＿航空公司专机前往＿＿＿＿，我们因能有机会为您服务感到非常荣幸。

祝您旅途愉快！谢谢！

Notes

［1］chartered flight：包机航班。

［2］Your Excellency：阁下。敬语，多用于外交场合。

［3］Chairman：主席；President：总统；Premier：总理；Prime Minister：首相。

二、客舱安全类广播（Cabin Safety Announcement）

安全是民航永恒的话题，也是航空公司的生命线，客舱安全类广播在朗读时需要准确无误，清晰明确，语气坚定。

（一）起飞前的安全广播

1. 电子设备使用规范（Electronic Devices Restriction）

Ladies and gentlemen,

Cabin doors have been closed. According to CAAC regulations, lithium power banks should be turned off. You may use your small portable electronic devices, such as mobile phones, after setting to airplane mode. Mobile phones without airplane mode, interphones and remote-control equipment are prohibited during the entire flight. Headsets and oversized laptop or tablet PC are prohibited in critical flight phases, such as taxiing, take-off, descent and landing. In order to ensure flight safety, cigarette and equivalent smoking are prohibited in this flight. Thank you！

女士们、先生们：

现在飞机舱门已经关闭。根据中国民航局规定，禁止使用锂电池移动电源，请您将电源始终关闭。小型便携式电子设备，如移动电话调至飞行模式后可全程使用。不具备飞行模式功能的移动电话、对讲机和遥控设备全程禁止使用。在滑行、起飞、下降和着陆等飞行关键阶段，禁止使用耳机和超过规定尺寸的手提电脑、平板电脑等设备。本次航班禁止抽吸香烟及同类产品，以确保飞行安全。谢谢！

Notes

［1］飞机上电子设备使用规范广播，主要目的是向乘客告知在飞行的各阶段电子设备的使用规定。一般电子设备被限制使用是为了避免干扰导航和通信设备(navigation and communication system）。

[2] CAAC: Civil Aviation Administration of China，中国民用航空局。

[3] lithium:（n.）锂元素。lithium power bank：锂电池充电宝。lithium battery：锂电池。

锂元素非常活跃，容易自燃，故不可在客舱使用，也不可以作为托运行李。

[4] airplane mode: 飞行模式，也作 flight mode。

[5] remote control equipment: 遥控设备。

[6] prohibit:（v.）禁止。类似表达如 forbid、not allowed 等。

[7] entire:（adj.）整个的。类似表达 whole。

[8] flight phase: 飞行阶段。例如: Usually the flight phases include taxiing-out, take-off, cruising, landing and taxiing-in. 通常飞行阶段有：滑出、起飞、巡航、降落、滑入。

[9] descent:（n.）下降。descent 的反义词是 ascent（上升）。

[10] equivalent:（adj.）相等的，相当的。（n.）对等的人（或事物）例如: It's our Greek equivalent of lasagne but nicer. 这是希腊式的千层面，但是更好吃。

2. 安全示范（Safety Demonstration）

Ladies and gentlemen,

Our cabin crew will now demonstrate the use of the life vest, oxygen mask and seatbelt, and show you the location of the emergency exits.

Your life vest is located in a pouch under your seat. When instructed to do so, remove it from the pouch, slip the life vest over your head.

Pass the straps around our waist and adjust at the front. Fasten the buckles and tighten it by pulling outwards.

To inflate the life vest, pull firmly on the red cord. Please perform this procedure only when leaving the aircraft.

To inflate further, blow into these mouthpieces.

Your oxygen mask is located in a compartment above your seat. It will drop automatically in case of decompression.

Pull the mask down firmly to activate the flow of oxygen.

Place the mask over your nose and mouth, and tighten it by pulling the end of the elastic strap. In a few seconds, the oxygen will begin to flow.

Your seatbelt contains two pieces. To fasten it, insert the metal fittings one into the other, and tighten it by pulling on the end of the strap.

Please keep your seatbelts securely fastened when seated.

There are _____ emergency exits on this aircraft. They are located in the front, the rear and the middle of the main cabin (and on the upper deck). Please do not touch the emergency operating handles unless specifically instructed by our crew members in the emergency situations.

The emergency indication lights are located along the aisle and at the exits. In the unlikely event of an evacuation, please follow the emergency indication lights to the nearest exit, and do not carry any hand luggage with you.

The safety instruction card is located in your seat pocket. Please read it carefully.

Thank you!

女士们、先生们：

现在客舱乘务员向您介绍救生衣、氧气面罩、安全带的使用方法和应急出口的位置。

救生衣在您座椅下面的口袋里，使用时取出，经头部穿好。

将带子从后向前扣好、系紧。

然后打开充气阀门，但在客舱内不要充气。

充气不足时，用嘴向人工充气管里充气。

氧气面罩储藏在您座椅上方，发生紧急情况时面罩会自动脱落。

氧气面罩脱落后，请用力向下拉面罩。

将面罩罩在口鼻处，把带子套在头上进行正常呼吸。

在您座椅上各有两条可以对扣起来的安全带，将带子插进带扣，然后拉紧。

当您就座时，请系好安全带。

本架飞机共有_____个应急出口，分别位于前部、后部、中部（及上舱），请不要随意拉动应急出口手柄。

在客舱通道上及出口处有应急照明指示灯，在应急撤离时按指示路线撤离，撤离时禁止携带任何行李。

在您座椅口袋里备有安全须知卡，请尽早阅读。

谢谢！

65

Notes

[1] 安全示范广播通常有乘务员进行同步动作示范，朗读时语言的速度需要与动作相配合，同时，关键信息需要重读。

[2] demonstrate:（*v.*）示范，演示。名词形式为：demonstration。

[3] pouch:（*n.*）袋子。

[4] waist:（*n.*）腰部。

[5] inflate:（*v.*）充气。名词形式为：Inflation。

[6] cord:（*n.*）绳子。

[7] automatically:（*adv.*）自动地。

[8] tighten:（*v.*）拉紧。

3. 后推后安全检查及口令（Safety Check and Command After Pushing Back）

Ladies and gentlemen,

As we are preparing for take-off, please put your seatback upright, **secure** your tray table and footrest, and put your armrests down. Please make sure that your seatbelt is securely fastened, and your window shades are fully open. All mobile phones must remain switched off or set to airplane mode. Portable electronic devices including laptops, tablets must be switched off and stowed properly throughout the flight. Meanwhile, lithium battery chargers must be turned off for the entire duration of this flight.

In case of an emergency, please follow the instructions given by our crew members. Do not carry your hand luggage with you during an evacuation. Cabin Crew, please start safety check.

Thank you!

女士们，先生们：

我们的飞机已经准备起飞，调直座椅靠背，放下座椅扶手，收起小桌板及脚踏板。请您系好安全带，打开遮光板，确认手机关闭或处于飞行模式，笔记本电脑、平板电脑等便携式电子设备关机并放置于行李架内或妥善存放。同时，全程禁止使用充电宝、锂电池移动电源为电子设备充电，并确保充电宝电源处在关闭状态。

为保证您和他人的人身安全，一旦发生紧急情况，所有旅客必须严格听从机组人员的指挥，在应急撤离过程中禁止携带任何行李，现在由乘务员进行客舱安全检查。

谢谢！

Notes

[1] secure:（*v.*）固定。

[2] lithium battery charger: 锂电池充电电源。

4. 安全员客舱安全广播（Broadcast about the Cabin Security by Safety Officer）

Ladies and gentlemen,

Attention, please! I am the security team leader of this flight. According to the requirements of the Civil Aviation Administration of China, it is my duty to inform all passengers of the cabin security of this flight.

According to the *Public Security Administration Punishments Law of the People's Republic of China* and the *Regulations of the People's Republic of China on Safety and Security of Civil Aviation*, you may be to fine penalty, security detention or even criminal punishment if you are caught with the following behaviours: damaging the on-board facilities and equipment, smoking, using mobile phones or other electronic equipment illegally, grabbing seats or luggage racks, interfering with flight attendants' work, and other behaviours that disturbs the normal order in the cabin.

According to relevant laws and regulations of the People's Republic of China, the passenger cabin is a public space, and will be subjected to audio and video collection.

Your cooperation and support are greatly appreciated. To ensure the safety of you and all other passengers, my team members and I, together with the entire crew, will perform our duties conscientiously. Thank you!

女士们、先生们：

大家好！我是本次航班的安全保卫组长。根据中国民用航空局的统一要求，现在进行客舱安全广播。

根据《中华人民共和国治安管理处罚法》和《中华人民共和国民用航空安全保卫条例》的有关规定，损坏机上设施设备、吸烟、违规使用手机和其他电子设备、抢占座位和行李架、干扰乘务组正常工作等扰乱客舱秩序的行为将会被处以罚款、治安拘留等处罚，严重者会被追究刑事责任。

同时，依据国家相关法律规定，飞机客舱为音视频采集公共区域。请您支持配合。

为了您和本次航班全体旅客的安全，我和我的组员及全体机组成员将认真履行安全职责，谢谢！

Notes

[1] security team leader: 安全保卫组长；security officer: 安全员。

[2] fine penalty: 罚款。

［3］detention:（*n.*）拘留。

［4］illegally:（*adv.*）非法地。

［5］interfere with: 干扰。

［6］audio and video: 音视频。

［7］perform one's duty: 履行职责。

5. 起飞前安全提醒（Safety Reminding for Takeoff）

Ladies and gentlemen,

As we are about to depart, please make sure that your seat belts are securely fastened.

Thank you!

女士们，先生们：

飞机很快就要起飞，请您再次确认您的安全带已扣好、系紧。

谢谢！

➡ 小知识 ⬅

Special Situations Prior to Take-off 起飞前特殊情况

1. 除冰（Deicing）

Ladies and gentlemen,

We have just been informed by the captain that our departure will be delayed, because ice may have formed on the aircraft due to the cold weather. The aircraft is now being deiced. There may be slight smell and smoke in the cabin. And it will be fine very soon, please don't worry and remain in your seats. We will keep you updated with any information as we receive it.

Thank you!

女士们、先生们：

我们刚刚接到机长通知，航班起飞将会推迟。因为天气寒冷，飞机上结冰了。目前，飞机正在除冰。舱内可能有轻微的气味和烟雾。我们将很快处理完成，请不用担心，请您坐在座位上不要走动。我们会随时向您告知最新消息。

谢谢！

Notes:

［1］deice:（v.）除冰。

［2］积冰的种类：clear ice（明冰）、rime ice（毛冰）、mixed ice（混合积冰）。

2. 飞机加油时的提示（Refueling）

Ladies and gentlemen,

May we have your attention, please? The aircraft is now being refueled. Mobile phones and other electronic devices are not allowed to be used. Laptops must be switched off and stowed in the overhead compartments. For your safety, please leave your seatbelt unfastened, remain in your seat and smoking is strictly prohibited. Kindly do not walk around in the cabin. Lavatories should not be used at this time. Thank you!

女士们，先生们：

请注意，由于飞机正在加油，请您不要使用手机等任何电子设备，手提电脑必须关机并放置在头顶上方的行李架内。为了您的安全，请解开安全带，并保持在座位上坐好。禁止吸烟。请不要在客舱内来回走动，卫生间暂停使用。谢谢！

Notes:

［1］refuel:（v.）加油。

［2］prohibit:（v.）禁止。

3. 因有旅客临时取消行程的清舱（Cabin Clearance Due to Last Minute Passenger Cancellation）

Ladies and gentlemen,

Due to last minute passenger cancellation, for security reasons, <u>A/B</u> , thank you for your cooperation.

A. (Passengers need not deplane) We will check the cabin now. Please assist the flight crew to identify your luggage.

B. (Passengers need to deplane) We will clear the cabin and cargo right now. Please take all your carry-on items and proceed to waiting hall. We will inform you to reboard after finishing thorough clearance.

女士们、先生们：

由于有旅客临时取消行程，为了飞行安全，<u>A/B</u> ，感谢您的理解与配合。

A.（旅客无须下机）我们将对客舱进行安全检查。请您协助确认行李。

B.（旅客需要下机）我们将对客舱和货舱进行清舱。请您带齐全部手提物品，到候机厅休息片刻。我们在完成清舱工作后将尽快通知您登机。

Notes:

[1] identify: (*v.*) 确认。

[2] cargo: (*n.*) 货物。

[3] thorough: (*adj.*) 完全的。

（二）起飞后的客舱安全广播

1. 飞行关键阶段客舱广播（飞机爬升阶段遇有旅客按呼唤铃时的广播）

Ladies and gentlemen,

As our aircraft is climbing, the cabin crew are not allowed to leave their jump seats. Lavatories cannot be used at this time. If you find anything abnormal about our flight safety, please press the call button continuously to inform us. If you need cabin service, we will attend to your call light in 20 minutes after takeoff.

Thank you for your understanding!

女士们，先生们：

由于飞机正处于爬升关键阶段（尚未达到巡航高度），很抱歉乘务员暂时不能离开座位，洗手间尚未开启使用。如果您需要向我们反馈与飞行安全有关的信息，请您连续按压呼唤铃；如果您需要客舱服务，请您保留呼唤铃，乘务员将在飞机起飞20分钟进入平飞阶段后，尽快回应您的呼叫。

感谢您的理解！

Notes

[1] jump seat: 乘务员座椅。

[2] observe: (*v.*) 观察到，注意到。

2. 检疫规定（通用）[Quarantine (General)]

Ladies and gentlemen,

Quarantine regulations of ×××(country) do not allow fresh fruit, flowers, meat products, dairy products or any other plant or animal products to be brought into the country. If any of those has been brought in to the flight, you can ask a flight attendant for help.

We'll now show you a video on "*Quarantine for Air Travelers*". Please watch the video carefully.

Thank you!

女士们、先生们：

按照×××（国家）的检疫规定，旅客不能携带水果、鲜花、肉类、奶类或其他动植物制品入境，如您已带上飞机，请您在落地前处理完成或交给乘务员处理。

我们还将为您播放一段检疫录像片，请您注意收看。

谢谢！

Notes

quarantine regulations: 检疫规定。各个国家有不同的检疫规定，乘务员需要在广播中进行介绍和提醒。

3. 入出境安全须知（Safety Instruction for Entering/Exiting China ）

Dear passengers,

May I have your attention, please?

According to the *Frontier Health and Quarantine Law of the People's Republic of China*, for your own health and that of others, we kindly remind you that: If you have any symptoms such as fever, cough, dyspnea, nausea, vomiting, diarrhea, headache, muscle pains, joint pains and rash, please contact our flight attendants as soon as possible, or you can report to the quarantine inspection officials when entering or exiting the country.

If you have any carry-on or checked baggage that contains the following articles, such as microbes, human tissues, biological products, blood and blood products, please declare at China Inspection and Quarantine authority and go through the required inspections. Without permission, you may not take the above items into/out of the country.

Insects and animals which might transmit infectious diseases, such as rodents, mosquitoes and cockroaches, are not allowed to be brought into the country.

You are kindly asked to follow these instructions. Any violation will incur the due legal responsibilities. For additional information, please contact the quarantine inspection officials.

Thank you for your cooperation and have a pleasant journey!

各位旅客：

请注意，根据《中华人民共和国国境卫生检疫法》，为保护您和他人健康，中国检验检疫提示您：如果您出现发热、咳嗽、呼吸困难、恶心、呕吐、腹泻、头痛、肌肉痛、关节痛、皮疹等，请及时告知乘务人员或入出境时向检验检疫机构申报。

如果您携带、托运了微生物、人体组织、生物制品、血液及其制品等，必须向中国检验检疫机关申报并接受检验检疫，未经许可，以上物品禁止入境、出境。

禁止携带鼠、蚊、蟑螂等可传播传染病的昆虫和动物入境。

如违反上述规定，您将承担相应法律责任。如需了解详细信息，请与中国检验检疫官员联系。

感谢您的合作与支持，祝您旅途愉快！

Notes

[1] symptom: (*n.*) 症状。描述症状 describe the symptom，例如：fever（发烧）、cough（咳嗽）、dyspnea（呼吸困难）、nausea（恶心）、vomit（呕吐）、diarrhea（腹泻）、joint pain（关节痛）、rash（皮疹）。

[2] quarantine inspection official: 检验检疫官。

[3] carry-on or checked baggage: 随身携带行李或托运行李。

[4] microbe: 微生物。

[5] human tissue: 人体组织。

[6] infectious: (*adj.*) 传染性的。

[7] rodent: (*n.*) 啮齿类动物，鼠。

[8] mosquito: (*n.*) 蚊子。

[9] cockroach: (*n.*) 蟑螂。

[10] incur: (*v.*) 招致，引发。

→ 小知识 ←

Special Situations After Take-off 起飞后特殊情况

1. 颠簸（Turbulence）

1）轻度颠簸，暂停提供热饮（Light Turbulence, Suspending Hot Drinks）

Ladies and gentlemen,

As we expect turbulent weather/Because of turbulence, please return to your seats and fasten your seatbelts. Kindly do not walk around in the cabin.

We will be suspending hot drink service until the aircraft is clear of turbulence. For your own safety, lavatories should not be used at this time. Passengers currently using lavatories should hold the handle firmly. Please take care of your children and check if their seatbelts are securely fastened. Infants should be taken out of bassinets and be seated with infant seatbelts fastened. Thank you for your cooperation!

女士们、先生们：

由于飞机即将遇到不稳定气流 / 由于受到气流影响，请您回到座位上并系好安全带。请不要在客舱内来回走动。

我们将暂时停止热饮服务，直到天气好转。为了您的安全，在颠簸期间，卫生间暂停使用。正在使用卫生间的旅客请扶好把手。请照顾好您的小孩并检查他们的安全带已系好。请父母将婴儿从摇篮中抱出并帮他们系好婴儿安全带。感谢您的配合！

Notes:

［1］turbulent:（*adj.*）颠簸的。

［2］suspend:（*v.*）暂停。

［3］bassinet:（*n.*）摇篮。

［4］infant seatbelt: 婴儿安全带。

2）中度或中度以上颠簸（Moderate or Severe Turbulence）

Ladies and gentlemen,

Our aircraft is now experiencing strong turbulence, and it will last for some time. Please be seated and fasten your seat belt. If you are traveling with your children, please take good care of them. Please be cautious while taking meals.

All cabin services will be suspended. For your safety, please do not use the lavatory currently.

Thank you!

女士们、先生们：

飞机受气流影响正在经历较强烈的颠簸，并将持续一段时间，请您尽快就座并系好安全带，请带孩子的旅客协助孩子系好安全带。正在用餐的旅客，小心餐饮烫伤。

在此期间，我们将停止客舱服务，洗手间暂停使用。

谢谢！

Notes:

［1］experience strong turbulence: 遭遇 / 经历强烈颠簸。

［2］cautious:（*adj.*）小心的。

［3］currently:（*adv.*）当前。

3）Severe Turbulence（重度颠簸）

（1）严重颠簸（Severe Turbulence）时广播词如下。

Ladies and gentlemen,

We have encountered some strong turbulence. Please take your seat and fasten your seat belt. Do not use the lavatories. Please grasp the overhead assistant bar or the assistant handle in the lavatory, in case you can't go back to your seats immediately. Cabin service will be suspended during this period. Thank you for your cooperation!

女士们、先生们：

我们的飞机正经历强烈的颠簸。请您尽快就座，系好安全带，洗手间停止使用。如果您不能及时回到座位，请抓紧行李架边缘的凹槽处，如果您在使用洗手间请抓紧洗手间内的扶手。在此期间，我们将暂停客舱服务。感谢您的配合！

（2）严重颠簸后（After Strong Turbulence）的广播词如下。

Ladies and gentlemen,

Due to _____, our aircraft has experienced some severe turbulence. We apologize for the inconvenience caused. If you have any discomfort, please contact our flight attendants.

Thank you for your understanding and cooperation!

女士们、先生们：

我们的飞机由于_____的原因，刚刚经历了严重颠簸。如果您的身体感到不适，请速与乘务员联系。

感谢您的理解与配合！

Notes:

［1］encounter:（*v.*）遇到，遭遇。

［2］grasp:（*v.*）抓紧。

［3］severe:（*adj.*）严重的。

2. 禁用电子设备（Stop Using Electronic Devices）

Ladies and gentlemen,

The captain has informed us that our navigation and communication system are being interrupted. The source of the signal could be your electronic devices./The captain will put/keep the aircraft in low visibility conditions.

Now, please power off all your electronic devices and keep them off until the aircraft has reached the safety altitude/the aircraft has landed/the cabin doors are opened.

Thank you for your cooperation!

女士们、先生们：

根据机长指示，我们飞机的导航及通信系统疑似受到机上便携式电子设备的干扰 /我们的飞机将在低能见度情况下运行。为了您的安全，请关闭所有电子设备电源，直到飞机进入巡航阶段 / 飞机着陆后 / 舱门开启。

谢谢您的合作！

Notes:

[1] interrupt:（v.）干扰。

[2] source of the signal: 信号源。

[3] low visibility: 低能见度。

[4] safety altitude: 安全高度。

3. 喷药（Spraying of Cabin）

Ladies and gentlemen,

The local authorities require the cabin of this aircraft to be disinfected with a non-toxic spray recommended by the World Health Organization. If you think the spray may affect you, please cover your nose and mouth. For passengers wearing contact lenses, you are advised to close your eyes during the spraying.

Thank you for your cooperation!

女士们、先生们：

_____（国家）有关当局要求在机舱内喷洒由世界卫生组织推荐的无毒性喷雾剂进行消毒。如您对喷雾过敏，请用纸巾捂住口、鼻。佩戴隐形眼镜的旅客，请暂时闭上眼睛。

感谢您的合作！

Notes:

[1] local authority: 地方当局。

[2] disinfect:（v.）消毒。

[3] World Health Organization: 世界卫生组织（WHO）。

[4] contact lenses: 隐形眼镜。

4. 防疫广播（Epidemic Prevention）

Ladies and gentlemen,

Please make sure to keep your mask on during the entire flight. Please clean your hands at any time and avoid touching your mouth, nose or eyes without washing your hands. You should put your used mask in the airsickness bag.

女士们、先生们：

　　机组特别提示您，请您全程戴好口罩，并随时做好手部清洁消毒，未经消毒避免接触口鼻和眼部。废弃口罩请置于清洁袋内，不得随意丢弃。

（三）着陆前的客舱安全广播

1. 着陆前安全检查（Safety Check Before Landing）

Ladies and gentlemen,

Our aircraft is expected to arrive in ×××(destination) in×××minutes, and we will be suspending our cabin service. We are now beginning our final descent, and flight attendants will conduct a safety check.

Please fasten your seat belt, stow your tray table (return your footrest to its initial position), adjust your seat back to the upright position, help us by opening the sunshades, and ensure large portable electronic devices, such as laptops, are powered off. Lavatories have been suspended. Thank you!

女士们、先生们：

　　飞机将于××分钟后抵达目的地××，我们将停止客舱服务。现在乘务员进行下降前的安全确认。

　　请您系好安全带、收起小桌板（及脚踏板）调直座椅靠背，打开遮光板，关闭并妥善存放笔记本电脑等电子设备。洗手间已停止使用。谢谢！

> **Notes**
>
> [1] conduct a safety check: 进行安全检查。
>
> [2] initial position: 最初的位置。
>
> [3] sunshade: 遮阳板。同样的表达还有 window shade, window blind。

2. 飞行关键阶段客舱安全广播（下降安全检查后有旅客按呼唤铃时）（Passenger Calls During Landing）

Ladies and gentlemen,

As we are descending, flight attendants are not allowed to leave their seats or to provide cabin services. (Lavatories can not be used at this time.) If you find anything about flight safety, please press the call button continuously.

　　Thank you!

空乘实用英语教程

女士们、先生们：

由于飞机正处于下降关键阶段，很抱歉乘务员不能为您提供客舱服务。（洗手间暂停使用。）如果您需要向我们反馈与飞行安全有关的信息，请您连续按压呼唤铃。

谢谢！

3. 着陆前安全确认（Safety Reminding for Landing）

Ladies and gentlemen,

Our aircraft will be landing shortly. Please make sure that your seat belts are securely fastened. Thank you!

Cabin crew, please prepare for landing.

女士们、先生们：

飞机很快就要着陆，请您再次确认您的安全带已经扣好、系紧。谢谢！

客舱乘务员请做好着陆前的准备。

➡ 小知识 ⬅

Special Situations Before Landing 着陆前特殊情况

机上有病人备降（Diversion for Patient）

Ladies and gentlemen,

May I have your attention, please? We have a very sick passenger in need of urgent medical treatment. The Captain has decided to land immediately at ××× airport, which is the closest to us. We expect to arrive there in approximately ×× minutes.

Thank you for your understanding and support!

女士们、先生们：

请注意！现在飞机上有一位重病旅客需要尽快抢救，为了保证病人的生命安全，机长决定临时降落在最近的 ××× 机场，飞机将在 ×× 分钟后到达。

非常感谢您的理解与支持！

Notes:

［1］in need of：需要。

［2］closest：(*adj.*) 最近的。也可用 nearest 表达。

（四）着陆后滑行时的安全广播

滑行期间制止旅客不安全行为 (Stopping Passengers' Unsafe Behaviors While Taxiing)

Ladies and gentlemen (passengers standing in the cabin),

Our airplane is still taxiing. For your safety, please do not open the overhead locker and take your seat as soon as possible. We will be brightening the cabin lights when the airplane comes to a complete stop. Thank you for your cooperation.

女士们、先生们（客舱中站立的旅客）：

飞机还未滑到指定停机位，为了您的安全，请您关闭行李架，立即就座。稍后我们将通过调亮客舱灯光来提示您飞机已经完全停稳。感谢您的配合！

➡ 小知识 ⬅

Special Situations After Landing 着陆后特殊情况

1. 机上有病人降落后（After Landing for Patient）

Ladies and gentlemen,

We have a very sick passenger in need of urgent medical treatment. Please remain in your seat and keep the aisle clear, so that medical personnel can provide on-board medical rescue as soon as possible (so that the sick passenger can disembark as soon as possible for further treatments). Thank you for your understanding and support!

女士们、先生们：

由于机上有一名重症病人需要急救，请您配合在座位上等候，保持过道通畅，以便于医护人员尽快登机实施医疗救护工作（以便病人尽快下机接受医疗救护）。非常感谢您的理解与支持！

Notes:

［1］rescue:（v.）救护。

［2］treatment:（n.）治疗。

2. 检疫官员登机评估疫情（Assessment of Quarantine）

Ladies and gentlemen,

The Quarantine and Inspection Service will be boarding the aircraft to assess the health condition of a passengers. Please remain in your seat and keep the aisles clear. The assessment will be carried out as quickly as possible and disembarkation will commence as soon as clearance is given by the Quarantine Officer. Thank you!

女士们、先生们：

检疫局官员即将登机评估每位旅客的健康状况，请您留在座位上并保持走道通畅。我们将在检疫官员完成评估程序后，尽快通知大家下机。谢谢！

Notes:

在发现疑似疫情航班落地后，检疫官员即将登机时广播。

（五）客舱紧急情况广播

飞行期间发生各种紧急情况时将会播放的广播，这些紧急情况包括客舱失火、客舱出现疑似爆炸物、客舱释压、遭遇劫机、寻求医疗救助、紧急下降、陆地/水上迫降等。客舱应急广播词内容如下。

1. 客舱失火（Fire in the Cabin）

Ladies and gentlemen,

We have encountered a minor fire in the front/center/rear section of the cabin and we are quickly containing this situation. Please keep calm and follow the instructions of the flight attendants. We will relocate passengers near the area of the fire. All other passengers do remain in your seats with your seatbelts securely fastened.

女士们、先生们：

现在客舱前/中/后部有一处失火，我们正在组织灭火。请大家不要惊慌，听从乘务员指挥，我们将调整火源附近旅客的座位，其他旅客不要在客舱内走动。

Notes

relocate:（v.）调整座位。

2. 灭火后（Fire Extinguished/Put off）

Ladies and gentlemen,

The fire in the cabin has been completely put out. Please remain calm. We will need to land at an alternative airport nearby for further check of this aircraft. The estimated arrival time is _____ a.m./p.m. We sincerely apologize for any inconvenience caused.

Thank you for your assistance and cooperation!

女士们、先生们：

我们已经结束了灭火工作。现在飞机处于良好状态，请大家不要惊慌。我们需要就近机场着陆以便对飞机进一步检查。预计到达备降机场的时间是上午／下午_____。 给您带来不便，我们深表歉意。

感谢您的协助与配合！

> **Notes** ───────────────────○
>
> alternative airport: 备降机场。

3. 客舱烟雾（Smoke in the Cabin）

Ladies and gentlemen,

Attention, please! It is smoky in the front/center/rear cabin. For your safety, please remain seated with your seatbelts fastened. Keep calm and quiet. Bend forward and cover your nose and mouth with a handkerchief or clothes. Please follow the instruction of the flight attendants.

女士们、先生们：

请注意：客舱（前／中／后部）有烟雾。为确保您的健康，请在座位上坐好并系好安全带。请保持冷静，请您低下头，弯下腰，用衣物、手帕捂住口鼻。请听从乘务员指挥。

> **Notes** ───────────────────○
>
> bend: (*v.*) 弯腰。

4. 客舱释压（Cabin Depressurization /Decompression）

Ladies and gentlemen,

Attention, please! Our aircraft is losing pressure and is now becoming depressurized. Please fasten your seat belt and pull an oxygen mask! Place it over your nose and mouth and breathe normally. Put on your own mask before helping others. Our aircraft will have an emergency descent. Please remain calm and follow the instructions from your flight attendants.

女士们、先生们：

现在客舱发生释压，请立即系好安全带。用力拉下氧气面罩，罩在口鼻处，正常呼吸。帮助别人之前，自己先戴好。飞机将紧急下降，大家不要惊慌，听从乘务员指挥。

> **Notes** ───────────────────○
>
> depressurize: (*v.*) 释压。

5. 释压后到达安全高度（After Depressurization）

Ladies and gentlemen,

Our aircraft has reached the safety altitude. You can now remove the oxygen masks and breathe normally. If you feel uncomfortable, please contact our cabin attendant.

Thank you for your cooperation!

女士们、先生们：

现在，飞机已到达安全高度，您可以摘下氧气面罩。如果您感到身体不适，请与我们的乘务员联系。

感谢您的配合！

6. 陆地 / 海上迫降（Emergency Landing/Ditching）

Ladies and gentlemen,

Attention, please! This is the chief purser. We are forced to make an emergency landing (ditching). The crew has been well trained to handle this type of situation. We assure you that you'll be safe with us. Please be seated and keep calm. And follow the flight attendants' directions.

女士们、先生们：

请注意，现在是乘务长广播。我们已决定采取陆地（水上）迫降，对于处理这种情况，我们全体机组人员都受过良好的训练，有信心、有能力保证你们的安全。请你们回座位坐好，保持镇静，注意听从乘务员的指挥。

Notes

［1］ditching: 水上迫降。

［2］well trained: 受过良好训练的。

7. 紧急着陆前广播（Before Emergency Landing/Ditching）

Ladies and gentlemen,

We will now make an immediate emergency landing (ditching). Remain calm. Fasten your seat belt securely. Brace yourself until the aircraft comes to a complete stop.

Thank you!

女士们、先生们：

飞机马上就要紧急着陆（着水），请保持冷静。请您系好安全带。保持防冲击姿势直至飞机完全停稳。

谢谢！

8. 安全紧急着陆后（Evacuation After Emergency Landing）

Ladies and gentlemen,

The aircraft has safely landed. Please remain seated and keep your seatbelt tightly fastened. Please keep calm and follow the instructions of the cabin attendants.

女士们、先生们：

现在飞机已经安全着陆，请大家保持安全带扣好、系紧，保持安静并听从乘务员的指挥。

9. 快速离机（Express Disembark）

Ladies and gentlemen:

It's necessary to disembark the aircraft as a precaution. Stairs are available and ready. Please follow the instructions of your cabin crew and leave all luggage onboard.

女士们、先生们：

我们需要尽快离开飞机。扶梯已准备就绪，请您听从乘务员的指挥，将所有行李物品留在飞机上。

Notes

precaution:（n.）预防。

➡ 小知识 ⬅

在飞机上，大多数时候我们听到的都是乘务员广播，但是有时机长也会进行广播。和亲切甜美的空乘广播相比，有时候机长广播会让乘客的空中体验更有"安全感"。

在空中客舱广播中，旅客往往对例行的乘务员服务广播关注度不高，而对偶尔的机长广播十分关注，这是因为乘坐航班的旅客普遍都有一个公众心理——"空中安全"。特别是第一次乘飞机的旅客，机长广播往往比服务广播更能带给旅客更多的安心。在实际运行中，由于机长在起飞、降落等关键阶段需要做好安全方面的工作，没有精力做机长广播，所以，一般机长广播多在平飞后进行。最常听到的是机长欢迎词广播，例如"我是本次航班机长，欢迎你乘坐××航空班机和我们一起前往×××，您今天所乘坐的飞机机型是×××，飞行高度是×××米，空中飞行时间大约×××小时×××分，在飞行航程中，请您在座位上坐好，务必系好安全带，再次感谢您选择××航班，祝大家旅途愉快！"

　　根据民航运行手册的规定，机长广播不是强制的，通常客舱广播由客舱经理或乘务员来做，在非正常情况下，机长会进行广播。例如，在夏秋季节雷雨多发，由于空中气流颠簸较多，或航路不通，或紧急情况，客舱乘务员的服务广播往往很难奏效，而此时的一次机长广播却会让旅客安静下来，究其原因，源自机长掌握着空中航路状态，乘务员所知晓的信息也来源于机长，再多的解释，都不如机长亲自告知。所以在此时，机长广播对航路情况作一个简单介绍或解释，往往会产生事半功倍的效果。近年来，随着航空市场的发展，公众对航空运输的认知度提高，乘飞机旅行更加普及，为争取时间或缩短旅途，或赴境外旅游，更多的人会选择飞机作为交通工具，为了使旅客在空中有限的时间里，体验到航空服务带来的特别享受，各航空公司对服务品牌予以高度重视、不断提升服务品牌，在全方位提供人性化的服务基础上，更加关注旅客的乘机感受。其中作为重点关注安全的机长广播，也被列为品牌服务的一项重要内容。如在机长广播中，有时也会听到某机长这样的广播："本次航班将飞越××，您可以观赏到××景观××"这样的广播多为机长自由发挥，将所乘航班的人文、地貌、地域风光予以介绍。除此之外，还有每逢重要传统节日的问候和祝福，或跨境归国航线上"欢迎您回到祖国……"，等等，短短的几句话，却温暖着旅客的心，此时的机长广播也是目前所提倡的，不仅使旅客的感受趋向人性化，也更加体现着大航空公司的服务风范，并成为航空公司品牌服务的亮点。

　　由于机长的职责主要是关注安全，机长广播的第一原则始终是为安全服务；在保证安全的前提下，助力空中服务工作，为品牌服务增光添彩，这是目前机长广播遵循的规则。虽然机长广播不是客舱广播的主体，但却发挥着举足轻重的作用，它始终在航班运行中关注着旅客的安危，更为飞行安全保驾护航。

　　（资料来源：中国民航网）

第六节　客舱广播练习

一、常规广播（Routine Announcements）

Practice 1

Ladies and gentlemen,

　　Welcome aboard Air China. For your safety and comfort, please take your assigned seat according to the numbers displayed under the overhead compartments. Please place your bags carefully in the overhead compartments or under the seats in front of you. Do not place them in the aisles or obstruct the emergency exits. If you need any assistance, we are glad to help you. Thank you!

女士们、先生们：

欢迎搭乘中国国际航空公司班机。为了您的舒适和安全，登机后请按照登机牌上的座位号就座。座位号位于行李架下方，找到座位的旅客请您尽快入座。请将您的手提行李稳妥地放置行李架内，或是您前座椅的下方。请不要在紧急出口旁、过道上放置行李。如果您需要帮助，我们很乐意协助您。谢谢！

Practice 2

Ladies and gentlemen,

This is China Eastern Airlines flight MU529 which is code shared with Japan Airlines bound for Nagoya. Please check your boarding pass once again and verify your flight number.

Thank you for your cooperation!

女士们、先生们：

本架飞机是飞往名古屋的中国东方航空公司的 MU529 航班，本次航班与日本航空实施代码共享。请各位旅客再次确认一下您的登机牌和航班号。

谢谢您的合作！

Practice 3

Ladies and gentlemen,

According to the CAAC regulations, smoking is prohibited on board during the whole flight. To ensure proper function of the navigation and communication system, please note certain electronic devices must not be used on board at any time. These devices include mobile phones, radios and remote-control equipment. All other electronic devices including portable computers, MP3, CD players and game players may be used except during take-off and landing.

Thank you for your cooperation!

女士们、先生们：

根据中国民航局规定，全程禁止旅客吸烟。为了保证飞行通信和导航系统的正常工作，请您在飞行的全过程中不要使用移动电话、收音机及遥控电子设备等。在飞机起飞后，手提电脑、MP3、数码播放机和游戏机可以使用，但必须在飞机下降前关闭，以确保飞行安全。

谢谢您的合作！

Practice 4

Ladies and gentlemen,

We are ready for departure. Please fasten your seatbelt, open the window shade, put the tray table in place, bring your seatback upright and unplug your headphones and electronic devices. The large portable electronic devices, such as laptops, should be stowed properly. Please ensure that small portable electronic devices, like cell phones, are switched to the airplane mode. Please do not smoke during the entire flight.

Thank you!

女士们、先生们：

飞机已经开始滑行，请您系好安全带，打开遮光板，收起小桌板，调直椅背，取下耳机及连接在座椅电源上的数据线，妥善存放笔记本电脑等大型便携式电子设备。手机等小型便携式电子设备请确认已切换至飞行模式。本次航班是禁烟航班。

谢谢！

Practice 5

Ladies and gentlemen,

I am the security team leader of this flight. Thank you for flying Spring Airlines. Chinese law and aviation regulations state any passenger who causes a disturbance, interferes with or causes damage to the aircraft or its equipment, or fails to comply with cabin crew instructions may be subject to fines or criminal charges. Let's make this a pleasant journey for everyone.

Thanks for your cooperation!

女士们、先生们：

我是本次航班的安保组组长，感谢您今天乘坐春秋航空班机。

根据中国法律和航空管制条例，扰乱、干扰或损坏飞机或其设备，或不遵守机组人员指示等扰乱客舱秩序的行为会被处以罚款，或追究其刑事责任。让我们共同营造安全、文明的乘机环境。

谢谢您的配合！

Practice 6

Ladies and gentlemen,

Good morning (afternoon/evening)!

This is your cabin manager/purser speaking. Welcome to China Eastern, a member of Sky Team Alliance.

This flight is bound for Paris (via Beijing). (which is code-shared with Air France.) Our

85

flight distance (from Shanghai to Paris) is 9274 km, and the flying time is 11 hours and 30 minutes. We are looking forward to making this flight an enjoyable and comfortable experience for all of you.

Thank you!

尊敬的各位旅客：

早上好／下午好／晚上好。

我是本次航班的客舱经理／乘务长。我谨代表全体机组人员欢迎您搭乘天合联盟成员中国东方航空班机。

本次航班前往巴黎（中途经停北京），（本次航班与法国航空公司实施代码共享）。从上海到巴黎的飞行距离为 9274 千米，飞行时间大约需要 11 小时 30 分钟。我们希望与您一起度过这段温馨而愉快的旅行。

谢谢！

Practice 7

Ladies and gentlemen,

Our aircraft has left Tianjin. We are going to serve beverage and (breakfast/lunch/dinner) refreshment shortly.

Please keep your seatbelts fastened when seated in case of sudden turbulence. Once again, portable power banks are not permitted during the entire flight. Please switch into airplane mode (and turn off the Wi-Fi function) while using your portable electronic devices. We will be by your side any time you need anything from us. We wish you a pleasant trip!

女士们、先生们：

飞机已经离开天津（已进入平飞状态）。我们即将为您供应饮料和（早餐／午餐／晚餐）便餐。

为了防止意外颠簸，就座时请系好安全带。再次提醒您，不要使用锂电池移动电源。请将便携式电子设备设置为飞行模式（并关闭无线网络功能）。如您需要服务，请随时告诉我们。祝您旅途愉快！

Practice 8

Ladies and gentlemen,

We will be serving you meal with tea, coffee and other soft drinks. Welcome to make your choice. Please put down the table in front of you. For the convenience of the passenger behind you, please return your seat back to the upright position during the meal service. Thank you!

女士们、先生们：

我们将为您提供餐食、茶水、咖啡和饮料。欢迎您选用。需要用餐的旅客，请您将小桌板放下。为了方便其他旅客，在供餐期间，请您将座椅靠背调整到正常位置。谢谢！

Practice 9

Ladies and gentlemen,

For your convenience of travel, we have prepared in-flight entertainment equipment for you. You can enjoy movies, music, games and e-books and other programs. The headsets are in the seat pockets in front of you. We wish you a pleasant journey!

女士们、先生们：

为了丰富您的旅途生活，我们在机上为您配备了娱乐设备，内置电影、音乐、游戏、电子书籍等多种娱乐设备。耳机放置于您前方座椅靠背的口袋中，祝您旅途愉快！

Practice 10

Ladies and gentlemen,

Our duty-free shop will be available soon. We accept cash cards and major credit cards. For further information, please refer to the sales magazine in your seat pocket.

Thank you!

女士们、先生们：

我们将开始售卖免税商品。我们接受现金提取卡和主流信用卡。您可以查阅您椅袋中的免税品售卖杂志获取详细信息。

谢谢！

Practice 11

Ladies and gentlemen,

For your convenience, we are now distributing landing forms. Before you go through Customs and immigration, it is necessary for you to fill in the forms required by the Government. In order to speed your passage through customs and immigration, please complete it before we land. If you have any questions about filling in the forms, please ask cabin attendants for help.

We will be very happy to assist you. Thank you!

女士们、先生们：

为了缩短您在机场的停留时间，现在请各位旅客填写入境卡和申报单。这些表格请在飞机落地前填好，填写好后请自行保管。落地后交给移民局和海关检查站。如果您需要帮助，请与客舱乘务员联系。我们很高兴对您进行协助。谢谢！

Practice 12

Ladies and gentlemen,

Our flight is expected to arrive at the destination airport at 10 : 15 a.m.

Now the ground temperature is 22 degrees Centigrade. As we will be landing shortly, please have your headsets ready for our collection. Thank you!

女士们、先生们：

本架飞机预计上午十点十五分到达目的地机场。现在地面温度为22℃。飞机即将下降，乘务员将到您面前收取耳机。谢谢！

Practice 13

Ladies and gentlemen,

Thank you for your support and understanding during the entire flight. As we are approaching the airport, the cabin crew will make a final check of the cabin to ensure that all baggage are stowed securely. Please return to your seat, fasten your seat belt, stow your tray table, open your window shade, put your seat-back in the upright position and take off your headsets. Meanwhile, please note where the nearest emergency exit is located.

We look forward to seeing you again on a future flight.

We wish you a pleasant journey! Thank you!

女士们、先生们：

感谢您的一路相伴，现在飞机已经开始下降，客舱乘务员将进行落地前安全检查。请您回到自己的座位，系好安全带，收起小桌板，打开遮阳板，调直座椅靠背，并取下耳机，回想一下离您最近的出口在哪里。

我们期待与您再次相逢。

祝您旅途愉快！谢谢！

二、特殊广播（Special Announcements）

Practice 14

Ladies and gentlemen,

This is your purser speaking. The Captain has just informed us that due to air traffic control, our aircraft cannot take off for this moment. Please remain in your seat. Further information will be provided as soon as it is available. (We will play video programs, and serve meals & beverages while we are waiting.)

Thank you for your patience!

女士们、先生们：

现在是乘务长广播。刚刚接机长通知：由于航路交通管制，飞机暂时无法起飞。请大家在座位上休息等候，如有进一步的消息，我们会尽快通知您。（在此期间，我们将为您播放录像节目并提供餐饮服务。）

感谢您的耐心等待！

Practice 15

Ladies and gentlemen,

This is your (chief) purser speaking. The Captain has just informed us that to ensure the safety of the flight, this aircraft will be deiced prior to take-off, and the flight will be delayed. Our aircraft is expected to depart at 10：30.

Thank you for your patience!

女士们、先生们：

这是（主任）乘务长广播。刚刚接到机长通知：为了确保飞机安全起飞，地面工作人员需要对飞机外表进行除冰，起飞时间将推迟至 10：30。

感谢您的耐心等待！

Practice 16

Ladies and gentlemen,

There are 3 passengers who have decided to cancel their trip after boarding this aircraft (have not boarded the aircraft).

According to safety regulations, we must make a thorough safety check of the cabin. Please take all your belongings, disembark and follow our ground staff to the lounge. We are very sorry for any inconvenience caused and thank you for your understanding and cooperation.

女士们、先生们：

由于 3 名旅客登机后又决定终止行程（机上缺少 3 名旅客）。现在，根据安全管理条例，我们将对客舱进行全面的清理和检查。请您带齐全部手提物品到候机室休息等候。对于由此给您带来的不便我们深表歉意。感谢您的理解与配合。

Practice 17

Ladies and gentlemen,

We are sorry to inform you that this flight has been cancelled due to the bad weather condition. We apologize for the inconvenience. Please take all your carry-on items and prepare to disembark. The further arrangement will be made by the ground staff.

Thank you for your understanding.

女士们、先生们：

很抱歉通知您，由于恶劣天气，今天的航班被取消。现在请您带好全部手提物品，准备下机。地面工作人员会为您做好航班取消后的后续安排。

感谢您的谅解！

Practice 18

Ladies and gentlemen,

Your attention, please. We urgently need the assistance of a doctor. If there are any medical professionals on board, please contact our flight attendants as soon as possible. Thank you.

女士们、先生们：

请注意，现在飞机上有一位患病的旅客，哪位旅客是医生或护士，我们需要您的帮助，请您尽快与我们联系。谢谢！

Practice 19

Ladies and gentlemen,

If any passenger has lost a wallet in the lavatory, please contact the flight attendant. Thank you.

女士们、先生们：

哪位旅客在洗手间丢失了钱包，请与乘务员联系。谢谢！

Practice 20

Ladies and gentlemen,

Due to the water supply system failure, we will be unable to offer hot drinks on today's flight. We apologize for this inconvenience. Thank you for your understanding.

女士们、先生们：

本架飞机由于供水系统出现故障，无法为您提供热饮，由此给您带来的不便，我们深表歉意。谢谢您的理解！

Practice 21

Ladies and gentlemen,

The captain has advised us that our navigation and communication system is being interrupted. The source of the signal could be your electronic devices.

Now, please switch off all your electronic devices and keep them off until the aircraft has reached the safety altitude/has landed and the cabin doors are opened. Thank you for your cooperation!

女士们、先生们：

根据机长指示，我们飞机的导航及通信系统疑似受到机上便携式电子设备的干扰。

现在，请您关闭所有电子设备电源，直到飞机抵达巡航高度 / 落地后舱门开启。感谢您的配合！

Practice 22

Ladies and gentlemen,

We are experiencing some turbulence. Please don't worry. But fasten the seatbelt tight and low. The lavatories shouldn't be used right now, and passengers in the lavatories, please hold the handrail.

Cabin service will be suspended during this period. Thank you.

女士们、先生们：

飞机受到气流影响，正在颠簸。请您不用担心，但请系好安全带。机上洗手间暂停使用，正在使用洗手间的旅客，请您抓好扶手。

我们将暂停客舱服务。谢谢。

Practice 23

Ladies and gentlemen,

We are putting out a minor fire that has broken out in the front (center/rear) of the cabin. Passengers sitting in the front (center/ rear), please follow the cabin attendants' directions. All other passengers please do not leave your seats. Smoking is prohibited.

女士们、先生们：

我们正在扑灭客舱前部 / 中部 / 后部爆发的小型火势。坐在火源附近的旅客，请听从乘务员指挥。其他乘客请不要离开自己的座位，不要吸烟。

Practice 24

Ladies and gentlemen,

The fire in the cabin has been completely put out. Please remain calm. We will need to land at an alternative airport nearby for further check of this aircraft. The estimated arrival time is 10:15 a.m. Thank you for your cooperation and assistance.

女士们、先生们：

我们已经结束了灭火工作。请大家不要惊慌。我们需要就近机场着陆以便对飞机进一步检查。预计到达备降机场的时间是上午 10 ：15。感谢您给予我们的协助。

Practice 25

Ladies and gentlemen,

Attention! Please sit down immediately. Pull an oxygen mask firmly toward yourself and place the mask over your nose and mouth and breathe normally. Put on your own mask first before assisting others. Please remain seated with your seat belt fastened until further instructed.

女士们、先生们：

请注意！请立即坐下，请将氧气面罩戴好，罩在口鼻处进行正常呼吸。协助他人前请先戴好自己的面罩。请坐好并系好安全带，等待后续广播通知。

Practice 26

Ladies and gentlemen,

May I have your attention, please?

According to *Frontier Health and Quarantine Law of the People's Republic of China*, if you have any symptoms such as fever, cough or breath difficulty, please contact our cabin crew as soon as possible. For further information, please refer to the instructions in the seat pocket in front of you.

Quarantine officials will carry out health inspection upon your arrival. Thank you for your cooperation!

女士们、先生们：

请注意！根据《中华人民共和国国境卫生检疫法》，如您有发热、咳嗽以及呼吸困难等症状，请及时与我们联系。请您仔细阅读座位前口袋内的须知以便获取更多信息。

本次航班抵达后，将由检验检疫机关对所有旅客进行入境检疫检查。谢谢您的合作！

Practice 27

Ladies and gentlemen,

According to the quarantine regulations of the Australian government, we will be spraying the cabin against insect infestation. If you are sensitive to this non-toxic spray approved by the World Health Organization (WHO), we recommend that you place a napkin over your nose and mouth during the spraying. Thank you for your cooperation!

女士们、先生们：

根据澳大利亚政府的检疫规定，现在，我们须在客舱内喷洒由世界卫生组织认可的无毒性喷雾。如您对喷雾过敏，请用纸巾捂住口鼻处。感谢您的合作！

Practice 28

Ladies and gentlemen,

Due to the unfavorable weather condition and low visibility at Shanghai Pudong International Airport, we have been ordered to circle over the airport until weather conditions improved. We will keep you informed of our progress. Thank you.

女士们、先生们：

由于上海浦东国际机场天气不好，能见度不符合降落标准，飞机暂时无法降落，我们需要在机场上空盘旋等待。进一步的消息，我们将及时通知您。谢谢！

Practice 29

Ladies and gentlemen,

Due to strong head winds, our arrival will be delayed by an additional 20 minutes. The new arrival time is 14：50. Thank you!

女士们、先生们：

由于受航路上的强逆风影响，飞机着陆时间比原计划推迟20分钟，我们将于14点50分到达。谢谢！

Practice 30

Ladies and gentlemen,

We are waiting for the air steps (air bridge/transit bus). For your safety, please remain in your seat for further information. Thank you.

女士们、先生们：

由于机场繁忙，我们的飞机需在此等待客梯（廊桥、摆渡车）到达，为了您的安全，请您在座位上稍等片刻，谢谢！

第3章
客舱情景

章前导读

本章为基于乘务员职业素养的客舱情景对话。将乘务员工作中的能力定位为核心词，从职业忠诚、团队合作、安全指导、服务意识、应急意识、交际沟通、劝说技巧、医疗急救、旅游引导、出入境常识等维度出发，明确乘务员在客舱服务中的价值引领，提升乘务员客舱服务的语言技巧和沟通技能，着力于交际能力、应变能力和解决问题的能力等实际工作中的岗位需求。同时，融入客舱文化常识和跨文化交际意识，兼顾语言的人文性和工具性，塑造具有职业认同感、岗位能力明确、外语表达能力突出的国际化民航高素质人才。

本章旨在提高学生对职业素养的认同。同时在职业精神和相关职业能力的指导下，有目的地完成客舱对话，拓展服务意识，掌握客舱文化，提升跨文化交际能力和沟通技巧。学生可以以客舱情景对话为依托，从知识、技能、情感三个方面提升自己的专业英语能力。

思政园地

青年学生应当努力掌握科学文化知识和专业技能，努力提高人文素养，以真才实学服务人民，以创新创造贡献国家。客舱情景对话的学习要求学生掌握客舱工作语境情景下客舱服务和客舱安全的规范表达内容和有效应答技巧，提升主动服务意识、谨记客舱安全要领。同时教师还应引导学生关注语言背后的文化背景，通过拓展理解，提升跨文化沟通技巧，增强文化自信，以培养学生对民航职业的认同感和人类命运共同体的关注。

第一节 职业忠诚

职业忠诚（professional loyalty）体现了乘务员对客舱工作的职业认知和职业操守。当代民航精神提出，所有民航从业人员应该具备：忠诚担当的政治品格，严谨科学的专业精神，团结协作的工作作风，敬业奉献的职业操守。乘务员首先要热爱这份职业，爱岗敬业，忠于职守，并将个人理想融于报效民航和中华民族伟大复兴的事业中。下面以有准备的陆地迫降和撤离为例。

Dialogue 1   Planned Emergency Landing and Evacuation（有准备的陆地紧急迫降和撤离）

（*CA=Cabin Attendant, PAX=Passenger*）

Purser's Announcement:

Ladies and gentlemen,

Due to mechanical difficulties, our left engine has stopped working. Our captain has decided to make an emergency landing. Please remain calm since all the crew members are well-trained to handle this situation. And our captain has full competence to land safely. We will do everything necessary to ensure your safety. Please follow our directions.

乘务长广播：

女士们、先生们：

由于本架飞机出现机械故障，左侧引擎失灵。机长决定进行陆地紧急迫降。请保持镇定，我们全体机组人员都受过良好的训练，我们的机长完全有能力将飞机安全着陆。我们有信心、有能力保证你们的安全。请听从我们的指令。

（*A cabin attendant is walking along the aisle to make cabin checks.* 一位乘务员在过道里做客舱检查。）

CA: Excuse me, sir. Please pass your food tray and all other service items for collection.

乘务员：不好意思，先生。请把盘子递给我，并把所有东西收好。

PAX: OK. I'm so nervous. Could you give me some details about the mechanical difficulties? Is it serious?

乘客：好的，我很紧张。您能就这个机械故障告诉我一些细节吗？严重吗？

CA: Don't worry, sir. We will ensure the safety of the passengers. Now please fasten your seatbelt, bring your seatback to the upright position and stow all tray tables. Please stow footrest and in-seat video units. Put all your baggage in the overhead compartment or under the seat in front of you.

乘务员：别担心，先生。我们会确保大家的安全。现在请系好安全带，将座椅靠背调直并且收起小桌板。请收起脚踏板和屏幕。将行李全部放到行李架上或者前方座椅下面。

CA: (*to another passenger*) Madam, please remove your earrings and high heeled shoes, for the sharp objects would hurt you during emergency landing.

乘务员：（对另一位旅客说）女士，请取下您的耳环、脱下高跟鞋，因为这些尖锐物品在紧急着陆时会伤到您。

Madam：OK, thanks for reminding me. I hope we can land safely.

女士：好的，谢谢提醒。希望我们能平安着陆。

CA: We will. Trust us.

乘务员：我们会的，请相信我们。

Purser's Announcement:

Ladies and gentlemen,

Now we will explain the brace positions against impact. Please follow the instructions and practice.

When you hear "Heads down, brace!", put your legs apart, place your feet flat on the floor, tighten the chin, bend forward, lean your head against the seatback in front of you and hold your head with your hands.

If there is no seatback in front of you or the space is far apart, bend forward and hold your legs with your hands.

While landing, there may be more than one impact, so keep your brace position until the aircraft comes to a complete stop. Now let's practice.

乘务长广播：

女士们，先生们：

现在乘务员将向您介绍两种防冲击的姿势，请跟随乘务员练习。

当您听到"低下头，全身紧迫用力！"的指令时，两腿分开用力蹬地，收紧下颚，身体前倾，将头抵在前方座椅靠背上，双手抱住头部。

如果前面没有或抵不到座椅靠背，弯下腰，将双手抱住两腿。

在飞机着陆时，可能会有多次撞击，保持防冲击姿势直到飞机完全停稳。现在，我们开始练习。

PAX: Excuse me, Miss. I didn't hear clearly what the announcement said. I'm in a bulkhead seat, so there is no seatback in front of me. What position should I take?

乘客：您好，小姐。我没听清广播里说的。我是隔板座位，所以我前面没有座椅靠背。我该做怎样的动作？

CA: Don't worry. I'll show you. Please bend forward and hold your legs like this.

乘务员：别担心。我为您演示，您像这样弯腰，双手抱住两腿。

PAX: Oh, I see. Like this?

乘客：哦，明白了。是这样吗？

CA：Perfect!

乘务员：非常好！

……

Purser's Announcement:

Ladies and gentlemen,

Please contact our flight attendant if you are an employee of airlines, law enforcement personnel, firefighter or military service personnel. We appreciate your assistance. Please cooperate as we relocate passengers according to the instructions from captain.

乘务长广播：

女士们、先生们：

请注意，如果您是航空公司的雇员、执法人员、消防人员或军人的话，请与乘务员联系，我们需要您的协助。同时，根据机长的要求，我们将调整一些人的座位。

（*Then two passengers came to the front cabin and found the purser.* 随后两名乘客来到前舱，找到了乘务长。）

PAX 1: Excuse me, purser. My name is Sophia. I worked as a cabin attendant in Singapore Airlines before. I'm ready to help when in need.

乘客1：乘务长，您好。我叫索菲亚，曾经做过新加坡航空公司的乘务员。需要时我随时准备好帮忙。

PAX 2: Purser, I'm a professional firefighter. You can call me Hans. What can I do for you?

乘客2：乘务长，我是一名职业消防员，我叫 Hans。我能帮你们做些什么吗？

Purser: Sophia, Hans, thanks so much for your participation. We will be asking you to change seats to better help those needing assistance or to be closer to an exit to help evacuate.

乘务长：索菲亚、汉斯，非常感谢你们的参与。我们将会要求你们更换座位以便更好地协助那些需要帮助的旅客，或在紧急出口协助旅客撤离。

PAX 1 and PAX 2: No problem. We'll be waiting for your instructions.

乘客 1 和乘客 2：没问题。我们等待您的指令。

Purser: Thanks again. I'll rearrange your seats soon and notify you some points for attention.

乘务长：再次感谢。我稍后马上调整你们的座位并告知你们一些注意事项。

（*The cabin crew arranged the work of helpers, secured all the cabin facilities. All cabin crew should have completed preparations and taken the seats after hearing the command from the cockpit crew "Be ready for landing, be ready for landing."* 乘务员给援助者安排好分工，固定好所有客舱设备。当听到飞行机组发出"完成准备、完成准备"指令时，全体乘务员完成准备并入座。）

…

Captain: Brace! Brace!

机长：防冲击！防冲击！

CA：Heads down! Brace! (keep issuing the command)

乘务员：低下头！全身紧迫用力！（反复叫喊）

（*When the plane comes to a complete stop.* 当飞机停稳后。）

Captain: Crew at your station! Crew at your station!

机长：机组各就各位，机组各就各位！

（*The cabin attendants release the seatbelts.* 乘务员解开安全带。）

CA: Keep calm! Follow instructions! (keep issuing the command)

乘务员：镇静！听指挥！（反复叫喊）

Captain: Evacuate! Evacuate!

机长：撤离！撤离！

（*The cabin attendants assess conditions and pull the inflation handle to activate the exit.* 乘务员评估出口外环境，拉充气把手、打开出口。）

CA：Release your seat belt! No baggage! No high-heeled shoes! Come this way! Jump! Slide!

乘务员：解开安全带！不要带行李！脱掉高跟鞋！到这边来！跳！滑！

……

PAX 1: Help... help me, please. I cannot release my seatbelt.

乘客 1：帮……帮我。我解不开安全带了。

CA: Lift up the top of the buckle, and pull out the metal link. Sir, hurry up.

乘务员：向上抬起锁扣的最上面，然后拉出金属连接片。先生，快点儿。

PAX 1: Oh, thank goodness. It works now.

乘客1：哦，谢天谢地，终于打开了。

CA: (*To some passengers trying to get their baggage*) Leave your bag behind, now. Evacuate! Evacuate!

乘务员：（对一些想要拿行李的旅客说）现在不要拿行李。撤离！撤离！

PAX 2: (*coughing*) I can't breathe... help me... the smoke!

乘客2：（咳嗽）我没法呼吸了……帮帮我……烟雾！

CA: Cover your nose and mouth. Keep low and follow the emergency track lights on the floor to the exit.

乘务员：捂住口鼻。低下身子，顺着地板上的应急路线灯到达出口。

PAX 2: Oh, I can't see anything.

乘客2：啊，我什么也看不见。

CA: Hold onto the person in front of you, and follow him to the exit. OK... Jump! Jump!

乘客：抓着您前方的人，跟着他向出口走。好的……准备跳！跳！

PAX 2: Oh, no, I feel frightened.

乘客2：哦，不，我害怕。

CA: Don't be scared. Follow my instructions. Keep your arms straight ahead, jump and slide!

乘务员：别怕。听我的指令。双臂向前伸直，先跳，然后滑下去！

(*Finally the crew succeeded in evacuating all passengers in time.* 最后机组成功地及时撤离了所有乘客。)

第二节 团队合作

团队合作（team work）是客舱乘务工作的有效保证。从驾驶舱机组人员到客舱人员，从客舱经理到乘务长，再到乘务员，每一项任务的实施都离不开个体的支撑。然后，个体又必须借助团队的力量保证任务高效、有序地开展。作为一名准乘务员，平时应该多参加一些集体或团队活动，增强集体意识，发扬奉献精神。下面以航前准备会和机组协调会为例。

Dialogue 2-A　Pre-flight Briefing（航前准备会）

(CP=Chief Purser, CA=Cabin Attendant)

CP: Good morning, everyone. I'm the chief purser in charge of this flight, Margaret. I'm very glad to fly with you from Shanghai to Vancouver.

主任乘务长：大家早上好，我是本次航班的主任乘务长，玛格丽特。很高兴和大家一起执飞上海到温哥华的航班。

CA: Good morning!

乘务员：上午好！

CP: Now let's get to know each other. Please raise your hand and introduce yourself when I call you by your name.

…

Then let's check our personal grooming and sync watches. Please make sure you've taken your valid license and health certificate with you.

主任乘务长：接下来我们相互认识一下。当我点到你名字时请举手并介绍自己。

……

下面我们来检查个人的仪容仪表并对一下时间，请确保自己带好了有效证件和健康证明。

CP: Well, let's go through some flight information. Our flight is AC 26 from Shanghai to Vancouver. Captain William is in command and the first officer is Richard. And we have a security guard whose name is Leo. Our aircraft type is Boeing 787-9. Now I'd like to arrange duty assignment and make clear responsibilities of every station, OK?

主任乘务长：好的，下面我们就航班信息进行介绍。我们今天的执飞的航班是 AC26，上海飞往温哥华。机长是威廉，副飞是理查德，安全员是里欧。我们的机型是波音 787-9。接下来我将对大家进行号位分工并明确相关职责，好吗？

All: Yes, all right.

全体成员：好的。

CP: Tina, you work as CS2 in business class. Jane, CS11 for you. Elizabeth, you are SS7 in premier economy class. And SS9 is Linda. SS8 is Alice. SS10 is Ivy, SS3 is Mary and Lily is SS5. Are there any questions about your working positions?

主任乘务长：蒂娜担任公务舱 2 号位，简在 11 号位。伊丽莎白担任 7 号位，在超级经济舱。琳达在经济舱 9 号位，8 号位是爱丽丝，艾薇担任 10 号位，玛丽在 3 号位，莉莉在 5 号位。对于号位分工大家有什么问题吗？

CA: No, that's OK.

乘务员：没问题。

空乘实用英语教程

CP: Now let's clarify the duties. Tina is responsible for R1 as well as the inspection and retraction of drinks, in-flight supplies in the C2 galley, and also takes charge of the cabin service and safety management in the R-aisle of the business class. Jane, you are responsible for L1 and the C1 galley as well as the L-aisle of business class. Elizabeth is in charge of R2, C2 galley and the R-aisle of the front of economy class. Linda is responsible for L2, the L-aisle of the front of economy class, the receiving, counting and handing over of hygiene supplies as well as entertainment portable equipment. Alice, you are responsible for R3, the R-aisle of the economy class and the inventory, sales and handover of the duty-free goods. Ivy is responsible for L3 and the L-aisle of the economy class. Mary, takes charge of L4, the galley in economy class and the rear of the economy class. Lily, is in charge of R4, the galley in economy class and R-aisle of the economy class. Have you got your duties clear?

主任乘务长：现在我们来明确下职责要求。蒂娜负责 R1 门和 C2 厨房饮料和机上供应品的检查、回收，同时也负责公务舱右通道的客舱服务和安全管理。简负责 L1 门、C1 厨房以及公务舱的左侧通道。伊丽莎白负责 R2 门、C2 厨房和经济舱前舱右边通道。琳达负责 L2 门，经济舱前舱的左边通道，卫生用品及娱乐便携设备的接收、清点和转交。爱丽丝负责 R3 门，经济舱右边通道和免税品的清点、销售和转交。艾薇负责 L3 门和经济舱的左通道。玛丽负责 L4、经济舱厨房以及经济舱的后部。莉莉负责 R4 门，经济舱厨房和右通道。大家都明白自己的职责了吗？

CA: Yes, we have.

乘务员：是的，明白了。

CP: Lily, a WCHR passenger will be sitting in the R-aisle side in the rear of the cabin. So please take good care of him. Do remember to introduce him the facilities on board around him, and remind him to disembark until the ground staff come to pick him up.

主任乘务长：莉莉，本次航班有一位轮椅旅客，他会坐在右通道那一侧，请照顾好他，一定要记得给他介绍周围的设施设备，并且提醒他落地后不要急着下机，等候地面工作人员来接他。

Lily: OK, I got it.

Lily: 好的，明白了。

CP: Now we'll check if you've been familiar with the flight routes information. What is the scheduled time of departure and arrival, Alice？

主任乘务长：现在我们就航线信息进行提问，看看大家是否已经熟知。爱丽丝，我们的计划起飞和到达时间是什么时候？

Alice: The scheduled time of departure is 9:55 a.m. Beijing time and the arrival time is 6:40 a.m. local time in Vancouver. The time difference is 16 hours.

Alice: 计划起飞时间是北京时间上午 9:55，到达时间是温哥华当地时间早上 6:40。两地时差是 16 小时。

CP: Good! Lily, what is the passenger number for today's flight?

主任乘务长：很好！莉莉，今天的航班人数是多少？

Lily: We have 15 in business class, 30 in premier economy class and 128 in economy class.

Lily: 我们有 15 名公务舱旅客，30 名超级经济舱旅客和 128 名经济舱旅客。

CP: Yes! Cabin safety is the most important issue for the flight. Please check the emergency equipment in your area after boarding. Linda, how many First Aid Kits are there on this plane?

主任乘务长：没错。客舱安全是航班最重要的方面。登机后请检查自己所负责区域的应急设备。琳达，本架飞机上有多少个急救箱？

Linda: There are four. They are located at the door of L1, L4, R4 and in the aft galley area.

Linda: 共有 4 个，分别在 L1、L4、R4 和后舱厨房区域。

CP: Great! Now Ivy, could you please tell us how to use the Halon Extinguisher?

主任乘务长：非常棒！艾薇，请说明一下海伦灭火器的方法，好吗？

Ivy: Hold the handle with the right hand, roll and pull out the safety bins with the left hand. Hold the bottle vertically 2 to 3 meters from fire source, aim at the bottom, press the trigger, and move to fight fire.

Ivy: 右手握住手柄，左手转动并拔出安全销。垂直握住瓶体，距离火源 2 至 3 米，对准火源底部，按下触发器，移动灭火。

CP: Right, thank you, Ivy. Now let's have a review of the evacuation procedures. Tina, could you talk about your responsibilities in land evacuation？

主任乘务长：是的，谢谢艾薇。现在让我回顾一下应急撤离程序。蒂娜，你能说说在陆地撤离时你的职责是什么吗？

Tina: OK, I'm CS2 for today's flight. I'm responsible for the front galley and stand in Row 11 of R-aisle for safety demo. I'm in charge of the clearance and security check from Row 11 to Row 20 of R-aisle. And I'm responsible for R1 door and evacuate from R1. The emergency item I should carry is flashlight.

Tina: 好的，我是今天航班的 CS2 号位。我负责前厨房的工作，站在右通道的第 11 排进行客舱安全演示。我负责右通道第 11 至 20 排的清舱和安全检查，负责右一门，并且从右一门撤离。陆地撤离时，我要携带的应急设备是手电筒。

CP: Thank you, and do hope that everyone will cooperate with each other as a team. Let's have a pleasant journey.

主任乘务长：谢谢，希望大家能够团队协作。旅途愉快！

Dialogue 2-B Crew Coordination Meeting（机组协同会）

Purser: Good morning, Captain! I'm the purser of today's flight. My name is Margaret. I'm very glad to fly with you today.

乘务长：机长您好，我是今天跟您一起执行航班的乘务长。我叫玛格丽特，很高兴今天和您一起执飞。

Captain: Good morning! Our flight number is AC 26 from Shanghai to Vancouver. My name is Michael.

机长：早上好！今天我们的航班号是 AC 26，上海到温哥华，我叫迈克尔。

Purser: How do we communicate with you and enter the cockpit under normal situation, Captain?

乘务长：机长，正常情况下我们与驾驶舱联络的方式是什么？我们如何进入驾驶舱？

Captain: Use the cabin interphone under normal situation. And you can enter the cockpit by pressing the pound sign and knocking the door three times under normal situation.

机长：正常情况下直接使用内话联络，进入驾驶舱按"#"键并敲三下门。

Purser: How do we contact each other under emergency？

乘务长：机长，请问紧急情况下如何联络？

Captain: Use emergency call button for emergency or hijacking. The emergency code is "Captain, your cappuccino is ready." in case of hijacking. Please follow abnormal procedure in the manual in emergency.

机长：遇到紧急情况或劫机，使用紧急呼叫按钮。万一遇到劫机，暗语是"机长，您的卡布奇诺咖啡准备好了"，紧急情况下执行手册里的非正常程序。

Purser: How is the weather on route today, Captain?

乘务长：机长，请问今天航路天气如何？

Captain: Due to strong winds and storms over the Pacific Ocean, we may encounter some turbulence during the flight.

机长：由于太平洋上有强烈风暴，预计我们途中可能会遇到气流颠簸。

Purser: What is the signal for turbulence, Captain?

乘务长：机长，颠簸的信号是什么？

Captain: "Fasten Seat Belt" sign on and one time ringing for slight turbulence, and you must pay attention. Two times for moderate turbulence and the cabin service should be suspended.

Margaret, can you confirm that your crew is familiar with the cockpit procedures？

机长：安全带信号灯亮起，一声铃代表轻度颠簸，客舱需要注意；两声铃代表中度颠簸，客舱需要暂停服务。玛格丽特，你可以确认乘务员们都熟悉驾驶舱程序了吗？

Purser: Yes, Captain. All crew members are familiar with the rules and procedures regarding the cockpit.

乘务长：是的，机长，全体乘务员都已熟悉驾驶舱相关规则和程序了。

Captain：Great! Thank you and have a good flight!

机长：很好！谢谢大家，飞行愉快！

第三节　安全指导

安全指导（safety instruction）是飞行中必不可少的环节。国际航空运输协会（IATA）对客舱安全有明确说明：客舱安全重在强调乘务员必须完成维持客舱安全的相关任务。这些任务是为了确保飞机在正常、非正常或紧急情况下，既能保证安全，又能兼顾效力和效率的运营。客舱人员在阻止大小事故发生上起着重要作用。民航系统提出了"三个敬畏"，即敬畏生命、敬畏职责、敬畏规章，也是对安全至上理念的一次致敬。下面以座位安排和安全检查为例。

Dialogue 3-A　Seat Arrangement（座位安排）

1. take a wrong seat（坐错座位）

(*CA=Cabin Attendant, PAX=Passenger*)

PAX 1: Excuse me, Miss?

乘客 1：不好意思，小姐？

CA: What can I do for you?/Can I help you?

乘务员：我能为您做点什么吗？

PAX 1: I think my seat number is 12B, but it's been taken.

乘客 1：我的座位号是 12B。但是已经有人坐在那里了。

CA: May I see your boarding pass, please?

乘务员：能看一下您的登机牌吗？

PAX 1: Here you are.

乘客 1：给你。

CA: I am afraid the lady might be in the wrong seat. / I'm afraid the lady might have taken a wrong seat. Please wait a moment.

乘务员：恐怕那位女士坐错座位了。请在这里稍等片刻。

CA: Excuse me, madam. May I see your boarding pass?

乘务员：对不起，女士。我可以看看您的登机牌吗？

PAX 2: Here you are.

乘务员：给你。

CA: I'm sorry. This is 36B, but your seat is 56B, in the rear of the cabin.

乘务员：对不起。这里是 36B，而您的座位是 56B，在后舱。

PAX 2: Let me check... Oh, I'm sorry, I'm in the wrong seat. I'll move.

乘客 2：让我看一下……哦，对不起，我坐错位子了。我立刻就换。

CA: Thanks a lot.

乘务员：十分感谢！

2. Narrow Legroom（座椅间距太窄）

(*CA=Cabin Attendant, PAX=Passenger*)

PAX: Excuse me, Miss. I want to change a seat. /May I take another seat? The legroom here is too narrow for me.

乘客：打扰一下，小姐。我想换个座位。/ 我能换个座位吗？这儿的座位空间太窄了。

CA: For the weight and balance of the plane, would you please take the assigned seat for this moment? I'll try to arrange it after take-off.

乘务员：为了飞机的配载平衡，请您先坐在指定位子好吗？起飞后我稍后将尽量为您安排。

PAX: OK, thanks.

乘客：好的，谢谢。

CA: Sir, I'm sorry there are no vacant seats on board.

乘务员：对不起，先生。我们没有空位子了。

PAX: Thanks anyway.

乘客：不过还是得谢谢你。

CA: There are some vacant seats in the rear row. Would you like to sit there?

乘务员：后舱那排有些空位子，您想坐那儿吗？

PAX: OK, thank you very much.

乘客：好的，非常感谢！

3. Sitting Together（座位调换）

(*CA=Cabin Attendant, PAX=Passenger*)

PAX: Excuse me, Miss. My friend and I have separate seats but we want to sit together. He is in 36C.

乘客：打扰一下，小姐，我和我的朋友的座位号不在一起，但我们想坐在一起。他坐在 36C。

CA: Well. I'll try to talk with the lady next to him to exchange seat with you.

乘务员：好的。我去和坐在他边上的女士商量一下，和您换个座位。

(*To the lady sitting next to the passenger's friend.* 对该旅客朋友旁的女士。)

CA: Excuse me, Madam. The man sitting in 36J would like to sit together with the passenger next to you. Would you mind changing seats with him?

乘务员：打扰了，女士。坐在 36J 的那位先生想和您邻座的这位乘客坐在一起。您介意和他调换下座位吗？

Madam: OK, no problem.

女士：没问题。

CA：Thank you so much, Madam.

乘务员：太感谢您了，女士。

(*To the passenger who wants to exchange seats.* 对刚才那位想调换座位的旅客。)

CA: Now you can sit with your friend.

乘务员：您现在可以和您朋友坐在一起了。

PAX: It's so kind of you.

乘客：您真好！

CA: My pleasure.

乘务员：很乐意为您服务。

4. Emergency Exit Seats（紧急出口座位）

CA: Excuse me, Miss. You are now sitting next to the emergency exit. According to the regulations, you are required to read the *Safety Instruction Card*. If you have any questions, please ask our flight attendant. The door beside you is an emergency exit. In normal situations you are not allowed to touch any part, especially this red handle to avoid unexpected accident. In addition, you are supposed to help us by opening this exit and assist other passengers to evacuate in case of emergency. Are you willing to sit here?

乘务员：打扰一下，女士。您现在所在的座位是飞机上的出口座位，根据有关规定，请您先阅读一下这张出口座位旅客须知，如果有任何问题，请向乘务员提出。您座位旁边的是飞机上的应急出口，在正常情况下，请您不要触动机门上的任何装置，尤其是这个把手，以免发生事故。另外，在紧急情况下，需要请您协助我们打开此门并协助其他旅客紧急撤离。您愿意坐在这里吗？

(*Situation A*)

PAX: No problem.

乘客：没问题。

CA: Please read the Safety Instruction Card in the seat pocket in front of you. Thank you for your cooperation.

乘务员：这个是紧急出口安全须知卡，请您在起飞前仔细阅读。感谢您的配合。

(*Situation B*)

PAX: Oh, I don't want to sit here.

乘客：啊，我不想坐在这里了。

CA: All right. I will manage to arrange another seat for you.

乘务员：我去想办法帮您重新安排一个座位吧。

Dialogue 3-B Security Check（安全检查）

(*CA=Cabin Attendant, PAX=Passenger*)

（*A passenger is using the mobile phone.* 一位旅客正在使用手机。）

CA: Excuse me, madam. Mobile phones cannot be used at this moment.

乘务员：打扰一下，女士。现在不可以使用手机。

PAX: Why?

乘客：为什么？

CA: Because it will interfere with the cockpit instrument and navigation system. So we ask all passengers to turn off their electronic devices or switch them to flight mode during take-off and landing.

乘务员：因为手机信号会干扰驾驶舱设备和导航系统。所以我们要求所有乘客在飞机起飞和着陆阶段关闭电子设备或者调成飞行模式。

PAX: OK, I see. I'll switch it to flight mode.

乘客：好的，明白了。我把它调到飞行模式。

CA: Thanks for your understanding. And would you please put your seatback to an upright position?

乘务员：谢谢您的理解。您能将座椅靠背调直吗？

PAX: Oh, I'm sorry. But how can I adjust it?

乘客：哦，对不起。但是我怎么调节呢？

CA: Just press the button on your armrest.

乘务员：只需要按一下座椅扶手上的按钮就可以了。

PAX: Is that right?

乘客：这样就可以了吗?

CA: OK. Please also keep your seat belt fastened.

乘务员：可以了。同时请您系好安全带。

PAX: Sorry, I don't know how to do it. Can you help me?

乘客：对不起，我不会操作。您可以帮帮我吗?

CA: Sure. Please inset the link into the buckle and pull on the loose end to tighten the belt. And if you need to release the seatbelt, just lift the flap and pull out the link.

乘务员：当然可以。请将连接片插入锁扣，然后抽紧另一头。如要解开，将锁扣打开并拉出连接片即可。

PAX: I see. Thank you.

乘客：我知道了。谢谢你。

(*Then A lady with a baby sitting next to this passenger asks.* 旁边带小孩的女士问道。)

Lady: Excuse me, the seatbelt is too short for both my baby and me.

女士：打扰了，安全带太短了，不够我和宝宝一起使用呀。

CA: Let me help you. Please hold your baby outside the seat belt. That will be comfortable for the baby.

乘务员：让我来帮您。请将孩子抱在安全带的外面，不要绑在孩子的身上。这样孩子会舒服些。

Lady:Oh, thanks. By the way, I want to go to the lavatory to change the diaper for my baby.

女士：是的，谢谢您。对了，我需要去趟洗手间给孩子换下尿布。

CA: Sorry, madam. The plane is about to take off and the lavatory has been suspended. You must remain seated with your seatbelt fastened and wait until the plane reaches its cruising altitude.

乘务员：对不起，女士。飞机马上要起飞了，洗手间已经暂停使用。您必须在座位上系好安全带，等飞机达到巡航高度后才可以使用洗手间。

PAX: I see, thank you.

乘客：明白了，谢谢您。

第四节　服务意识

　　客舱服务工作是乘务员工作的主要内容。服务意识（service awareness）的培养离不开具体的服务工作。服务意识贯穿于航班起飞前、起飞中、起飞后的整个过程。服务意识不仅体现在对服务内容的了然于心，也体现在对服务细节、旅客心理和差异化服务等方面。作为一名准乘务员，平时需要从细节入手，将爱心、关心、细心、耐心融入服务过程。下面以行李安排、设备使用、客舱餐饮、免税品销售服务为例。

Dialogue 4-A　Baggage Arrangement（行李安排）

1. No Vacant Locker（行李架已满）

(CA=Cabin Attendant, PAX=Passenger)

CA: Excuse me. May I help you with your baggage, Miss?

乘务员：先生，需要我帮您放行李吗？

PAX: Yes, the overhead locker here is full and I've tried to put it under the seat, but it doesn't fit.

乘客：好的，行李架已经满了，我试着放在座位下面，但放不下。

CA: Would you mind if I put it in the front of the cabin?

乘务员：您不介意我帮您把行李放到前舱吧？

(Situation A)

PAX: Thanks. But there is something I will need during the flight. May I take it out?

乘客：谢谢你，但包里有些东西我要用。我可以取出来吗？

CA: OK. You may take it out and stow it under the seat in front of you.

乘务员：哦，您可以取出来放在您前排座位下面。

(Situation B)

PAX: No, I don't want to put my baggage in other places.

乘客：不，我不愿意把我的行李放在其他地方。

CA: OK. Then I'll try my best to make room for you soon. We are very sorry for the inconvenience.

乘务员：好吧！我尽量给您腾出地方帮您放，很抱歉给您带来了不便。

PAX: That's OK.

乘客：没关系。

2. Over-sized /Scattered Baggage（行李过大 / 散乱）

(CA=Cabin Attendant, PAX=Passenger)

CA: Excuse me. Whose bag is it?

乘务员：不好意思，请问这是谁的包？

PAX: It's mine. Is there a problem?

乘客：是我的。有什么事？

(*Situation A*)

CA: Your bag is too big for the overhead locker. I'm afraid you have to check it in. I will contact the ground staff for you. Do you have any valuables inside?

乘务员：您的箱子太大了，行李架都关不上了。我来联系地面工作人员办理托运。您箱子里有贵重物品吗？

(*Situation B*)

CA: There is not enough space for your baggage here. I need to rearrange it.

这里已经不够放您的行李了。我需要重新整理一下。

PAX: OK.

乘客：好的。

CA: Thank you for your understanding.

乘务员：谢谢您的理解。

Dialogue 4-B　The Use of the Equipment on Board（机上设施的使用）

(*CA=Cabin Attendant, PAX=Passenger*)

CA: Hello, sir. Can I help you?

乘务员：您好，先生。有什么需要帮忙的吗？

PAX: Yes. It's very hot and stuffy in the cabin.

乘客：是呢。客舱里又热又闷。

CA: Sir, you can turn the knob here to open the air ventilator and adjust the direction you like.

乘务员：您可以转动这个旋钮来打开通风口，并且调整到您想要的方向。

PAX: I see. Let me try. OK, it's all right now. By the way, can I recline the seatback now?

乘客：明白了。我试试看。好的，这下可以了。对了，现在我可以将座椅靠背倾斜了吗？

CA: Yes, please feel free to adjust your seatback to a more comfortable position. Just press the button on your armrest and lean backward at the same time.

乘务员：是的，您可以随意调节椅背到较舒适的位置。只要按下扶手上的按钮，同时身体向后靠就行了。

PAX: OK, thank you very much.

乘客：好的，非常感谢。

(*After a while, cabin attendants are distributing/handing out earphones.* 过了一会儿，乘务员开始发放耳机。)

PAX: Could you give me a pair of earphones?

乘客：可以给我一副耳机吗？

CA: Certainly. Here you are.

乘务员：当然可以。给你。

PAX: Thanks. But I don't know how to use it.

乘客：谢谢。但是我不知道如何使用。

CA: Don't worry. Let me show you. Put the earplugs into your ears and put the plug into the socket on your armrest. The volume and channel buttons are located on the armrest. You can turn to whichever channel you like and adjust the volume by pressing the plus or minus sign.

乘务员：别担心。我演示给您看。将耳塞插入您的耳朵，将插头插入扶手上的插座孔里。控制声音和频道的按钮都在扶手上。您可以调到您喜欢的任意频道，按增加或减少键调整音量。

PAX: Oh, I got it. Thanks a lot.

乘客：哦，我明白了。谢谢！

CA: You are welcome.

乘务员：不客气。

Dialogue 4-C　Meal and Drink Service（餐饮服务）

1. Snacks（小吃、点心）

(*CA=Cabin Attendant, PAX=Passenger*)

CA: Good morning, sir/madam! We are going to serve you snacks. May I put down your tray table?

乘务员：女士 / 先生，早上好！我们现在为您提供餐饮服务。可以为您把小桌板放下来吗？

PAX: Sure.

旅客：好啊。

CA: We have prepared peanuts/cookies/sandwiches. Here you are.

乘务员：我们为您准备花生 / 饼干 / 三明治。给您。

PAX: Thank you.

旅客：谢谢。

CA: And what would you like to drink? /What kind of drinks do you prefer? We only serve tea, coffee and mineral water for short flights.

乘务员：请问您想喝点什么饮料？短航线我们只提供热茶、咖啡，以及矿泉水。

PAX: Just water, please.

旅客：水就可以。

2. Beverage Service（饮料供应）

(*CA=Cabin Attendant, PAX=Passenger*)

PAX: What kind of drinks do you have on board?

乘客：飞机上有什么饮料？

CA: We have green tea, black tea, mineral water, mango juice, orange juice, Coke, Sprite and coffee. Which would you prefer/care for?

乘务员：我们有绿茶、红茶、矿泉水、芒果汁、橙汁、可乐、雪碧和咖啡，您想喝点什么？

PAX: A cup of green tea, please.

乘客：一杯绿茶吧，谢谢。

CA: OK, how would you like tea, light or strong?

乘务员：好的，您想要泡淡点还是浓点？

PAX: Light, please.

乘客：淡一点，谢谢！

CA: Here you are. Be careful, and it's hot.

乘务员：给您。请小心，有点儿烫。

PAX: Thanks.

乘客：谢谢。

CA: I'm happy to be at your service. If you'd like to refill your tea, please don't hesitate to call me.

乘务员：很高兴为您服务。如果您需要续茶，请随时叫我。

3. Vegetarian Food（素食）

(*CA=Cabin Attendant, PAX=Passenger*)

PAX: Excuse me, are there any meals available?

乘客：有吃的吗？

CA: We have fish rice and beef noodles. Which would you like?

乘务员：我们有鱼肉米饭和牛肉面，您要吃哪种？

PAX: Do you have vegetarian food?

乘客：你们供应素食吗？

CA: We do carry pre-ordered vegetarian meals for passengers who have booked prior to their flight. Did you book them?

乘务员：我们确实为预订了素食餐的旅客准备了素食。您有预订吗？

PAX: No, I'm afraid I didn't.

乘客：恐怕没有。

CA: Well, I could check to see if we have any spare meals for you. Would you like me to do that?

乘务员：嗯，我可以去帮您看看还有没有，好吗？

PAX: Yes, please. That would be great.

乘客：好的，那太好了。

CA: I'll be back in a moment.

乘务员：我一会儿就回来。

(*A moment later.* 过了一会儿。)

CA: Sorry, there's no vegetarian meal left on board. But we have fruits and desserts, would you like some instead?

乘务员：抱歉，机上已经没有素食餐了。但是我们有水果和甜点，您要不要来点儿？

PAX: OK, that's fine, thank you!

乘客：好的，行，谢谢！

CA: You're welcome.

乘务员：不客气。

4. Baby food（婴儿餐）

(*CA=Cabin Attendant, PAX=Passenger*)

PAX: Do you have baby food on board?

乘客：机上有没有婴儿餐？

CA: Yes. I will get it for you at once. / No, but would you like some bread and fruit instead for your baby?

乘务员：有的，我去给你拿。/ 没有，但是我们有些面包和水果。您要给小孩子拿点儿吗？

PAX: OK, thanks.

乘客：好的，谢谢。

PAX: Excuse me, miss. Could you help me prepare some milk?

旅客：能帮我准备点儿奶吗？

CA: Certainly. How much milk powder and water should I combine?

乘务员：没问题。需要加多少奶粉多少水？

PAX: Please add 3 spoons of milk powder and 2/3 bottle of water.

乘客：请加 3 勺奶粉，加水加到满瓶的 2/3。

CA: OK, I'll be back soon.

乘务员：好的，我马上回来。

客舱应急意识（emergency awareness）就是乘务员能对客舱特殊情况做出"未雨绸缪，防患于未然"的准备。它包括对航班延误或取消的处理，突发情况和特殊情况的有效应对。乘务员除了具备良好的服务能力和应急能力外，还应具备较强的心理素质。通过对问题的重视，乘务员能找到有效的解决方案，达到让旅客身心都舒畅或愉悦的目的。

下面以航班延误和投诉处理为例。

Dialogue 5-A　Delayed Flights（航班延误）

(*CA=Cabin Attendant, PAX=Passenger*)

PAX: Why don't we take off?

乘客：我们为什么没起飞？

CA: I'm sorry to tell you that this flight has been delayed due to the mechanical problem.

乘务员：很抱歉，由于机械故障，本次航班已经延误。

PAX: You mean...

乘客：您是说……

CA: I am afraid we will have to stay here overnight.

乘务员：恐怕我们要在这儿过夜了。

PAX: Oh, no. What time is it?

乘客：不是吧，现在几点了？

CA: It's 10:20 p.m. But don't worry. We'll provide free food and accommodation for every passenger.

乘务员：现在是晚间10点20分。是的，请不要担心。我们将为每位旅客提供免费食宿。

PAX: But when and how can I get back to Beijing?

乘客：但是我们什么时候才能到北京？怎么回北京呢？

CA: We will arrange buses to Beijing tomorrow morning.

乘务员：明天早上将安排大巴车让大家返回北京。

PAX: How long does the trip take?

乘客：那路上要多久？

CA: About one and a half hours.

乘务员：一个半小时左右。

PAX: That sounds reasonable.

乘客：哦，听上去还行。

Dialogue 5-B　Dealing with Complaints（投诉处理）

1. Miss the Meal Serving（供餐遗漏）

(CA=Cabin Attendant, PAX=Passenger)

CA: Excuse me, sir/madam. Do you enjoy your meal? /How do you like your meal? /What do you think of your meal?

乘务员：先生 / 女士，用餐愉快吗?

PAX: No, I have not even got it yet. I have been waiting for 10 minutes, and it seems that the attendant forgot it.

旅客：别提了。我的餐还没上呢！我已经等了 10 分钟了，乘务员好像是把我给忘了。

CA: I fully understand your feelings, sir/madam; and I apologize for this inconvenience. /I'm sorry for this mistake. I will be back with your meal soon, OK?

乘务员：我完全理解您的感受，我为给您造成的不便道歉。我这就去厨房，很快就回来，好吗?

PAX: OK.

旅客：好的。

CA: (*A moment later.*) Please enjoy your meal, sir/madam.

乘务员：（过了一会儿。）请慢用。先生 / 女士。

PAX: Thank you.

旅客：谢谢。

CA: My pleasure.

乘务员：不客气。

2. Explanation and Comfort（解释与安抚）

(CA=Cabin Attendant, PAX=Passenger)

PAX: Where is my drink?

乘客：为什么我还没饮料呢?

CA: Sorry, madam. You were sleeping just then. I didn't want to wake you up. What would you like to drink?

乘务员：对不起，刚才您在休息，我不想吵醒您，您想喝点什么?

PAX: A cup of coffee, please.

乘客：来杯咖啡吧。

CA: Black or white?

乘务员：您要黑咖啡还是奶咖啡?

PAX: Black, please.

乘客：黑咖啡。

CA: OK, I'll get it for you at once.

乘务员：好的，我马上给您拿。

CA: (*The attendant comes back later.*) Sir/Miss/Madam, here is your black coffee.

乘务员：（过了一会，乘务员回来了。）先生 / 女士 / 小姐，您的黑咖啡。

PAX: Thanks.

乘客：谢谢。

CA: Would you like something to eat? We have chicken rice and beef noodles.

乘务员：您想吃点什么吗？我们有鸡肉米饭和牛肉面条。

PAX: I'd like some chicken rice.

乘客：我想吃点鸡肉米饭。

CA: OK, please wait a moment.

乘务员：好的，请稍等。

3. Mistakes During Meal Service（送错餐）

(*CA=Cabin Attendant, PAX=Passenger*)

PAX: Excuse me. I want chicken rice, not noodles!

乘客：打扰一下，我要的是鸡肉米饭，不是面条！

CA: I'm terribly sorry for the mistake. I'll change it for you at once.

乘务员：真是太抱歉了，我马上给您换一份。

(*The attendant comes back soon.* 乘务员很快回来了。)

CA: Here you are.

乘务员：给您。

PAX: Thank you.

乘客：谢谢。

CA: My pleasure.

乘务员：很高兴为您服务。

Dialogue 5-C   Looking for Lost Item（寻找丢失的物品）

(*CA=Cabin Attendant, PAX=Passenger*)

PAX: I can't find my mobile phone.

乘客：我找不着我手机了。

CA: When and where do you think you lost it?

乘务员：您是什么时候在哪里发现不见的？

PAX: I'm not sure.

乘客：我也不确定。

CA: Would you please offer us some details about your mobile phone?

乘务员：您的手机是什么样的呢？

PAX: It's a Huawei Nova 8, black in color.

乘客：一个黑色的华为 Nova 8 手机。

CA: We'll make an announcement about that. We'll contact you later.

乘务员：我们帮您做一个寻物的广播吧，稍后联系您。

Purser's Announcement:

Ladies and gentlemen,

May I have your attention, please? We are looking for a black Huawei mobile phone. If anyone's found one, please contact our flight attendant immediately, or press the call button overhead.

乘务长广播：

女士们、先生们：

请注意，现在广播寻物启事，如有旅客拾到一个黑色华为手机，请立刻与乘务员联系，或按压头顶上方的呼唤铃。

CA: (*a moment later*) Sorry, we haven't found it onboard. Please write down your name, address, phone number and a detailed description of your mobile phone. If we get it, we will contact you as soon as possible. Or when you arrive, you can contact the Airport Lost and Found Office by dialing this number: ××××××××.

乘务员：（片刻后）对不起，我们没有找到您的手机，您能写下您的姓名、联系地址、电话和您物件的明细吗？我们找到后会尽快联系您。或者您可以在到达后打电话给机场失物招领咨询，电话号码是 ××××××××。

PAX: It's so nice of you.

乘客：你真是太好了。

CA: You are welcome.

乘务员：不客气。

第六节 沟通技巧

沟通技巧（communication skills）注重与不同旅客打交道的策略和技巧，也涉及因服务对象不同而产生的语言多元化，表达多层次，以及内容丰富性。乘务员除了能够熟练掌握语言策略，还应熟悉旅客的心理特征，做到游刃有余。平时可以通过辩论、演讲等形式提高自己的表达能力和沟通技巧。下面以登机和头等舱服务为例。

Dialogue 6-A　Boarding（登机）

(*CA=Cabin Attendant, PAX=Passenger*)

CA: Good morning/ afternoon/evening. Welcome aboard!

乘务员：早上好 / 下午好 / 晚上好。欢迎乘机。

PAX: Good morning/afternoon/evening. Where can I find my seat?

乘客：早上好 / 下午好 / 晚上好。我的座位在哪里？

CA: May I see your boarding pass, please?/Could you show me your boarding pass, please?

乘务员：能看一下您的登机牌吗？

PAX: Here you are.

乘客：给您。

CA: Your seat number is 40A, a window seat, in the middle of the cabin. This way please. The seat number is shown/indicated on the edge of the rack.

乘务员：您的座位是 40A，靠窗，在客舱中部。请走这边。/ 请跟我来。座位号位于行李架的边缘。

PAX: Thank you. And when will we take off? And how about the time to land?

乘客：谢谢。请问我们什么时候起飞，什么时候落地呢？

CA: We will take off at 9:50 a.m. and land at 6:40 a.m. local time in Vancouver.

乘务员：我们将于早上九点五十起飞，到达温哥华的时间是当地时间早上 6：40。

PAX: Thanks.

乘客：非常感谢。

CA: You're welcome.

乘务员：不客气。

(*A passenger is blocking the way in the cabin. / A passenger is standing in the aisle.* 一位旅客挡住了客舱通道。)

CA: Excuse me, sir/ madam/miss. Would you please step aside / make room for others to go through?

乘务员：对不起，您能靠边一些以便他人通过吗？

PAX: Oh, sorry.

乘客：哦，对不起。

CA: Thanks for your cooperation.

乘务员：谢谢您的合作。

Dialogue 6-B　First Class Service（头等舱服务）

1. Priority of Boarding（优先登机）

(CA=Cabin Attendant, PAX=Passenger)

CA: Welcome aboard! Good morning, Miss Lee.

乘务员：欢迎登机！李女士，早上好。

PAX: Good morning!

乘客：早上好！

CA: Miss. Lee, I'm the cabin attendant for the first class in this flight. My name is Jane, and I'm very honored to be at your service. Let me help you stow your bag in the overhead compartment.

乘务员：李女士，我是本次航班的头等舱乘务员。我叫简，很高兴为您服务。我帮您把包放到行李架上吧。

PAX: OK, thanks.

乘客：好的，谢谢。

CA: Would you mind if I hang up your coat?

乘务员：请问要将您的衣服挂起来吗？

PAX: No problem. Here you are. Thanks.

乘客：好的，给您，谢谢。

CA: Miss, could you please keep the valuables by yourself?

乘务员：女士，请您自己保管您的贵重物品好吗？

PAX: I will take my wallet and mobile phone out.

乘客：那我取出钱包和手机吧。

CA: OK. I will return your coat before descending.

乘务员：好的，下降前我会给您把衣服拿来的。

2. Distribution Service（派送服务）

(CA=Cabin Attendant, PAX=Passenger)

CA: Miss, you might feel cold later. This is a blanket for you. And we provide slippers for the passengers in the first class. Would you like to change to slippers now? It's good for a long flight.

乘务员：女士，怕您等会儿觉得凉，先给您一个毯子。另外我们为头等舱旅客提供拖鞋，您现在要换拖鞋吗？这对长时间乘坐飞机有好处。

PAX: OK，thanks.

119

乘客：好的，谢谢。

CA: Here is the slippers bag and the shoehorn. You can put your shoes in the slippers bag.

乘务员：这是您的鞋袋和鞋拔。您可以将您的鞋子存放在鞋袋里。

PAX: Thanks, how thoughtful you are!

乘客：谢谢，您的服务真周到。

（*A moment later.* 过了一会儿。）

CA: Miss, here is the warm towel for you.

乘务员：女士，请用热毛巾。

PAX: Thanks.

乘客：多谢!

CA: Would you like to read a newspaper or magazine, Miss? We have *China Daily*, *National Geographic*, *Time* and *Reader's Digest*.

乘务员：您要看报纸、杂志吗，女士？我们有《中国日报》《国家地理》《时代周刊》和《读者文摘》。

PAX: I'd like the latest issue of *Time*.

乘客：我要最新一期的《时代周刊》吧。

CA: Here you are.

乘务员：给您。

PAX: Thanks.

乘客：谢谢。

3. Entertainment Service（娱乐服务）

(*CA=Cabin Attendant, PAX=Passenger*)

CA: Excuse me, Miss. Would you like me to demonstrate how to use the in-flight entertainment system for you?

乘务员：女士，请问需要我为您演示机上娱乐系统操作吗？

PAX: Sure, go ahead.

乘客：当然，好啊。

CA: This is our portable multimedia device designed exclusively for our first-class passengers. Let me turn it on. There are a variety of programs for you to select and enjoy.

乘务员：这是我们专为头等舱旅客准备的多媒体播放器。我来打开它。系统里有很多节目可供选择观看。

PAX: Great!

乘客：太棒了！

CA: Click MODE, then AUDIO for music, and VIDEO for movies. From this menu, you can choose pop music, light music, classic music, symphony, jazz, folk and so on; and you can also select literary film, war film, detective film, romance film, suspense film, action film, documentary, comedy, tragedy, science fiction, disaster, thriller, cartoon and so on. You can enjoy any movie or music on the menu as you like.

乘务员：点击 MODE 键，指向 AUDIO 有各种音乐，指向 VIDEO 有许多电影。在节目菜单上，有流行音乐、轻音乐、古典乐、交响乐、爵士乐、民歌等供您选听；还有文艺片、战争片、侦探片、爱情片、悬疑片、动作片、纪录片、喜剧、悲剧、科幻片、灾难片、惊悚片、动画片等供您选看。您可以欣赏菜单上的任何电影或音乐。

PAX：Sounds good. That's a variety of selections. Thanks.

乘客：听上去不错。选择很多。谢谢。

CA: It's my pleasure to serve you. Enjoy your time. Press the call button whenever you need any help, please.

乘务员：很荣幸为您服务。请您随心欣赏。如有需要请按呼唤铃。

第七节　劝说技巧

劝说技巧（persuasive tips）主要是通过乘务员运用口头表达能力帮助旅客解决实际问题，化解客舱危机。除了能言善辩，乘务员还需要掌握客舱语言与心理服务的一些小技巧。乘务员不仅可以通过巧舌与言辞赢得旅客对服务的认同，也能让旅客的心理得到满足。下面以免税品销售为例。

Dialogue 7　Duty-free Sales（免税品销售）

(*CA=Cabin Attendant, PAX=Passenger*)

(*A cabin attendant comes with a trolley along the aisle.* 乘务员推着推车经过通道。)

PAX: Excuse me, miss. What duty-free items do you have?

乘客：您好，小姐，请问有哪些免税品啊？

CA: We have cigarettes, liquor, cosmetics, jewelry, perfume, watches, silk scarves, etc.

乘务员：我们有香烟、酒、化妆品、珠宝、香水、手表、丝巾等。

PAX: Could you recommend perfumes for me? I'd like to buy a light perfume for my twenty-year old daughter's birthday.

乘客：您可以为我推荐一下香水吗？我想为我20岁的女儿买一款清淡的香水作为生日礼物。

CA: There are two kinds of perfume for you. Both are 50 ml. This one is Miss Dior Blooming Bouquet. The other one is Chanel Coco Mademoiselles.

乘务员：有两款供您选择，都是50毫升。这款是迪奥小姐花漾淡香氛，这款是香奈儿可可小姐香水。

PAX: I guess she likes the Miss Dior Blooming Bouquet. How much does it cost? Do you have a discount?

乘客：我想她喜欢迪奥小姐花漾淡香氛这款。多少钱，有折扣吗？

CA: Sorry, madam. We don't have any discount. All the items are sold at marked prices on board. It's 130 dollars.

乘务员：抱歉，女士，我们没有折扣。机上销售的商品都是明码标价的。这款香水是130美元。

PAX: OK, I see, I'll take it.

乘客：好的，明白，我就要这个了。

CA: How would you like to pay? You can pay in cash or by credit card.

乘务员：您怎么支付呢？现金或信用卡都可以。

PAX: By credit card. Here's my credit card and my frequent flyers card, too, for the points.

乘客：刷信用卡吧。这是我的信用卡，还有我的常旅客卡，可以积分。

CA: Thank you. Would you like a receipt, or just the credit card print-out?

乘务员：谢谢！您需要收据吗，还是信用卡小票就行？

PAX: I need the receipt too, please.

乘客：收据也要的，谢谢。

CA: No problem. Here's your receipt. Here are your cards and this is your gift.

乘务员：没问题。这是您的收据，您的卡和购买的礼品。

PAX: Thanks a lot.

乘客：非常感谢。

CA: My pleasure.

乘客：不客气。

第八节 医疗急救

医疗急救（medical first aid）是乘务人员应对客舱旅客突发事故的有效途径。它需要乘务员掌握机上常见疾病和医疗事故的有效应对策略。除了有危机意识以外，乘务员还应具备相关的动手能力。平时可以积累一些常见疾病和药品的英文表达，同时熟悉医疗急救的步骤和对策。通过医疗急救，乘务员能够更加懂得生命的意义，用大爱去服务每一位旅客。下面以医疗服务为例。

Dialogue 8-A　Medical Service（医疗服务）

1. A passenger with airsickness（晕机旅客）

(*CA=Cabin Attendant, PAX=Passenger*)

PAX: Sir, I feel like vomiting and I'm dizzy. I'm afraid I have got airsickness.

旅客：先生，我想呕吐，也有点头晕。我可能晕机了。

CA: I'm sorry to hear that. But don't worry. Here is an airsickness bag and let me get you a glass of water and a pillow. I'll remove your armrest; put your seatback to a lower position and open your air vent. Please just lie down and relax.

乘务员：很抱歉听到这个消息，但是不必担心。小姐，这是给您的呕吐袋，我再给您拿杯热水和枕头，顺便给您放下扶手，调整靠背和打开通风孔。您可以躺下休息会儿。

（*After a while.* 一会儿之后。）

CA: Miss, here is a glass of hot water and an airsickness tablet. And you can lie on this pillow so that you can feel a little better.

乘务员：女士，这是给您准备的热水和晕机药。您可以靠在枕头上休息，这样感觉会好点。

PAX: Thanks a lot. You're so thoughtful.

乘客：多谢，您真是太周到了。

2. A passenger catching a cold（患重感冒的旅客）

(*CA=Cabin Attendant, PAX=Passenger*)

CA: Hello, madam. Can I help you? You don't look very well.

乘务员：女士，您好！请问有什么需要帮忙的吗？您看起来不太舒服。

PAX: I have caught a cold. I can't help sneezing. And I have a slight headache, a sore throat and a runny nose.

旅客：我好像感冒了，一直打喷嚏。头有点疼，嗓子也不舒服，一直流鼻涕。

CA: Oh, madam, Do you have medicine with you?

乘务员：女士，您有随身携带感冒药吗？

PAX: Yes, it's in my bag in the overhead compartment.

旅客：有的，在我包里，在行李架上。

CA: OK，I'll get your bag down for you and bring you a glass of warm water. A moment, please.

乘务员：好的，我帮您把包取下来。再给您准备杯热水，请稍等。

(*The cabin attendant passed a glass of water to the madam, and also brought her a blanket and pillow.* 乘务员将水递给这位女士，还为她准备了毛毯和枕头。)

CA: Madam, here is the warm water for you. And I also got you a blanket and a pillow, you can take a rest after taking the medicine. If you have any request, please feel free to press the call button.

乘务员：女士，这是给您的热水。我还给您拿来了毛毯和枕头，您服药后可以休息一会儿。如果有需要，请随时按呼唤铃。

PAX: Thanks. You are so considerate.

乘客：谢谢。您真是太贴心了。

3. A passenger suffering from earache（耳朵疼痛的旅客）

(*CA=Cabin Attendant, PAX=Passenger*)

(*A passenger pressed the call button.* 一名乘客按压了呼唤铃。)

CA：What can I do for you, sir?

乘务员：先生，有什么可以帮您的吗？

PAX: I feel pain in my ears. / I'm suffering from earache.

乘客：我觉得耳朵疼。

CA: This is due to the change in air pressure. It's common during the flight. You can relieve it by chewing gum or swallowing saliva.

乘务员：这是由于气压的变化造成的。在飞行中很常见。您可以通过咀嚼口香糖或吞咽口水来缓解疼痛。

4. A passenger with a scald（烫伤的乘客）

(*CA=Cabin Attendant, PAX=Passenger*)

CA: Sir, your tea please. Watch out! It's very hot.

乘务员：先生您的茶，请当心，很烫喔。

PAX: OK... (Passenger distracted)... Ouch! My arm... feels like it is burning!

旅客：好的（伸手接，但未拿好）哎哟！我的胳膊，烫死了！

CA: I'm terribly sorry, sir. This way please. You need ice compress right now.

乘务员：天哪，实在对不起，先生。请您先跟我来，您急需冰敷降温。

PAX: It really hurts!

旅客：痛死了！

CA: I'm sorry sir. We should pay more attention when serving hot drinks. How do you feel now? (*While applying burning ointment.*)

乘务员：真对不起，先生。给您热饮的时候我应该更加小心才是。您感觉怎么样了？（敷烫伤药。）

PAX: It's not so bad.

旅客：还好吧。

CA: Don't worry, sir. After applying ice compress and burning ointment, you would feel better. I'm really sorry!

乘务员：别担心先生，及时冰敷降温和涂药膏后，您就不会那么疼了。真的很抱歉。

PAX: Hey, it's not your fault! And thank you!

旅客：没事，也不是你的错。谢谢！

CA: I'm at your service. I will be back later.

乘务员：随时为您效劳。稍后再来看您。

Dialogue 8-B　Serious Medical Incident（严重医疗事件）

PAX (Passenger): Hey, Miss, come quickly. There's a man back here. He's unconscious.

乘客：喂，快过来啊，女士。后面有个人，他已经失去意识了。

Lily: OK, where is he? Ivy, grab the oxygen and a defibrillator from the medical kit and get Alice to call Margaret, to advise her of a medical emergency.

Lily: 哦，他在哪里？艾薇，你拿下医疗箱里的氧气瓶和除颤器，另外让爱丽斯呼叫玛格丽特，告诉她有医疗紧急情况。

Ivy: OK.

Ivy: 好的。

Alice: Hello, Margaret. This is Alice here from Economy cabin. We have a medical emergency on board...

Alice: 你好，玛格丽特。我是经济舱的爱丽斯。我们这里有医疗紧急情况……

Lily: Hello, can you hear me? (*to the lady next to him*) Are you travelling with this passenger?

Lily: 您好，能听见我说话吗？（对他旁边的女士说）您是和他一起的吗？

Lady: I'm his wife. Oh, my goodness, I think he's had a heart attack. He said he had a bit of indigestion—that was all. He stood up to go to the toilet and then he collapsed.

女士：我是他的妻子。哦，天呐，我想他是心脏病发作了。他前面说他有点消化不良——就没说别的了。然后他起身去洗手间，然后就晕倒了。

（ *The chief purser Margaret came over.* 主任乘务长玛格丽特赶过来了。）

Margaret: Oh, he's very pale. He's not breathing. Let's get him on the floor now... Ivy, loosen his tight clothing and keep his airway unblocked... Oh, he's breathing again. (*To his wife*) Has this ever happened before?

Margaret: 哎呀，他的脸色很苍白。他已经停止了呼吸。我们现在快让他躺在地上……艾薇，解开他的衣领，保持他的呼吸道畅通。……哦，他又有呼吸了。（对他的妻子说）以前有发生过这样的情况吗？

Lady: No.

女士：没有啊。

Margaret: Ivy, help me get the mask over his head. (*To the sick man*) Can you hear me?

(*To other passengers*) Please move away and return to your seats. He needs as much air as possible. Sit down, please. Thank you. Ivy, I think we need a doctor. Can you make an announcement immediately?

(*To his wife*) Is he on any medication?

Margaret: 艾薇，帮我给他戴上氧气面罩。（对病人说）您能听到我说话吗？

（对其他乘客说）请大家离开，回到自己的座位上。他需要尽可能多的空气。请大家坐下来，谢谢！艾薇，我觉得我们需要医生了。你能马上播广播吗？

（对他的妻子说）他有在服药吗？

Lady: Yes, he's a diabetic so he has injections for that. Is he going to be all right?

女士：有的，他患有糖尿病，他有注射药物。他会好吗？

Margaret: Don't worry. We're taking care of him. How old is he?

Margaret: 别担心。我们在照料他。他多大年龄了？

Lady: Sixty-five.

女士：65 岁。

Lily: Is he in good health usually?

Lily: 他平时身体状况好吗？

Lady: Yes, but he's been very tired recently.

Lady: 不错的，但他最近很累。

Purser's Announcement:

Ladies and gentlemen,

There is an urgent medical need here. If there is a doctor on board, please tell the cabin attendants immediately by pressing your call button. Thank you!

乘务长广播：

女士们、先生们：

这里有个医疗紧急情况。如果机上有医生，请您立刻按下呼唤铃告诉乘务员。谢谢！

Doctor: I'm a doctor. What's the problem?

医生：我是医生，有什么问题？

Lady: Oh, thank goodness!

女士：哦，谢天谢地！

Margaret: Hello, doctor, thank you for coming forward. This passenger is unconscious and he stopped breathing for a few seconds. We administered CPR for two minutes and he's breathing again, although his pulse is very weak and his breathing is shallow. We're just administering oxygen...

Margaret：您好，医生，谢谢您赶过来。这名乘客失去意识了，刚还停止了几秒钟的呼吸。我们给他做了 2 分钟的心肺复苏，他又恢复了呼吸。不过他的脉搏还很虚弱，呼吸也很微弱。我们刚刚给他吸了氧……

(The doctor examined the sick man and recommended immediate hospitalization. Then the chief purser informed the captain. 医生对病人检查后建议立即入院。随后主任乘务长通知了机长。*)*

Captain: So what is the situation with the passenger?

机长：这名乘客的情况怎么样了？

Margaret: We have a doctor on board who is with the passenger at the moment. However, it's a very serious situation. The doctor has said the passenger is going into cardiac arrest and has requested the aircraft should divert to the nearest hospital urgently.

Margaret：现在有位医生在陪着这名乘客。但是，情况很严重。医生说这名乘客会心脏骤停并要求飞机立刻备降最近的医院。

Captain: All right. You're absolutely certain?

机长：好的。你完全确定吗？

Margaret: Yes, Captain.

Margaret：是的，机长。

Captain: Is the passenger travelling with anybody else?

机长：这名乘客有同行的人吗？

Margaret: His wife is with him. She's highly stressed and anxious.

Margaret: 他的妻子和他一起的。她现在压力非常大，忧心忡忡。

Captain: All right, I need the passenger's details immediately. I'll contact ATC and make the necessary arrangements. And I'll be back in touch with you in a minute.

机长：好的，我马上需要这名乘客的具体信息。我会和塔台联系，做好必要的安排。稍后我和你联系。

Margaret: OK.

Margaret: 好的。

（*A moment later.* 片刻之后。）

Captain's Announcement:

Ladies and gentlemen,

I'm the Captain William. This is an important announcement. We have a serious medical situation on board and we need to divert to Narita, the nearest airport, as soon as possible. The cabin attendants will now prepare the cabin for landing. I anticipate being on the ground within the next 15 minutes. After landing at Narita, you must remain on board. I do apologize for any inconvenience this diversion may cause. However, I'd like to thank you for your cooperation and understanding. After landing at Narita, we will keep you regularly updated with our plans for your continued flight today.

机长广播：

女士们、先生们：

我是本次航班的机长威廉。下面播送一则重要通知。我们机上出现严重的医疗情况，我们需要尽快备降到最近的成田国际机场。乘务员现在将做着陆准备。预计15分钟后将着陆。在成田国际机场降落后，请您在座位上坐好。对这次备降给您造成的不便，我们深表歉意。感谢您的配合和理解。到达成田后，我们将定时向您告知我们今天航班后续的安排。

（*After the plane landed and the emergency services took charge of the patient, who was transferred to hospital. The flight resumed an hour later. It was later reported that the patient was in a stable condition in hospital in Narita.* 飞机着陆后，地面应急服务部门负责接管病人，将病人转入医院。一小时后，航班重新起飞。后来据报道病人在成田的医院病情稳定。）

第九节 旅游引导

旅游引导（travel guide）主要包括乘务员对候机楼设施、中转和目的地城市旅游信息的掌握。乘务员除了需要一定的地理常识之外，还应具备相应的航班信息知识。乘务员在平时的生活中可以关注世界地理和旅游景点的一些内容，便于和旅客进行深层次的交流。下面以中转和目的地指引为例。

Dialogue 9-A Transfer（中转）

1. About transfer information（中转航班信息）

(CA=Cabin Attendant, PAX=Passenger)

PAX: When will we arrive in Beijing?

乘客：请问我们什么时候能到北京？

CA: About 13：20.

乘务员：13：20 左右。

PAX: Oh, I am afraid I might miss my transfer flight.

乘客：我恐怕会赶不上我的中转航班了。

CA: What's the flight number and departure time?

乘务员：您的中转航班起飞时间及航班号是多少？

PAX: The flight number is 8L9901. And it will take off at 14：50. I have two pieces of checked-in luggage.

乘客：航班号是 8L9901，14：50 起飞。而且我还有两件托运行李。

CA: Sir, please don't worry. There is over an hour for transfer.

乘务员：先生，请别担心。您有一个多小时的转机时间呢。

PAX: The flight number is 8L9901, which will take off at 14：00. I paid 1000 Yuan for the ticket.

乘客：航班号是 8L9901，14：00 起飞。我付了 1000 元买的机票。

CA: I am sorry to hear that. But please don't worry, miss. We will contact our ground staff to help you. They can make an endorsement to another flight and provide free food and accommodation for you.

乘客：很抱歉。但请不要担心，我们会联系地面人员来帮助您。他们会为您更改另一个航班，并为您提供免费食宿的。

PAX: Oh, thank you very much indeed.

乘客：实在太感谢了。

CA: It's my pleasure.

乘务员：不用客气。

2. Stopover at a Transit（中转停留）

(*CA=Cabin Attendant, PAX=Passenger*)

（ Passengers are waiting at the terminal。旅客下机等候。）

PAX: How long shall we have to wait at the terminal and why?

乘客：我们需要在候机楼等多久？为什么要下去等呢？

CA: About 20 minutes. That's because the airplane needs cleaning and refueling.

乘务员：大概需要等待 20 分钟的时间。因为飞机需要清洁和加油。

PAX: Oh, I see. Shall I take everything with me?

乘客：哦，我知道了。所有的东西都要带下去吗？

CA: No. You can leave your luggage on board and please put it into the overhead locker. But do take your boarding pass and valuables with you.

乘务员：不用的。您可以把行李留在飞机上，但请把它们放到行李架内。登机牌和贵重物品请您一定随身携带。

PAX: OK. Thanks.

乘客：好的，谢谢。

CA: You are welcome. And please pay attention to the re-boarding broadcast.

乘务员：不客气。请您留意再次登机的广播。

(*Waiting on board.* 旅客不下机等候。)

PAX: Where can I smoke?

乘客：我在哪里可以吸烟呢？

CA: Sorry, sir. Smoking is not permitted during the whole flight.

乘务员：对不起，先生，您不能在飞机上抽烟。

PAX: Why?

乘客：为什么？

CA: Because it is a regulation of CAAC (Civil Aviation Administration of China) .

乘务员：这也是中国民用航空局的一个规定。

PAX: Well, I got it.

乘客：好吧，我知道了。

Dialogue 9-B　Final Destination（目的地）

(CA=Cabin Attendant, PAX=Passenger)

（Arrival time and information of destination city. 到达时间和目的地城市信息。）

PAX: Excuse me, when will we arrive in Vancouver and what is the temperature there?

乘客：女士，请问我们什么时候能到温哥华，温哥华的地面温度是多少？

CA: Oh, we will arrive at 6:40 a.m. local time in Vancouver. Vancouver time is 16 hours later than Beijing time. And the temperature is 25 degrees Centigrade, 77 degrees Fahrenheit.

乘务员：我们将于温哥华当地时间早上6：40到达，温哥华时间比北京时间晚16小时。地面温度是25℃，77 ℉。

PAX: I see, thank you. This is my first visit to Vancouver. Could you give me a brief introduction of this city?

乘客：明白了，谢谢。这是我第一次来到温哥华。您可以给我简单介绍下这个城市吗？

CA: Certainly. Vancouver is located on the Pacific Coast in southwestern British Columbia, Canada. It is a major port city and an important economic center in Canada. It's also the political, cultural, tourism and transportation center of Western Canada. In addition, Vancouver hosted the Winter Olympic Games in 2010.

乘务员：当然可以。温哥华位于加拿大不列颠哥伦比亚省西南部太平洋沿岸，是加拿大的主要港口城市和重要经济中心，也是加拿大西部的政治、文化、旅游和交通中心。另外，2010年冬奥会也在温哥华举办。

PAX: Oh, I'm looking forward to the visit of this metropolitan city. Could you recommend me some scenic spots in Vancouver?

乘客：哦，我太期待接下来对这个国际都市的参观了。您可以向我推荐下温哥华的景点吗？

CA: Yes, it has lots of tourist attractions, such as Stanley Park, Capilano Suspension Bridge, Gastown, Granville Island and so on. And you can pay a visit to the prestigious university— University of British Columbia, where you can enjoy the enchanting campus scenery.

乘务员：好的，温哥华有很多旅游景点，例如斯坦利公园、卡皮兰诺吊桥、煤气镇、格兰维尔岛等。您还可以参观知名学府——英属哥伦比亚大学，那里可以欣赏到迷人的校园美景。

PAX: It sounds fantastic. Thank you so much for your information.

乘客：听上去太棒了。非常感谢您提供的信息。

CA: It's my pleasure. Wish you have a pleasant trip in Vancouver.

乘务员：很荣幸。希望您在温哥华旅途开心。

（*45 minutes later.* 45 分钟后。）

Purser's announcement:

Ladies and gentlemen,

We have just landed at Vancouver International Airport. Please don't release your seatbelts until the plane comes to a complete stop. Please make sure you've taken all your belongings when you disembark.

乘务长广播：

女士们、先生们：

本架飞机已经降落在温哥华国际机场，请等飞机完全停稳后，您再解开安全带。下机时记得带好您所有的手提物品。

PAX: Excuse me, miss. How far is the downtown from the airport?

乘客：你好，请问机场离市中心有多远？

CA: Fifteen kilometers, sir/ madam/ miss.

乘务员：15 千米，先生 / 女士 / 小姐。

PAX: How can I get to the downtown area from the airport?

乘客：请问我从机场怎样到达市区呢？

CA: You can take a taxi or the airport shuttle bus or the Sky Train. And you may consult the information counter. They'll be able to help you.

乘务员：您可以乘坐出租车，也可以乘坐机场大巴或者天车，您可以咨询机场问讯处。他们会帮您的。

PAX: Thanks. By the way, how much will it cost if I take a taxi?

乘客：谢谢，顺便问一下，打车大概多少钱？

CA: The taxi fare will be about 40 Canadian Dollars.

乘务员：车费大约要 40 加元。

PAX: Thanks so much.

乘客：太感谢了。

CA: My pleasure. Now the air bridge has just been put in this position. You can get your belongings ready for disembarkation. Please make sure nothing is left behind.

乘务员：愿意效劳。现在登机廊桥已到位，您可以拿着行李下飞机了。请确保没有东西落下哦。

PAX: Thank you so much for all you've done for me. I'm deeply impressed by this flight.

乘客：感谢您为我做的一切，让我这次的机上之旅十分难忘。

CA: We're so glad you've enjoyed the flight and it's a great honor for us to be at your service. We look forward to serving you again in the future.

乘务员：您旅途愉快令我们非常高兴，很荣幸为您服务。期待将来再次为您服务。

PAX: Thank you. Good bye.

乘客：谢谢，再见。

CA: See you! Have a nice day!

乘务员：再见！祝您开心！

第十节　出入境常识

出入境常识（customs, immigration & quarantine knowledge）主要涉及乘务员在出入境时候需要自身了解的内容以及国际旅客在出入境时候需要了解的一些常识，具体包括海关、边检和检疫三大块内容：海关主要是控制现金、违禁品、国宝等物件的出入；边检主要管控旅客出入境的目的；检疫主要是做好人和动植物的健康检查。下面是以 CIQ 表单填写为例。

Dialogue 10　CIQ Forms Filling（表单填写入境卡、海关申报单、检验检疫 / 健康卡）

(*CA=Cabin Attendant, PAX=Passenger*)

Purser's Announcement:

Ladies and gentlemen,

We've prepared the entry cards and the customs declaration forms of Canada. Please fill them out before landing. Thank you.

乘务长广播：

女士们、先生们：

我们准备了加拿大的入境卡和海关申报表。请在落地前填写好。谢谢！

CA: Sir, these are CIQ forms for you. Please fill them out before arrival.

乘务员：先生，这是您的 CIQ 表格。请在落地前填好。

PAX: What does CIQ mean? And I've been through quite a few flights before but have never been asked to do so.

乘客：CIQ 是什么意思？另外我之前乘坐过好几次飞机，从来没有让我填写过这些啊。

CA: CIQ means Customs, Immigration and Quarantine. In an international flight, you should do so to keep a record of your travel and help you pass Customs and Quarantine. While in domestic flights, we needn't fill these forms.

乘务员：CIQ 指的是海关、入境和检疫。在国际航班上，您需要填写这些表单从而保持您的入境记录并有助于您通过海关和检疫的检查。而在国内航班上则不要写填写这些。

PAX: Oh, I see. Shall I fill them out on board?

乘客：哦，明白了。那我是要在机上填好吗?

CA: You'd better do so in order to shorten the time of going through the Customs, Immigration and Quarantine.

乘务员：为了缩短您办理海关、入境和检疫的手续的时间，您最好在飞机上把它们填好。

PAX: OK, thanks.

乘客：好的，谢谢！

(*After the cabin attendant handed out all the forms, she patrols the cabin to see if anyone needs help.* 乘务员发完表单后，巡视客舱看看是否有乘客需要帮助。)

PAX: Hello, Miss. I find it difficult to fill out these forms. I've never filled them before and I can't see the fine prints clearly.

乘客：您好，小姐。我觉得填写这些表格很困难。我从来没有填过，也看不清楚上面印的这些小字。

CA: Don't worry. Let me help you. You can fill out the forms from the very beginning of the block by printing in capital letters. Here please write your surname and given name, your date of birth and nationality.

乘务员：别担心。我来帮您。您可以用大写印刷体从表格的开头开始填写。这里请填上您的姓和名字、出生日期和国籍。

PAX: It's OK.

乘客：好了。

CA: Then your passport number, country of origin and flight number here.

乘务员：然后这里填上您的护照号码、原住地和航班号。

PAX: Let me see. My passport number is 009438658. Country of origin, it's China. And the flight number is AC26. Am I right?

乘客：我来看一下。我的护照号码是 009438658。原住地是中国。航班号是 AC26. 我填得对吗?

CA：Yes. Then the city where visa was issued and the date issued.

乘务员：对的。然后是签证签发地和签发日期。

PAX: A moment, please... OK, it's done. What's next?

乘客：请稍等……填好了。接下来填什么？

CA: Next is your purpose of this trip.

乘务员：接下来是填您此次出行的主要原因。

PAX: Oh, we just go to Canada for touring.

乘客：哦，我们是去观光旅行的。

CA: In that case you should tick the "Personal" box. Then your duration of stay in Canada and your accompanying number. The last is your signature.

乘务员：这样的话，您就在"个人"这里打钩。然后是您在加拿大的停留天数和随行人数。最后是您的签名。

PAX: OK, it's done. Many thanks.

乘客：好的，完成了。太感谢了。

CA: It's my pleasure.

乘务员：不客气。

第4章
职业演讲

章前导读

本章为职业演讲。空乘英语教学的目标之一是培养和提高空乘人员应用英语进行沟通交流的能力。演讲与修辞则是实现上述能力的有效手段。事实上，英语演讲是英语综合能力的体现，它不仅强调以语言为载体，以交际为目的，更注重交际过程中各种专业知识、技能和文化背景的综合运用。

本章内容结合空乘职业相关的主题演讲而设计。首先，就英语演讲的本质做了简要介绍。其次，考虑到职业主题演讲的特殊性，从演讲前的准备、演讲稿的撰写、演讲时的技巧三个方面提出了相应的对策。最后，对具有代表性的空乘职业话题进行了罗列和汇总。这些内容涵盖空乘职业素养、客舱安全、服务意识、求职面试等诸多方面，并就每个主题列举了相应的演讲范文。

通过学习本章知识，学生一方面可以强化职业认知，增强职业认同感，另一方面还可以提升英语综合能力，从而适应未来工作岗位对其英语交际能力提出的挑战。另外，英语演讲能力的提升，还可以为学生在毕业后的求职、晋升以及在国外生活等多种语境下用英语进行交流打下良好的基础，并提升其综合素养。

思 政 园 地

青年的人生目标各有差异，职业选择也有不同，但理想信念不可动摇。只有把自己的小我融入祖国的大我之中，与时代同步伐、与人民共命运，才能更好地实现人生价值。作为一名民航人，立足客舱"小世界"，服务民航"大世界"。乘务员通过职业演讲可以加强职业认同感，领悟"三个敬畏"，弘扬民航精神，传播正能量，确立正确的人生观、世界观、价值观。训练演讲的过程，就是要用正确的思想观点说服人，用美好的情感打动人，用优美的语言及优雅大方的仪表感染人，从而引起听众的共鸣。

第一节 英语演讲本质

英语演讲是指在公众场所，以英语为载体，以体态语言为辅助手段，针对某个具体问题，鲜明、完整地发表自己的见解和主张，阐明事理或抒发情感，进行宣传鼓动的一种语言交际活动。

在西方，演讲的历史可以追溯到古希腊时期。亚里士多德的《修辞学》（rhetoric）是最早的系统阐释修辞原理的著作，这种修辞学既是一种研究演说的技艺（演讲术），也是一种研究散文写作的理论。当时的人们就是用演讲和辩论的方式交流哲学上的思辨，并决定公众事务。在我国，演讲的历史也是源远流长，《论语》、魏晋高士谈玄的诘辩之术、南朝刘勰的《文心雕龙》都是古代口才、修辞之学的巨著。

随着时代的发展，现在人们所说的演讲早已不再局限于政治、宗教领域，而是将演讲归类为公众交流（public communication）。一场成功的演讲首先需要考虑的是听众和主题，其次才是语言能力和表达技巧。

一、听众

听众（audience）是演讲信息的接收方。演讲虽然是以口头单向传递的形式呈现，但在信息交流的过程中却是演讲者与听众之间的心理对话（mental dialogue）。因此，一次成功的演讲实际上是演讲者与听众双向交流的动态过程。没有听众参与和支持的演讲只是演讲者一个人的自我表演，将失去交际的目的。成功的演讲者应当在演讲过程中时刻留意听众的反馈，如肢体语言、面部表情等，从而实时调整演讲的节奏。听众专注的神情、认真地聆听、热情的掌声、积极的互动都会对演讲者产生正面的鼓励，使演讲更具感染力和互动性。

二、主题

主题（topic）是演讲的话题，它直接影响了演讲内容和演讲形式。职业主题演讲将话题固定在某一具体的职业领域，对于该行业的从业者而言更具知识储备方面的优势。但演讲者仍需要根据给定的演讲主题进行细致的前期准备工作，充分搜集有关资料，选取更具说服力的论据，同时将题目进行细化和具体化，避开自己不熟悉的内容，充分发挥自己专业背景的优势，使语言更加生动形象。

三、语言能力

语言能力（language competence）是指演讲者对演讲时所用语言的驾驭程度。很多演讲者用母语进行演讲时口若悬河，而用非母语演讲时却战战兢兢，究其根本原因是语言能力影响了演讲者的发挥。因此，演讲者平时就应注重英语基本功的提升，养成阅读大量原文的好习惯。阅读是一个循序渐进的过程，同时也是培养思维的过程，对提高口头表达能力和书面表达能力都是至关重要的。一名成功的演讲者通常需要同时掌握写作、会话和表演三个方面的技能，其中会话技能是最基本也是最重要的。这也是目前空乘人员亟待提升的核心技能之一。

当然，虽然一些演讲者能讲一口地道的英语，但一上台难免就紧张得说不出话，甚至做出一些不当动作，而直接影响了演讲的顺利展开。因此，良好的心理素质也是语言能力得以正常发挥的前提条件之一。要想克服怯场，培养良好的心理素质，演讲前可以多进行模拟训练，适应演讲环境，充分做好演讲前的准备工作，演讲时才能更好地表现自己，取得更理想的演讲效果。

四、表达技巧

表达技巧（presentation techniques）是演讲者在演讲时运用的辅助直接语言表达的手段，包括口头语言、肢体语言与道具。口头语言是指演讲者对其声音的使用技巧，包括音量、语调、语速、重音、停顿、连读、情感等因素。每个人的音色生而不同，因为不是每个人都有播音员一般的嗓音条件，但对语言技巧的恰当运用能弥补音色上的不足，从而取得理想的演讲效果。

肢体语言主要是指演讲过程中的非语言技巧，如眼神、体态、手势、面部表情等。道具指搭配在一起的各种设计元素，主要包括图表、照片、文字、实物、模型、音视频资料等。随着科技的日新月异，道具的呈现方式日趋多样化，目前常见的做法是通过幻灯片（PPT）的形式将多种资料整合，并在演讲时配合演讲者逐一呈现。精心设计的道具往往能对演讲起到锦上添花的作用，并在一定程度上弥补演讲者语言能力的不足。

总之，英语演讲，实际上与其他语言的演讲一样，其本质都是交流，而这种交流活动需要演讲者和听众共同参与和积极配合。

第二节 演讲前的准备

充足的准备是演讲取得成功的前提条件。这种准备既包含了外在的准备，如收集整理资料、撰写演讲稿、准备得体着装等；也包含了内在的准备，如心态的调整和放松。

一、收集整理资料

根据准备时间的不同，可以将演讲分为命题演讲（topics speech）和即兴演讲（prompt speech）。命题演讲在演讲前有更加充裕的时间紧扣话题进行准备，如写好演讲稿或者演讲大纲。而即兴演讲需要演讲者语言修养高，文化知识丰富，对古今中外、天南海北、历史典故、风土人情等各类知识都有所储备和了解，如政治、经济、文化、教育等，并且具备超强的记忆力、想象力、敏捷的思维能力以及丰富的语言表达方式。

俗话说："巧妇难为无米之炊。"无论是命题演讲和即兴演讲，当确定了主题后，演讲者都需要围绕演讲主题组织材料，这些材料既有理论的，又有实际的，必须两者结合，才能真正做到言之有物。

一般而言，职业演讲的主题围绕某一特定领域，因此对于熟悉本行业的演讲者而言，获取材料的途径有直接材料、间接材料和创见材料三类。

（1）直接材料是在生活、工作、学习中通过个人观察、体验、感受、调查、研究得到的材料，如演讲者本人的学习感悟、实习经历等。

（2）间接材料是从书籍、报刊、文献中借鉴的材料，如调研报告、案例研究等。

（3）创见材料是在获取直接材料和间接材料的基础上经过归纳、研究、分析而得出的新材料。使用创见材料时需要格外注重材料的客观性，因为只有真实的材料才具有说服力，能够增强演讲的可信度。

收集材料对于演讲而言十分重要，它是充实演讲主题，充分论证观点的有利条件。材料越充分，思路就越开阔，论据就越充分，就越能清晰地阐明观点。因此，演讲者要养成阅读的好习惯，除了锻炼自己利用有关资源与材料（如图书、报纸、杂志或网络资源等）的能力，还应注重收集资料的能力。

当然，收集后的梳理和筛选同样重要。从实用的角度来说，可以将材料归类整理，如笑话、趣事、名人名言、有趣的数据等。一般情况下，所选材料需要紧扣主题，并且具有针对性和代表性。只有具有代表性的典型材料才能深刻揭示事物本质，才能在演讲时说服观众、鼓动人心。因此，演讲者还需具备对资料的观察分析能力和较强的逻辑思考能力。

二、撰写演讲稿

演讲的成功与否很大程度上取决于演讲稿的好坏。有人认为，演讲只需要写个提纲，登台时临场发挥就行，不需要完整的准备；也有人认为，完整的演讲稿会使人囿于文辞，从而无法根据现场听众的反馈适时调整演讲的节奏，其实不然。纵观历史上成功的演讲，大多都是提前准备好完整的演讲稿的。演讲者通过撰写演讲稿（write speeches），能够更加清晰地梳理自己的思路，最后在演讲时，再试图忘记一切，根据拟定的演讲框架，上演一台精彩的脱口秀。

虽然演讲稿是书面语，但由于演讲活动本身的口语特性，撰写时语言应当简洁易懂，同时符合演讲者的身份。由于职业演讲的特殊性，演讲者最好是这个行业的专家或至少是从事这个行业的相关人员。如果让一位非专业人士来讲，不仅有很大的难度，也难以服众，演讲内容的可信度也大打折扣。

一篇好的演讲稿通常由正确的选题、合适的结构与得体的修辞等方面组成。首先是要确定演讲的题目，演讲者应当根据自己的知识储备和经历来确认自己是否能驾驭演讲的话题。其次就是寻找切入点，将题目进一步细化和具体化，写出演讲稿的提纲，构思和组织演讲框架。就内容而言，演讲稿要主题鲜明，表达完整；就文章组织结构而言，演讲稿要思维清晰，逻辑性强；就语言而言，演讲稿要有感染力、形象生动。写作时可根据需要，有效且正确地使用英语写作方法和技巧，如恰当地运用明喻、暗喻、夸张等各种修辞方法，用词要准确，尽量避免使用生僻、模糊、晦涩的字词。总之，既要考虑演讲的对象，注意演讲的措辞，但又要简明扼要、有理有力、结构紧凑。许多著名的演说家的不朽之作都有振奋人心、扭转乾坤般的力量，从《我有一个梦想》（*I have a dream*），到《葛底斯堡演说》（*Gettysburg Address*），再到"克林顿在北大的演说"，不少句子都成为不朽的佳句，值得认真研读。

三、准备得体着装

有些演讲者对演讲的内容精雕细琢，对演讲的技巧烂熟于胸，但对演讲时的个人形象及穿着打扮不以为意。殊不知蓬头垢面，不修边幅的个人形象会给听众留下不重视、不专业的印象，直接影响演讲的效果。但演讲者千种模样，万般风采，有精神矍铄的老学者，有妙语连珠的教师，也有口若悬河的法庭律师，还有能言善辩的公关小姐。不同的职业和年龄，表现出来的举止修养都不尽相同。那么演讲时应该如何规范着装呢？

一般而言，演讲者可以根据活动的公开信息判断出席活动的正式程度，甚至可以直接向活动主办方询问相关着装的具体要求。在没有把握或者无法确认的情况下以正式着装为宜，以表达对活动的重视。因此，绝大多数场合，人们对演讲者的形象可以概括为以下几点。

（1）Dark colored suits or dresses.（身着深色西装／套装。）

（2）White shirts or dresses.（穿朴素的白衬衫或上衣。）

（3）Ties or scarves.（戴领带或丝巾。）

（4）Black shoes, freshly polished.（脚上穿着锃亮的黑色鞋子。）

（5）Very little jewelry, worn discreetly.（尽量不佩戴首饰，如果要戴的话需要小心谨慎。）

（6）Calm, slow gestures and slow movements.（动作镇定自若。）

虽然这些对于专业化形象要求更高的空乘人员而言，并不算什么，但无论演讲者是什么身份，演讲前均要进行一番打扮。当然，演讲的着装要求也不是完全千篇一律的。一方面，要根据演讲的场合决定，场合越正式，服饰就越要正规；另一方面，也要根据演讲者的身体形态、个性爱好、年龄职业、风韵涵养做到整洁、得体、大方，要通过打扮告诉听众"这就是我，这才是我"。

四、调整心态

怯场（stage fright）是每位演讲者或多或少都会产生的正常心理现象，它是一种紧张、害怕甚至恐惧的心理，具体可以表现为演讲前的焦虑甚至失眠，演讲时的心跳加快、声音发颤、头脑空白、语无伦次等。不妨回顾一下，当你站在台上演讲时，是否曾经有过下列行为。

（1）Hands in pockets.（把手插在口袋里。）

（2）Increased blinking of the eyes.（眨眼次数过多。）

（3）Failure to make eye contact.（与听众没有眼神交流。）

（4）Licking and biting of the lips.（舔嘴唇或吸嘴唇。）

（5）Finger tapping.（敲叩手指。）

（6）Fast, jerky gestures.（手势又急又快。）

（7）Cracking voices.（声音粗哑。）

（8）Increased rate of speech.（讲话速度过快。）

（9）Clearing of the throat.（清嗓子。）

（10）Buttocks clamped tightly together.（臀部绷得太紧。）

这些都是演讲时常见的紧张的典型特征。这种紧张的情绪也不完全是负面的，与之相反，适度的紧张（positive nervousness）能促使演讲者做出更充分的准备，从而达到更好的演讲效果。

因此，演讲者首先需要暗示自己，演讲前的紧张是一种正常的心理现象；其次，找到适合自己的调节方法，如演讲前多进行模拟演讲，提高自己的心理素质。当然，在演讲时也可以通过一些技巧，更快地帮助自己消除紧张心理，从而在演讲时更加自信（gain confidence）。可以通过以下方式提高自己的自信心。

（1）Breathe in deeply and breathe out slowly for some times.（调匀呼吸，深吸气，慢呼出。）

（2）Smile and glance at the audience.（面带微笑看向听众。）

（3）Start slowly, with your shoulders back and your chin up.（开始发言时语速慢一点，身体保持着昂首挺胸的姿态。）

（4）Open your speech by saying something very frankly.（开场白说得真诚坦率。）

（5）Wear your very suitable clothes.（穿适合自己的衣服。）

（6）Say something positive to yourself.（在心里鼓励自己。）

第三节 撰写演讲稿

撰写演讲稿的第一步就是列提纲。一份结构清晰的演讲提纲能帮助演讲者厘清思路，从而在写讲稿时思路更清晰、连贯、有条理。

首先需要明确的是演讲的目标（objectives）。一般而言，演讲有四种目标。

（1）To offer information.（提供信息。）

（2）To entertain the audience.（娱乐听众。）

（3）To touch the audience.（动之以情。）

（4）To move to action.（说服行动。）

其次需要确定的是演讲的主要论点（main points）。一般而言，主要论点有 2～3 个就够了，论点太多会使演讲者很难在短时间内阐述清楚，从而难以给听众留下深刻印象。

最后需要将主要论点与搜集到的材料有条理地组织起来，或直接分为 1、2、3 几点，或可以从地理上划分为东、南、西、北，或可以通过比较与对比、我方与他方、正面与反面逐一展开，总之可以通过综合运用不同字母 / 数字、缩进格式等表明并列关系与从属关系，使提纲逻辑清晰，结构分明。例如：

A. First major point

    a. First sub-point

        a) Material 1

        b) Material 2

    b. Second sub-point

        a) Material 1

          i. Example 1

          ii. Example 2

iii. Example 3

   b) Material 2

B.Second major point

…

列完提纲后就是演讲稿的正式写作了。一般而言，演讲的开头（beginning）即开门见山，演讲者既要一下子抓住听众，又要提出自己的观点，因此常用的方法如下。

（1）To tell a story (about yourself).（讲个（自己的）故事。）

（2）To acknowledge the occasion of the gathering.（感谢听众的到来。）

（3）To pay the listeners a compliment.（称赞听众。）

（4）To quote.（引用名人名言。）

（5）To use unusual statistics.（引用不同寻常的数据。）

（6）To ask the audience a challenging question.（向听众提出具有挑战性的问题。）

（7）To show a video or a slide.（播放视频带或使用幻灯片。）

正文部分则需综合、灵活地运用各种方法娓娓道来，将所准备的材料说明用于支持自己的论点，从而感染听众。英语演讲稿正文撰写八招如下：运用排比、用词准确、营造亲切、巧妙引用、脉络清晰、慎用俚语、善用幽默、使用修辞。

无论演讲的内容有多少，结尾（ending）都十分重要。好的结尾可以起到画龙点睛的效果，否则功亏一篑。一个精心设计的结尾或再次强调主要论点，或得出最终结论，或展望未来，因此常用的方法有以下七种。

（1）To repeat your opening.（呼应开头。）

（2）To summarize your presentation.（概括演讲内容。）

（3）To close with an anecdote.（以趣事结尾。）

（4）To end with a call to action.（以号召行动结尾。）

（5）To ask a rhetorical question.（以反问结尾。）

（6）To make a statement.（以陈述结论结尾。）

（7）To show an outline of your presentation.（展示演讲大纲。）

第四节　演讲技巧

完成演讲稿只是演讲的序幕，要进行成功的演讲还需进行严格的训练，并且要掌握演讲的有关知识和技巧。对于演讲过程的准备和优化主要可以从以下三个方面进行：一是关注演讲时与听众的交流，提升演讲信息传递的效率；二是回顾专业演讲录像视频，尽可能地提升演讲的表现力；三是善用辅助道具，使演讲结构更清晰，语言更生动形象，更易被听众理解。

那么演讲时应当如何与听众交流呢？（How to communicate with the audience?）一方面要让听众在理解的基础上接受演讲者表达的观点，因此需要注意以下六点。

（1）A message worth communicating.（要有值得交流的观点。）

（2）Gain the listeners' attention: capture their interest and build their trust.（能吸引听众的注意：使之感兴趣并获取信任。）

（3）Emphasize understanding.（让听众能听懂。）

（4）Obtain their feedback.（听取反馈意见。）

（5）Watch your emotional tone.（注意声调要有感情。）

（6）Persuade the audience.（说服听众。）

另外，还需要注意与听众的眼神交流（eye contact），具体做法可以如下所述。

（1）Move your eyes slowly from person to person, and pause two or three seconds with each listener.（看向听众并慢慢移动眼睛，平均在每个人身上停留两到三秒。）

（2）Look at people straight or look at the bridge of their noses or chins.（眼睛直视听众，或者看着他们的鼻梁或下巴。）

（3）Look for the friendlier faces and smile at them one by one, then move on to the more skeptical members and also smile at them one by one.（先找出那些看起来比较友善的听众，逐次朝他们微笑；然后眼神转向那些面露疑色的听众，逐次朝他们微笑。）

（4）Imagine the audience in bathrobes in case you are nervous.（如果感到紧张，不妨想象听众身着浴衣的样子。）

提升演讲表现力的有效方法之一就是反复观看专业类演讲视频录像，如 CCTV 杯和爱立信杯等英语演讲比赛等。在观看的过程中，领会演讲要领、借鉴演讲技巧、模仿演讲姿势，并按照比赛评分标准进行严格的模拟训练。训练时观察自己在演讲时是否满足以下几个方面的要求。

（1）演讲内容：主题鲜明，表达完整。

（2）组织结构：思维清晰，逻辑性强。

（3）演讲气势：感情充沛，有表现力。

（4）英语语音：发音规范，音调标准。

（5）心理素质：反应敏捷，回答准确。

（6）仪容仪表：着装整洁，仪态大方。

同时，注意演讲过程中要避开以下不足之处。

（1）Speaking too rapidly.（语速过快。）

（2）Speaking in a monotone.（说话语气单调。）

（3）Using too high a vocal pitch.（声音太细。）

（4）Talking and not saying much.（"谈"得太多，"说"得太少。）

（5）Presenting without enough passion.（感情不够充分。）

（6）Talking down to the audience.（对听众采取一种居高临下的姿态。）

（7）Using too many "big" words.（夸张的词汇用得过于频繁。）

（8）Using abstractions without giving concrete examples.（抽象概念太多而不辅以具体事例加以说明。）

（9）Using unfamiliar technical jargon.（使用听众不熟悉的专业术语。）

（10）Using slang or profanity.（使用俚语或粗俗语。）

（11）Disorganized and rambling performance.（演讲思路不清晰，缺乏逻辑性。）

（12）Indirect communication (beat around the bush).（语言不够精练，没有紧扣主题。）

演讲的辅助道具有很多，如话筒、手势、提词卡等。如果能熟练掌握它们的正确使用方式，就能为演讲锦上添花。

（1）How to use the microphone?（使用话筒的方法如下）。

① You must speak up and project your voice even if you are using a microphone.（即使是使用话筒，演讲时也要声音响亮，运气发声。）

② Your voice should be resonant and sustained when you speak.（余音绕梁，不绝于耳。）

③ Pitch your voice slightly lower than normal. Listeners tend to associate credibility and authority with a relatively deep voice.（音调略低于正常讲话的状态，因为听众往往认为低沉的嗓音更具有可信度与权威性。）

④ Try to end declarative sentences on a low tone without, however, trailing off in volume.（尽量用降调结束陈述句，但不要降低音量。）

⑤ Slow down.（放慢语速。）

（2）How to use gestures?（使用手势的方法如下）。

① Make sure all your gestures are smooth and natural.（采用的手势都应当流畅自然。）

② Don't put your hands in your pockets.（不要把手插在口袋里。）

③ Let your hands and arms drop naturally to your side, gently fold both index fingers together, without wringing or gripping your hands in any way.（将手和手臂自然地在身体两侧下垂，轻微屈起食指，不要扭在一起或握紧拳头。）

④ Let your hands do what they want to do as long as they don't go back into your pockets or make obscene gestures.（双手自然摆放，但不要放在口袋里或在听众面前做一些令人讨厌的手势。）

⑤ Point at imaginary objects and don't point at others with your index finger.（手指可以象征性地指向想象中的物品，但不能直接用食指当面对着人指。）

⑥ Size or quantity can also easily be shown by expanding or contracting the hands.（如果需要说明物品大小或数量，可以通过双手向外扩大或向内压缩的手势表示。）

⑦ Gracefully show your audience the appropriate number of fingers by holding your hands at a 45-degree angle from your head.（如果需要描述具体数字，可以举起手，与头部成45°角，优雅地展示出来。）

⑧ To emphasize physical size such as length and width, hold your hands out in front of you widely apart to move them up and down.（如果想要强调长、宽等尺寸大小，可以将双手分开向前伸，通过上下移动来说明。）

（3）How to use note cards?（使用提词卡的使用方法如下）。

① Number your cards on the top right.（在卡片的右上角标上序号。）

② Write a complete sentence on both your first and last card.（在第一张和最后一张上写上完整的句子。）

③ Write up to five key words on other cards.（其他卡片上最多写五个关键词。）

④ Use color to mark the words you want to emphasize.（用颜色来标记自己想强调的词。）

⑤ Remind yourself at a particular spot to check the time.（在特定位置做好标记，提醒自己查看时间。）

在演讲过程中，万一忘词（brownout），千万不要以惊慌失措、张口结舌、抓耳挠腮或重复上一句话等表现提醒听众自己忘词了。忘词是只有演讲者本人才可以知道的秘密，只要你表现得足够从容镇定，并迅速找出替代语句，是不会有人发现的。况且，即使临时想到的替代语句使句子间衔接得不够紧密，只要不影响整体表达，也无关紧要。因为听众是善忘的，他们只会记住那些有记忆点的内容。如果事先准备了提词卡，那就更好办了。你只需要微微一笑，换下一张卡片，继续接下来准备的内容即可。当然你会遗漏一部分内容，但是没有人会注意到这一点。听众只会责怪自己没有跟上你的思路。

第五节　演讲话题汇总

在本节中，我们对具有代表性的空乘职业话题进行了汇总，内容涵盖空乘求职面试、职业素养、服务意识、民航精神等方面，并就每个主题列举了相应的范文。以下是各主题的名字。

（1）How to Succeed at an Airline Job Interview?（如何通过航空公司的面试？）

（2）Preparations for an Airline Job Interview.（浅谈航空公司面试准备。）

（3）My Reflection on *Chinese Captain*.（影片《中国机长》观后感。）

（4）The Importance of English for Air Crew.（小议英语对机组人员的重要性。）

（5）My Understanding of Three Respects.（浅析"三个敬畏"。）

（6）Teamwork Spirit for Cabin Attendants.（试析空乘人员的团队合作精神。）

本节列举的每篇演讲范文都有一个明确的主题和目标，这也是在撰写演讲稿的过程中首先需要明确的，如"How to Succeed at an Airline Job Interview""Preparations for an Airline Job Interview"目的在于为听众提供信息，以帮助读者在航空公司的面试中取得好的成绩；"Teamwork Spirit for Cabin Attendant"目的则在于说服听众，让读者认识到团队合作精神的重要作用，并从现在起开始树立团队合作精神等。在演讲稿的开头，范文会通过一些特定的话语，来吸引听众，如"My Reflection of *Chinese Captain*"中通过询问听众是否看过电影来引起听众的思考和注意；"My Understanding on *Three Respects*"中通过引用电影中的金句，起到将听众带入主题的效果。在演讲稿的正文中，范文均围绕主题设定了2～3个论点，使演讲的过程逻辑更清晰，重点更明确，听众更易接受；如"The Importance of English for Air Crew"中列举了对于空乘人员而言，英语能力较强可以提升服务效果、减少安全事件发生、反映学习及沟通能力三个论点。

一、范文1

How to Succeed at an Airline Job Interview?

Hello, everyone. The topic of my speech today is "*How to Succeed at an airline job interview?*", which is crucial to us due to the ongoing outbreak of COVID-19.

First of all, it is necessary to make a good first impression. As the interview time is quite short, it is suggested to dress appropriately, behave decently, and wear natural makeup. Females can dress in short white sleeves and black skirts, while males can wear short sleeves and black trousers. Honestly speaking, it is not necessary to be beautiful to do well in an airline job, but an ideal candidate shall not make passengers feel uncomfortable.

Secondly, candidates should be fluent in oral English. A prepared English self-introduction is not enough. Moreover, the second-round interview is to read English announcements aloud and answer some questions in English. Therefore, it is vitally important to build a solid language foundation in daily study, especially the oral session. A suggested method is to find an English native speaker to be your language exchange partner and improve your pronunciation by practicing.

Last but not least, it is also important to keep calm and remain smiling during the whole interview. These are two basic qualifications for cabin attendants, so it's worth spending time rehearsing in front of a mirror. After all, practice makes perfect. Use a camera to record your rehearsal if necessary, and you will know how to improve your speech more clearly.

It's not easy to excel at an airline job interview at this particular moment, but if you can master the above three points, you shall have more opportunities compared with other candidates. That's all for speech today. Thank you for your attention.

参考译文：

如何通过航空公司的面试

大家好。我今天演讲的主题是"如何通过航空公司的面试"。这对于我们民航专业的学生来说是至关重要的，尤其是在新冠肺炎全球传播，各航空公司招聘名额有限的特殊时刻。

要想面试取得成功，第一就是要给面试官留下好的第一印象。由于面试时间较短，我们应该要保证面试时着装和举止得体，妆容自然大方。女性可以穿白色短袖和黑色短裙，男性可以穿黑色短袖和裤子。老实说，通过航空公司的面试并不一定需要本人长得漂亮，然而一个合格的准空乘至少不应当让乘客看着不舒服。

第二是面试者需要英语口语流利。仅仅是准备好一篇英语自我介绍是远远不够的，因为在第二轮面试中，面试者还需要用英语播报客舱广播词及回答常见问题。因此，在日常英语学习中需要打好坚实的语言基础，尤其是对口语方面的训练至关重要。我的建议是你可以找一个以英语为母语的人作为语言交换伙伴，通过反复练习来不断改善你的发音，使语音语调听起来更地道。

第三是在整个面试过程中保持冷静和微笑也很重要。由于这是空乘人员的两个基本素质，因此花一些时间对着镜子多多练习是值得的，毕竟，体态和表情方面的训练也是熟能生巧的。如果觉得有必要的话，还可以用摄像机记录你在练习演讲时的样子，这样你将更明确该如何改进自己的演讲表现。

在当下这个特殊的时刻，通过航空公司的面试似乎并不容易，但如果你能掌握以上三点面试技巧，你将比其他面试者有更多的机会取得成功。今天的演讲到此为止，感谢您的关注。

二、范文 2

Preparations for an Airline Job Interview

Distinguished judges, ladies and gentlemen, and my dear fellow students, good morning! In my opinion, it is not easy to prepare for an airline job interview as the competition is quite fierce. To have a better chance to win, I think we can improve ourselves from the following three aspects.

First and foremost, we should try our best to improve our English. As vocabulary is one of the basic elements of language, we should spend a fixed period every day to memorizing words. In addition, we should pay attention to using grammatically correct sentences and oral practice so that we can pass the related English exams and leave a deep impression in the English interview session.

Second, we should maintain a correct posture in everyday life to form a good habit. Attention should be paid to the way we walk, stand, and sit. Never sit with legs apart. The interviewers will observe our behavior during the whole interview, so that we should avoid those bad subconscious behavior.

Third, we should prepare the interview materials and speech content beforehand. The documentation used in the interview may include résumé, graduation certificate, English certificate, Mandarin certificate, computer certificate, etc. These materials will give the interviewer a better and quicker understanding of us. Besides, prepare a brief self-introduction and answers to the commonly asked questions in advance. An impressive self-introduction should highlight our advantages in a certain position, while frequently, asked questions are based on our own experience and views.

All in all, to prepare for an airline interview, we can make progress in the above three points: English ability, behavior in the interview process, as well as materials and speech prepared in advance. Thank you for listening. Goodbye.

参考译文：

浅谈航空公司面试准备

尊敬的评委们，女士们、先生们，亲爱的同学们，大家上午好！在我看来，由于航空公司的面试竞争非常的激烈，要想有更高的胜算，我们必须好好准备。准备工作可以从以下三个方面来进行。

第一，我们应该尽力提高自己的英语水平。由于词汇是语言的基础，因此我们应该每天固定花一些时间用于背单词。此外，还需要注重语法正确性和口语练习，这样才能取得有关的英语考级证书，并在英语面试环节给评委们留下深刻的印象。

第二，我们平时就要养成好习惯，保持正确的体态。在日常生活中，我们不仅要关注走路和站立的方式，还要注意自己的坐姿，坐姿状态下严禁两腿分开。由于评委们会在整个面试过程都时刻留意我们的行为举止，因此我们要避开所有下意识的不良行为。

第三，我们需要事先准备好面试材料、自我介绍和应答话术。面试中使用的材料大致包括简历、毕业证书、英语证书、普通话证书、计算机等级证书等。随身携带这些材料可以让评委们更全面和更快地认识自己，使面试过程更顺利。此外，还可以提前准备一份简短的自我介绍和常见面试问题的答案。一段令人印象深刻的自我介绍通常需要突出自己在这个职位上的优势，而在提前准备常见面试问题的答案时则应基于自己过去的人生经历和真实想法来进行。

总之，我们可以从以上三个方面入手，为航空公司面试提前做好准备。提高英语水平，关注行为举止，以及事先准备好相关面试材料、自我介绍和应答话术。谢谢大家，再见。

三、范文3

My Reflection on *Chinese Captain*

Have you seen the film *Chinese Captain*? If not, I strongly recommend it to you. Because you will be deeply moved by the miraculously heroic deeds of CAAC Heroic Crew and be proud of Civil Aviation Spirit just like other film watchers.

The film *Chinese Captain* was adapted from a successful alternate landing of Sichuan Airlines. It was a real case that had happened to Flight 3U8633 on May 14th, 2018. When the plane was flying over 10,000 meters, the right-hand side of the cockpit window burst suddenly, making the cabin depressurized and the temperature dropped to more than −40℃ Captain Liu Chuanjian, who was responsible for the safety of all the passengers, air crew and the plane, however, was fearless in such bad conditions, and eventually landed the plane safely relying on his excellent expertise and psychological quality. In the meantime, all crew members united as one in the emergency landing and together created the miracle.

There are a thousand Hamlets in a thousand people's hearts. From my point of view, I would like to share with you some of my feelings from the following three aspects:

First, the crew members were worthy of the honorary title of CAAC Heroic Crew, for they had created a miracle in the name of life. In fact, the difficulty of Sichuan Airlines' alternate landing can be classified as "world class". However, Captain Liu's amazing perseverance changed the impossible into the possible. It took merely 27 minutes from alternate landing confirmation to safe landing, with 128 passengers on board survived. Obviously, he handled the situation well and stayed calm when facing the emergency, which resulted from day-to-day training and a strong sense of responsibility for civil aviation.

Second, we still need to be alert to safety issues. It is fortunate to land successfully, but what's more important is the problems exposed behind the case. Safety is a lifeline and also the bottom line. Nothing is too trivial, for too much is at stake upon the celestial. As a prospective cabin attendant, we should learn from the past, summarize experience, and take preventive measures to create a safe environment for the passengers.

Third, greatness comes from ordinary, thus we should inherit this kind of heroic spirit. Though captain Liu is a hero, he is also just an ordinary member in his own post. We should not only learn from the heroic deeds and carry forward the heroic spirit, but also actualize the spirit in our ordinary work and take full responsibility for the safety of passengers' lives. In other words, we should not only learn skills in a down-to-earth way, but also deepen the understanding of our job and establish a sense of responsibility for dedication and service.

These are some of my thoughts after watching the film *Chinese Captain*. I hope it'll give you some inspiration, too. Thank you.

参考译文：

影片《中国机长》观后感

你看过《中国机长》这部电影吗？如果还没有，我强烈推荐你去看一看。因为看过之后，我相信你会和其他人一样被中国民航英雄机组的事迹所感动，为中国民航精神而感到自豪。

电影《中国机长》是根据川航 3U8633 航班成功备降的真实事件改编的。2018 年 5 月 14 日，当川航 3U8633 飞到万米高空时，驾驶室的右座前挡风玻璃突然爆裂，舱内瞬间失压，气温骤降至 -40℃ 以下。刘传健机长在如此恶劣的条件下，靠着过硬的飞行技术和心理素质，怀着对全体乘客和机组人员生命安全高度负责的责任意识，让飞机安全降落。在迫降全程，全体机组成员临危不乱，团结一心，共同创造了这次奇迹。

对于这部电影，也许每个人都有各自的看法和理解。我想要与各位分享一下我的三点感悟。

第一，他们以生命的名义创造了一个奇迹，是当之无愧的"中国民航英雄机组"。在真实事件中，川航备降的艰难程度堪称"世界级"。然而机长刘传健凭借惊人的毅力，把看似不可能的事变成了可能。飞机从确认备降到安全着陆只用了 27 分钟，机上 128 名乘客得以生还。这一切与机组人员临危不惧的心态及正确的处置流程密不可分。在这看似不可能的背后，是全体机组成员日复一日的训练和对于民航事业的高度责任感。

第二，我们仍需警惕安全问题。英雄值得赞誉，成功迫降也是万幸，但背后暴露的问题也必须正视。安全是一道生命线，更是底线。航空安全无小事，任何细小的疏忽都有可能造成巨大的损失。作为一名准民航人，我们应当吸取教训，总结经验，防患于未然，为广大人民群众营造一个安全、放心的乘机环境。

第三，伟大出自平凡。因此平凡的我们也应该充分继承这种英雄精神。机长刘传健固然是英雄，但他也是在自身岗位上平凡的一员。我们不仅要学习英雄事迹，弘扬英雄精神，更重要的是把这种非凡英雄精神带到平凡的工作岗位中，真正做到敬畏生命。这就意味着，在平凡的本职工作中，既要脚踏实地学本领，也要加强对自身工作岗位的理解，树立奉献与服务的责任意识。

以上是我对《中国机长》这部电影的一些感悟，也希望能带给你一些启发。谢谢！

四、范文 4

The Importance of English for Air Crew

According to the statistics in 2019, about 25% of the candidates failed in the English session during the campus interview. There's no doubt that English has become one of the major obstacles for us to get an airline job, but why do airline companies attach so much importance to English? I hope this speech can give you some inspiration.

Firstly, as a universal language in the world, English is a necessary tool for cabin attendants to talk with foreign passengers on board. It is very common to meet foreign passengers during cabin service. In some international routes, foreign passengers may account for more than half of the total. No matter what the passenger's mother tongue is, it is a basic tacit understanding to communicate in English. Therefore, if the cabin attendant can speak fluent English, it will not only make the service process smoother, but also give passengers a better experience. In recent years, with the improvement of China's international level and the increase of international routes, the scene of English service is becoming more common, and the demand for air crew to provide English service is also increasing year by year. Thus, many airline companies attach importance to English ability and take it as one of the important admission criteria.

Secondly, air crew's mastery of English may directly affect aviation safety. A NASA research shows that more than 70% of aviation safety problems were caused by language communication among people. Among those problems, the communication between pilots and controllers is one of the most important causes for flight accidents. Therefore, for pilots, especially international aviation pilots, to be proficient in using English for communication is the basic guarantee of flight safety. For flight attendants, English is not only used to provide basic cabin service, but also to remind passengers timely and accurately in case of danger. In the cabin broadcast words, using English to introduce "how to use oxygen mask" and "how to adopt brace position" is not only a compulsory course for flight attendants, but also an important communication content to ensure passengers' safety.

Thirdly, flight attendants' English ability can indirectly reflect their learning ability and communication ability. For most non-native speakers, the process of learning English is not an overnight achievement, which requires a great deal of energy. Meanwhile, to practice English needs to speak with others to improve one's communication skills. Therefore, for airlines, the selection of people with good English is not only about their ability to use English for service, but also their exceptional learning and communication abilities. This kind of candidates is more likely to do outstanding work and create more value in the work.

At the end of the speech, I will give you a brief review of my speech. In the process of recruiting air crew, airlines often attach great importance to English ability due to the following three reasons. First, flight attendants with excellent English ability can serve foreign passengers better. Second, English communication ability will directly affect aviation safety. Third, flight attendants with good English are likely to be strong in their learning ability and communication ability. That's all for my speech today. Thank you.

参考译文：

英语对机组人员的重要性

一项 2019 年的统计结果表明，在校园面试中因为英语环节未通过的面试者占 25% 左右。毫无疑问，英语成为很多学生获取航空公司工作的最大限制，那为什么各家航空公司都如此关注英语水平呢？希望这篇演讲能给你一些启发。

首先，英语作为世界通用语言之一，是我们与外国乘客在机上交谈时的必备工具。空乘人员在进行客舱服务时，遇到外国乘客是非常常见的。在一些国际航线中，甚至可能出现半数以上的外国人。当外国人与中国人交流时，无论他的母语是什么，一种基本的默契就是使用英语进行沟通。倘若空乘人员能使用流利的英语进行客舱服务，不仅能让服务流程更加顺畅，也能给乘客更好的乘机体验。近几年，随着我国国际化水平的提升及国际航线的增多，英语服务的场景也越来越普遍，让机组人员提供英语服务的需求也逐年提升，因此很多航空公司越来越看重英语能力，并把英语能力作为录取的重要标准之一。

其次，机组人员对于英语能力的掌握可能会直接影响航空安全。NASA 的一项研究表明，70% 以上的航空安全问题的发生都源于交流过程中的语言沟通。在这些问题中，飞行员与机场管制员之间的沟通问题，是飞行事故发生的最主要的原因。所以对于飞行员，尤其是国际航空的飞行员而言，能熟练使用英语进行沟通，是飞行安全的基本保证。而对于空乘人员，英语不仅用于提供基础的客舱服务，更重要的是在危险发生时，能更及时准确地提醒乘客。在客舱广播词中，使用英语介绍"如何佩戴氧气面罩"或"如何采取防冲击姿势"既是空乘人员的必修课，也是保护乘客安全的重要沟通内容。

再次，英语能力可以间接反映一个空乘人员的学习能力及沟通能力。对于多数非英语母语的人而言，学习英语的过程都不是一蹴而就的，它需要投入较多的精力。同时，作为一项语言技能，练习英语的过程也是对沟通能力的锻炼。因此对于航空公司而言，选拔英语好的人，看重的不仅是其使用英语进行服务的能力，更看重的其实是他们的学习能力和沟通能力。这类应聘者在入职后往往能在工作岗位上有更突出的表现，从而创造更多的价值。

最后，我们一起回顾一下本次演讲。航空公司在招聘机组人员的过程中，往往十分看重英语能力，主要原因有三：其一，具备优秀英语能力的空乘人员能更好地为外国乘客服务；其二，英语沟通能力直接影响航空安全；其三，具备优秀英语能力的空乘人员通常也同时具备较强的学习能力和沟通能力。以上就是我今天演讲的全部内容，谢谢大家。

五、范文 5

My Understanding on *Three Respects*

There is such a scene in the movie *Chinese Captain*. After the plane landed, the captain solemnly said, "Respect life, respect rules, respect responsibilities." These *Three Respects* are the aspirations and pursuits of us civil aviation personnel. Today I want to share with you my own understanding on the *Three Respects*.

First, respect life. Life is fragile in front of those natural and man-made disasters. However, when people work together to save lives, fight together to protect them, and mourn for the lost ones, they realize that life is not only strong and powerful, but also noble and sacred. Respecting life is to be responsible for safety and lives, be true to our original aspiration and keep our mission firmly in mind. When passengers fly with us above the sky, it means that they fully trust us and even entrust their lives to us. Only when we have respect for life, can we treat every command cautiously, perform every task carefully and take each flight seriously.

Second, respect rules. There is an old Chinese saying that nothing can be accomplished without norms or standards. As far as civil aviation regulations are concerned, every position and employee are faced with several or even dozens of rules and regulations that need to be understood and mastered. These rules and regulations, though seeming cumbersome, are constantly summed up and refined from the experience and lessons of blood. Only by respecting and abiding by them can we minimize all kinds of mistakes and potential risks.

Third, respect responsibilities. Respecting responsibilities means to keep in mind that everyone's work is a part of the system security, and any mistake may cause serious consequences, for too much is at stake upon the celestial. In order to avoid dangerous accidents, we must be in awe and carry out tasks with a high sense of responsibility. On the one hand, it is necessary to improve our professional ability; on the other hand, cultivate the work ethics of abiding by the laws and regulations and being rigorous and meticulous. Only by doing these two aspects well, are we more prepared to solve problems at critical moments.

These are some of my thoughts of *Three Respects*. What's your understanding?

参考译文：

浅析"三个敬畏"

电影《中国机长》中有这样一幕——飞机降落后，机长郑重地说："敬畏生命，敬畏规则，敬畏责任。"这"三个敬畏"可以说是我们民航人的心声和追求，今天我想和大家分享一下我对"三个敬畏"的理解。

第一，敬畏生命。在天灾人祸面前，生命是如此脆弱。但是，当人们齐心协力拯救生命，为保护生命而战斗，为逝去的生命而哀悼时，我们就会意识到，生命不仅强大有力，而且崇高神圣。敬畏生命就是为安全负责，为生命负责。当乘客乘坐飞机在万米高空飞翔时，就是充分信任我们，并将他们的生命托付给了我们。我们只有带着对生命的敬畏之情，才能真正做到谨慎地对待每一个指令、小心地执行每一次任务、认真地对待每一次航班。

第二，敬畏规则。中国有句老话，"没有规矩，不成方圆"。就民航规章而言，每一个工种、每一个员工都面临着几条甚至几十条需要理解和掌握的规章制度。这些规章制度是从血的经验教训中不断总结提炼出来的，虽然烦琐，但只有敬畏和遵守，才能最大限度地减少各种错误和潜在风险。

第三，敬畏责任。敬畏责任就是要时刻牢记，每个人的工作都是系统安全的一部分，任何失误都可能造成严重后果。为了避免危险事件的发生，我们要心怀敬畏，带着高度的责任感去执行任务。一方面要提高业务能力，另一方面要加强作风建设，培养遵纪守法、严谨细致的工作习惯。只有做好这两个方面，才能在关键时刻解决问题。

以上就是我对"三个敬畏"的一些粗浅理解，不知道你是怎么想的呢？

六、范文 6

Teamwork Spirit for Cabin Attendants

Good morning, everyone! It's my great honor to stand here today to share with you my speech on the teamwork spirit for cabin attendants. Teamwork spirit is applicable to all the air crew, which can help to improve the efficiency of the team. Therefore, teamwork spirit is one of the key capabilities for a cabin attendant.

On the one hand, good teamwork spirit of cabin attendants can give passengers a better flight experience. In general, each flight attendant is assigned to be responsible for a fixed area to accomplish routine tasks. Parts of CA's job is to respond in time when any passenger from the assigned area presses the call button. However, in real situations, the number of passengers asking for face-to-face communication may differ from one area to another. If each CA focuses merely on his/her own work, it will lead to the untimely response of passengers' demand, making them dissatisfied. Therefore, teamwork spirit is the key when facing the dilemma. As a member of the team, each member must put team interests before individuals'. So, give your colleague a hand if necessary and don't be shy to ask others for help. Only by mutual understanding and cooperation can we give passengers the best flight experience.

On the other hand, teamwork spirit can enhance members' sense of responsibility and of belonging to the air crew. Good teamwork spirit is conducive to the formation of a harmonious atmosphere, where team members can encourage and learn from each other. Under the guidance of a good leader, everyone in the team has a sense of ownership and willing to contribute to make the team better. No wonder in such an atmosphere, the service quality of the flight will be greatly improved.

In conclusion, teamwork spirit needs the efforts of everyone in the team. Let's start from now on, strengthen communication with people around us, and let teamwork spirit go deeper into the heart of every civil aviation personnel.

参考译文：

空乘人员的团队合作精神

大家上午好，今天我很荣幸能够站在这里与大家分享我的演讲——空乘人员的团队合作精神。团队合作精神适用于所有空乘人员，它可以有效提升团队的效率。因此，团队合作精神是空乘人员的核心素养之一。

空乘实用英语教程

一方面，空乘人员良好的团队合作精神可以给乘客带来更好的乘机体验。一般而言，每名空乘人员在客舱服务中都有自己负责的区域和需执行的常规任务。与此同时，如果他们负责的区域有乘客按了呼唤铃，也必须及时响应。但在实际的服务过程中，每个区域内有需求的乘客数量是不平均的，从而导致有的空乘人员很忙，有的则相对不那么忙。如果每位空乘人员只顾做好自己负责的工作，就会导致乘客需求响应不及时，从而破坏乘客对本次航班的整体印象。而团队合作精神是解决此类问题的良药，因为它要求每位成员将团队利益放在个人利益之前。因此，如果你看到同事有需要的话，应当主动帮忙；而当你需要其他人协助时，也不要羞于开口。只有整个机组成员间都互相理解与合作配合，才能带给乘客最好的乘机体验。

另一方面，团队合作的精神可以增强每位成员的责任感和归属感。良好的团队合作精神有利于形成融洽的团队氛围，成员之间可以相互学习与鼓励。在领导者的正确引导下，团队中的每个人都具备"主人翁"意识，自愿为集体做贡献，使团队变得越来越好。毫无疑问，在这样的氛围中，航班的服务质量也将大幅提高。

总之，团队合作的精神需要来自团队中每一个人的努力，让我们从现在做起，加强与身边人的沟通，让团队合作精神深入每个民航人的心中。

练习：

通过本章的学习，现在你知道如何高效完成一次职业演讲了吗？接下来就是实践的时刻了，请从以下十个话题中任选一个，完成一次正式的演讲。注意演讲前的准备内容、演讲稿的撰写要求以及演讲时的策略技巧。如果条件允许的话，可以多找一些观众来聆听你的演讲，听听他们的反馈意见。要知道，纸上得来终觉浅，绝知此事要躬行。

（1）Cabin Attendants' Duties during Four Phases（飞行四阶段中空乘人员的职责）

（2）My Civil Aviation Dream（我的民航梦）

（3）Safety Always Takes the First Priority（安全第一）

（4）How to Do Cabin Service in an Efficient Way（试论如何高效进行客舱服务）

（5）The Most Important Qualities of Cabin Attendants（空乘人员最重要的品质）

（6）How to Control your Emotion during Cabin Service Work（客舱服务时如何控制情绪）

（7）Emergency Awareness in Each Flight（试论飞行时的应急意识）

（8）How to Deliver Attractive Announcements in Cabin（怎样做客舱广播才能更吸引人）

（9）One Thousand Miles Begins with a Single Step（千里之行，始于足下）

（10）Professionalism and the Roles of Cabin Attendants（浅谈空乘人员的职业素养）

第 5 章
技能测评

章前导读

　　本章是对学生乘务英语能力的综合考核。从听、说、读、写等语言考核的基本维度着手，在借鉴航空公司考核内容和试题的基础上，结合空乘专业专门用途英语的知识体系和结构，有梯度、有难易、有重点的设计题型，展开测试和评估。这些测试和评估兼顾了语言学中语音学、词汇学、语义学、语用学等范畴，同时侧重社会语言学中客舱这一主要语域和场景，着重功能英语的语用表达，旨在考核乘务员职业素养中的英语应用能力。

　　考虑到校企合作的乘务员职业技能大赛以及《民航乘务员国家职业标准》的四、五级标准中对乘务员英语能力的要求，本章中的试题主要包括了书面测试（written test）和口头测试（oral test）。具体题型包括选择（choices）、判断（true or false）、翻译（translation）、情景问答（situational questions）、广播词编播和朗读（cabin announcement making & reading）等。

　　这些测试题目旨在测试学生对乘务专业英语的理解和表达能力，同时对接岗位和行业考核，兼顾校企合作和行业内技能大赛中对英语考核的内容和标准。本章汇总了相应的题库，供学生有目的地选择、练习、强化，达到应试考试和素质教育相结合的目的。在重点提高学生英语朗读、表达和沟通能力的同时，提高其知识储备量，提升其学习兴趣，达到学习效果和考核目标相一致，真正做到紧贴岗位、学以致用、文化拓展的多重考核目标。教师也可以有目的、有针对性地选择做过程性评价或结果性评价。

思政园地

　　新时代的中国青年要在学习中增长知识、锤炼品格，在工作中增强才干、练就本领。乘务员的外语能力体现在听、说、读、写、译的各个方面。过硬的外语能力不仅能提高自身的语言思维能力，也能拓展国际视野。教师在测评中，除了考查学生的英语基本功外，还可结合民航常识、飞行历史、航空地理、服务礼仪等方面进行双语能力的考核，以此提升乘务员的综合素养，夯实业务本领。

第一节　测试大纲

　　按照空乘专业专门用途英语的知识结构，结合行业知识，我们可以大致设定三个层次的考核级别，分别为初级目标、中级目标和高级目标。每一目标又涵盖了交际功能英语、航空通识英语和客舱专门用途英语三大板块。

　　在初级目标中，交际功能英语主要包括乘务员在客舱服务交际中的迎客与送别，客舱相关服务和应急内容的介绍，对旅客相关问讯的解答，客舱服务场所和使用设备的指引，对特殊旅客和两舱旅客的服务邀请，对不同旅客的帮助和问题解答，对应急出口位旅客和机上援助者的致谢，对航班延误或服务过失等情况的致歉和请求原谅，对特殊情况的解释和说明，对便携式电子设备和卫生间使用等的允许，澄清客舱发生的事实，祝贺旅客生日，对旅客的观点表示认同和反对，劝说旅客服从客舱指令，乘务员自身介绍等。结合常用的功能英语句型，融入客舱服务情景。

　　初级的航空通识英语主要包含机场指示语，乘务员能够熟悉机场图例及其含义；也包括航空安全常识，如旅行证件的准备、机上常见疾病的处理、民航常见机构（如CAAAC、ICAO、IATA）的全称。通过掌握这些基础知识，可以更好地对民航业的背景有个初步的了解。

　　初级的客舱专门用途英语包括正常的客舱广播编播。这些情景主要涵盖了登机、起飞、安全演示、电子设备使用、客舱颠簸、餐饮服务、娱乐服务、落地前提示等按照正常飞行旅程设置的广播词。在朗读广播词的过程中，要熟悉发音规则、掌握必要的连读、失爆、停顿等技巧，使播音亲切自然。同样，对于广播词中所涉及的主要国家、地区的英文名需要知道读音，同时对不同航空公司的英文读音和代码也要有所了解。

在中级目标中，交际功能英语主要包括客舱服务中的"破冰"沟通，这需要乘务员掌握一定的心理沟通技巧。同时，乘务员需要掌握特殊旅客的服务用语，特别是委婉语的使用。当然，这需要兼顾语用的目标。另外，还需要对旅客突发问题的应对有一定的沟通策略，对于航班延误或取消、返航或备降等非正常情况，或者直接来自旅客对于服务的投诉进行有效处理。对于头等舱和商务舱旅客，需要选择特定的服务用语，在表达上注意差异化。对于应急情况的说明，乘务员需要表明立场和观点。在与不同国籍、身份的旅客沟通时，乘务员要考虑话题的合适性、敏感性、政治性等因素，注意沟通的策略。

中级的航空通识英语包括对民航不同岗位名称和职责的认知。乘务员可结合附录中的机场图例，给旅客做出正确的引导和说明。对于特殊旅客的分别，需要掌握特殊旅客名称、服务设施等相关表达。同时，对于航空公司英文名，需要有一定的系统了解，包括其所属的航空公司联盟，如国航属于星空联盟（Star Alliance）、东航属于天合联盟（Sky Team）等，也需要对航空公司的基地有所了解。

中级的客舱专门用途英语主要包括三块内容：客舱特殊情况广播、客舱理论知识、客舱情景英语。其中特殊广播主要涉及航班延误、中转、返航等非正常情况的表达，指导国际旅客入境卡的填写，熟悉客舱医疗事故中药品和设施名称等内容。通过掌握这些专业知识，可以更好地认识乘务员的职业定位和职责。

中级的客舱理论知识可包括机组人员构成及职责，客舱设备名称表达，安全检查相关设备名称，餐饮名称，特殊餐食代码，西餐菜单解读，晕机等常见疾病的处理。如机组人员构成，乘务员需要知道不同机型的人员匹配；熟悉客舱应急设备的表达；熟悉特殊餐食代码和西餐的组成等；应对常见机上疾病。

中级的客舱情景英语主要包括航前准备会、登机与指引、行李摆放、安全检查、派送服务、儿童与婴儿服务、机上娱乐、免税品销售、落地前准备等。这是客舱服务的核心组成部分，也是服务的重点内容。

高级的交际功能英语涉及客舱服务中禁忌语的使用，客舱突发事件的协商谈判，客舱瞬息万变的各种情况的应对和处理，跨文化交际能力的培养和提升，与外籍空勤人员沟通策略的掌握，英式和美式英语的使用差别的对比认知等。这部分内容需要乘务员在上述初级中级的基础上，对语言使用和文化背景有更进一步的深化和理解。

高级的航空通识英语主要包括了不同国家的检查检疫（CIQ）常识，乘务员需要注意的异同点。同时，对民航组织和机构的主要工作需要有一定的了解。乘务员需要熟悉世界主要机场和代码，并对机场的级别做出一定的判断。在航空公司企业文化上，需要对其营销理念、服务策略有一定的认知，如对新航的优质服务、春秋的低成本服务等，列举出案例。

高级的客舱专门用途英语主要包括三块内容：客舱应急广播及城市介绍、客舱理论知识、客舱情景英语。其中客舱应急广播主要包含：陆地撤离、水上撤离、客舱失压、起火、防冲击姿势等。城市景点介绍主要涵盖了不同城市的景点介绍，包括对名胜和历史知识的认知等。通过掌握这些专业知识，可以更好地对客舱安全有更深入的了解。

高级的客舱理论常识主要包括酒类常识、应急设备名称、急救药品名称、问题旅客。如红酒的名称、产地与特征；掌握客舱应急设备的主要用途、急救药品的名称和用途、问题旅客的解决方案等。与初级和中级相比，其理论知识更为细化和具体。

高级的客舱情景英语主要包括除了常见特殊旅客外其他特殊旅客服务（如遣返旅客、心理障碍旅客等）、升舱与降舱、特殊餐服务、设备故障、特殊情况处理、严重医疗急救、心理安抚策略、机上与地面信息交接。这些都是服务和应急的特殊情况，乘务员需要掌握熟练的语言表达，具备强大的心理素质，精通沟通策略，这样才能游刃有余、有的放矢。总之，高级阶段是建立在初级和中级阶段基础上的提升和拓展。

空乘英语测试大纲简表如表 5-1 所示。

表 5-1　测试大纲简表

等级	项　　目	内　　　　容
初级	交际功能英语	迎客与告别、介绍、问询、指引、邀请、给予帮助、致谢、致歉、请求原谅、解释、说明、允许、澄清现实、祝贺、认同与反对、劝说、自我介绍
	航空通识英语	机场指示语、航空安全常识、民航组织和机构缩写
	客舱专门用途英语	A. 客舱常用广播：登机、起飞、安全演示、电子设备使用、客舱颠簸、餐饮服务、娱乐服务、落地前提示等 B. 主要国家和地名英文名、主要航空公司英文名
中级	交际功能英语	破冰沟通、特殊旅客用语、委婉语使用、旅客突发问题应对、投诉处理、不正常航班沟通、头等舱旅客服务用语、表明立场与观点、聊天话题选择等
	航空通识英语	民航相关岗位人员表达、候机楼指引英语、民航旅客种类表达、航空公司英文名
	客舱专门用途英语	A. 客舱特殊情况广播：延误、中转、返航、入境卡填写、常见医疗急救等 B. 客舱理论常识：机组人员构成及职责、客舱设备名称表达、安全检查相关设备名称、餐饮名称、特殊餐食代码、西餐菜单解读、晕机等常见疾病的处理 C. 客舱情景英语：航前准备会、登机与指引、行李摆放、安全检查、派送服务、儿童与婴儿服务、机上娱乐、免税品销售、落地前准备等
高级	交际功能英语	禁忌语使用、协商谈判、客舱应变技巧、跨文化交际、外籍空勤沟通、英式英语和美式英语主要差异
	航空通识英语	CIQ、危险品常识、民航组织和机构常识、世界主要机场名称、航空公司企业文化
	客舱专门用途英语	A. 客舱应急类广播词及城市介绍：陆地撤离、水上撤离、客舱失压、起火、防冲击姿势、城市景点介绍等 B. 客舱理论常识：酒类常识、应急设备名称、急救药品名称、问题旅客 C. 客舱情景英语：其他特殊旅客服务、升舱与降舱、特殊餐服务、设备故障、特殊情况处理、严重医疗急救、心理安抚策略、机上与地面信息交接

第二节 书面测试

一、Written Test 1

I. Choice (1' × 50=50')

1. Your seat number is 16A, the _____.

    A. single seat　　B. window seat　　C. middle seat　　D. aisle seat

2. The first issue that airlines should consider is _____.

    A. flight safety　　　　　　　　　　　　　　　B. high-quality service

    C. flight safety and quality service simultaneously　　　D. profitability

3. Due to Ivy's good performance, she will be _____ to the purser next mouth.

    A. postured　　B. projected　　C. promoted　　D. protected

4. I am awfully sorry for my _____.

    A. kindness　　B. friendliness　　C. carelessness　　D. carefulness

5. For the period of take-off and landing, the seat must _____.

    A. keep its position　　　　　　B. return to the upright position

    C. be fastened by the seat belts　　D. be returned to the upright position

6. The remote controller which underneath the screen _____ all functions of your personal entertainment system.

    A. include　　B. included　　C. including　　D. includes

7. Would you like some _____ or grapes to go with your cheese?

    A. cracks　　B. crash　　C. crackers　　D. crashes

8. For _____ tea, we have English breakfast and Earl Grey, which one would you like?

    A. green　　B. black　　C. red　　D. scented

9. If a passenger hurts and breaks his leg, it is called _____.

    A. chills　　B. asthma　　C. fracture　　D. fever

10. The correct way to take nitroglycerin tablets for heart disease is to _____.

    A. put them under the tongue　　B. chew and swallow

    C. swallow with water　　D. swallow with juice

11. If a passenger is burned by hot coffee, cabin attendant will turn to use _____.

    A. ointment　　B. scissors　　C. PBE　　D. cushion

12. If there are patients with mild burns or scalds, which of the following methods can you

162

空乘实用英语教程

第5章　技能测评

use to relieve the pain?

    A. Talking painkillers.

    B. Flushing with cool water or use ice, burn ointment.

    C. Wrapping.

    D. Puncturing blisters.

13. For wheelchair passengers, the general principle is to have them _____ .

    A. board the aircraft first and disembark later

    B. board the aircraft first and disembark first

    C. get on the plane and get off first

    D. get on and off the plane later

14. The age of unaccompanied children is _____ .

    A. 6–12 years old   B. 5–10 years old

    C. 5–12 years old   D. 6–11 years old

15. The cabin luggage can be placed in the _____ .

    A. toilet   B. aisle   C. cloakroom   D. galley

16. The time for land evacuation is _____ .

    A. 60 seconds   B. 90 seconds   C. 120 seconds   D. 150 seconds

17. The corporate logo of Air China is _____ .

    A. Kapok   B. Blue Sky Egret   C. Swallow   D. Phoenix

18. Which meal is provided for an unaccompanied minor?

    A. CHML.   B. BBML.   C. HFML.   D. LSML.

19. Which statement of the special meal is correct?

    A. Kosher meals need to be booked at least 48 hours in advance.

    B. Fruit meal can replace diabetic meal.

    C. Child meal is offered to passengers who are under 2 years old.

    D. BLML is provided for diabetic passengers.

20. The English abbreviation for First Class is _____ .

    A. F   B. Y   C. E   D. C

21. In cocktail Bloody Mary, there is Vodka and _____ .

    A. tomato juice   B. apple juice   C. pear juice   D. kiwi juice

22. The national flower of China is the _____ .

    A. peony   B. jasmine   C. rose   D. tulip

23. Heathrow International Airport (LHR) is located in _____ .

A. Paris, France   B. Berlin, Germany   C. London, Britain   D. Rome, Italy

24. The abbreviation of "中国民用航空局" is _____.

    A. CCAC   B. CCAR   C. CAAC   D. CATA

25. Cabin announcements are made to passengers on the ground or in the air, through the aircraft's _____.

    A. communication system   B. power system

    C. Warning system   D. flight management system

26. Which country is B787 airliner assembled in?

    A. France.   B. Britain.   C. United States.   D. Russia.

27. The longest river in the world is _____.

    A. the Nile   B. the Mississippi   C. the Volga   D. the Amazon

28. The free baggage allowance for domestic flights in first class is _____.

    A. 40   B. 30   C. 20   D. 50

29. In the flight number "MU5305", MU stands for _____.

    A. Shanghai Airlines   B. China Eastern Airlines

    C. Southwest Airlines   D. Air China

30. The headquarters of China Southern Airlines is located in _____.

    A. Beijing   B. Shenzhen   C. Guangzhou   D. Shanghai

31. The _____ is responsible for the management and use of the onboard first aid kit, emergency medical kit and hygiene kit during flight operations.

    A. captain   B. purser   C. flight doctor   D. cabin attendant

32. Before the flight takes off, the flight attendant should _____ in addition to the cabin security check.

    A. open the oven and prepare the meal trolley

    B. secure and check kitchen supplies, trolleys and tool boxes

    C. change the seats of passengers according to their needs

    D. switch on the water boiler and prepare the drinks supply

33. Which one is the sign of rapid decompression?

    A. Light coming in from the edge of the cabin door or overwing window exit.

    B. A whistling sound.

    C. Earache.

    D. Cold air rushing into the cabin and a drop in cabin temperature.

34. All aircraft are _____ with inflatable escape slides.

    A. equal   B. qualified   C. equipped   D. equivalent

35. The pre-flight checklist made by the pilot includes the following except _____.

    A. time en-route   B. weather   C. meal preparation   D. safety and security

36. In water evacuation, passengers should sit _____ on the life raft.

    A. near the bow   B. at the sides   C. at random   D. evenly

37. Among the following items, passengers are not allowed to bring _____ into the cabin.

    A. expensive musical instruments   B. firearms, swords and knives

    C. lithium power banks   D. laptop computers with wireless Internet access

38. The international standard time is _____.

    A. Beijing time   B. Paris time   C. Greenwich time   D. Tokyo time

39. The convention that is regarded as the constitution of aviation is _____.

    A. The Paris Convention   B. The Rome Convention

    C. The Warsaw Convention   D. The Chicago Convention

40. "采取防冲撞姿势" 的正确表达是 _____.

    A. donning procedures   B. manual inflation handle

    C. assume bracing positions   D. exit seat criteria

41. The English expression for "撤离滑梯人工充气手柄" is _____.

    A. manual inflate handle   B. release handle

    C. knife   D. pump

42. Sorry, sir. I completely understand _____ you feel, but we don't have pills for coldness on board.

    A. which   B. what   C. that   D. how

43. Excuse me, would you like me to _____ your overcoat?

    A. hang up   B. put up   C. hang on   D. put down

44. Which symbol refers to smoke hood (PBE)?

    A.   B.   C.   D.

45. In the event of fire and smoke in the cabin, the cabin crew guide passengers to stay low covering their mouths and noses so as to _____.

    A. protect the eyes   B. avoid inhaling toxic gases

    C. avoid panic   D. relax themselves

46. The fire on board mostly takes place in the _____.

    A. luggage racks   B. cockpit   C. galley   D. lavatory

47. If the flight departs at 20:30 Beijing time on Tuesday, the flight time is 11 hours and the time difference is known to be +2 hours, it'll arrive at _____ Sydney time.

    A. Wednesday 7:30 a.m.   B. Wednesday 8:30 a.m.

    C. Wednesday 9:30 a.m.   D. Wednesday 5:30 a.m.

48. A passenger buys a carton of cigarettes, a bottle of perfume and a wallet on board. The price of a carton of cigarettes is US \$13, a bottle of perfume is US \$90 and a wallet is US \$39. The exchange rate is 1 US \$ = 0.8 €. The traveller pays €200 and the cabin attendant should give him € _____ back.

    A. 25   B. 46.4   C. 86.4   D. 7.25

49. Auxiliary Power Units (APU) means _____.

    A. 运营控制中心   B. 辅助动力装置   C. 航空管制   D. 舱门预位

50. Which information is NOT printed on the entry card?

    A. Nationality.   B. Flight No.   C. Passport No.   D. Religion.

II. True or False (1′×50=50′)

1. The symbol means Customs.   (   )

2. The international code for the Canadian dollar is CAN.   (   )

3. The sale of duty-free goods on board is only available on international flights.   (   )

4. Flights of 6 hours or more are called international long-haul flights.   (   )

5. The world can be divided into 24 time zones, each spanning 7.5° longitude.   (   )

6. "Scald" means "烫伤".   (   )

7. STCR stands for "担架旅客".   (   )

8. "Crash ax" means "救生斧".   (   )

9. "Immigration officer" means "边检官员".   (   )

10. "Maximum weight allowance" means "免费行李额度".   (   )

11. The expression for "流控" is air traffic volume control.   (   )

12. The expression for "客舱释压" is "ditching".   (   )

13. "Black tea" means "黑茶".   (   )

14. "Cocktail" refers to "金酒".   (   )

15. "Appetizer" means "甜品".   (   )

16. "Eggplant" means "咸蛋".   (   )

17. "Sparkling water" means "气泡水". ( )

18. "Entrée" means "主菜". ( )

19. The expression for "希望您喜欢今天的晚餐" is "Hope you enjoy your lunch today." ( )

20. The change of air pressure in the cabin during flight is the cause of ear distress. ( )

21. When moving in the life raft during water evacuation, people should stay low and crawl. ( )

22. The crew's command at the exit in water evacuation is: "One by one, jump, slide." ( )

23. Air China is a member of Star Alliance. ( )

24. "PVG" is the three-character code for Shanghai Hongqiao International Airport. ( )

25. Pregnant women should fasten their seatbelts around the waist. ( )

26. Boeing 747 is a single aisle aircraft. ( )

27. The letter "A" means the row in the seat number "25A". ( )

28. Tonic water belongs to alcoholic drinks. ( )

29. Those who need to manage blood sugar would take BLML. ( )

30. Usually a full inflation of the slide will take about 2 seconds. ( )

31. Bordeaux is a famous beverage brand of Germany. ( )

32. Checked baggage is carried in the cargo hold of the plane. ( )

33. The first priority of cabin attendants' job is ensuring the safety. ( )

34. KSML is a kind of medical meals. ( )

35. The main body of the aircraft is called fuselage. ( )

36. VLML does not contain egg or dairy products. ( )

37. If a passenger feels airsick, you should relocate his/her seat to the back of the cabin. ( )

38. All Nippon Airways is a Korean airline. ( )

39. Rio de Janeiro is the capital of Brazil. ( )

40. The flight attendants belong to the cockpit crew. ( )

41. Cabin attendants require passengers to open the window shade before take-off or landing mainly because they want passengers to enjoy the outside view. ( )

42. The London time is also called Greenwich Mean Time (GMT). ( )

43. There is only one bracing position for impact in emergency. ( )

44. Lobster is a kind of seafood which all passengers can eat. ( )

45. Children under 5 years old can take the plane by themselves. ( )

46. Spaghetti is one of the Chinese delicacies. ( )

47. Green Channel means "Goods to Declare". ( )

48. Nausea and airsickness are common diseases on board. ( )

49. The number of the cabin attendants for each flight is the same. ( )

50. Portable lithium power banks can be used during the whole flight. ( )

二、Written Test 2

I. Choice (1′ × 50=50′)

1. You are required to fill out the Entry Card for _____ China.

    A. leaving   B. entering   C. going   D. coming

2. Which one of the following does NOT belong to the sharp or loose objects?

    A. Jewelry.   B. Hair clips.   C. Pencils.   D. Paper cash.

3. We have already _____ the temperature. It will be warmer in a few minutes.

    A. adjusted   B. changed   C. got   D. took

4. For movies, we have a _____ selection for you, many of which are new releases.

    A. many   B. much   C. some   D. wide

5. Overhead bins must be securely closed and _____ during aircraft movement.

    A. retracted   B. located   C. remained   D. latched

6. Don't worry. We will broadcast and _____ a doctor for you.

    A. bring   B. search   C. look   D. look for

7. Many airports now use special cameras to detect travelers with a fever in order to _____ them _____ traveling on an airplane.

    A. produce; from   B. provide; with   C. supply; for   D. prevent; from

8. During a first aid, _____ will be used for CPR.

    A. PSU   B. PBE   C. AED   D. ELT

9. What should be done in case of serious injury or illness on board?

    A. Observe the patient's vital signs and state of consciousness.

    B. Decide whether to give oxygen according to the situation.

    C. Promptly report to the captain, call for a doctor by PA.

    D. All of the above.

10. What should not be done when a passenger gets airsick?

A. Give the passenger an airsickness bag.

B. Open the ventilator.

C. Let the passenger hold his breath to prevent vomiting.

D. Have the airsick passenger look at the ceiling.

11. What are the key points of in-flight first aid for stroke?

A. Remove the pillow or use a lower pillow.

B. Keep quiet.

C. Inhale oxygen.

D. All of the above.

12. Infants are allowed to take the flight after _____ days of birth.

    A. 15   B. 14   C. 90   D. 30

13. China Southern Airlines joined _____ on Nov. 15th, 2007, becoming the first Chinese mainland airline to join an international airline alliance.

    A. Sky Team   B. One world   C. Star Alliance   D. Phoenix Miles

14. Each adult passenger on board is allowed to carry _____ infants.

    A.1   B.2   C.3   D.4

15. The cargo section of airliner is usually located at _____.

    A. the front part   B. the belly part   C. near the wings   D. near the tail

16. Which meal is suggested for Jewish people?

    A. MOML.   B. VGML.   C. DBML.   D. KSML.

17. Which one of the following titles ranks the top according to duties?

    A. CP   B. CS   C. PS   D. FS

18. The best serving temperature for white wine is _____ °C.

    A. 8–12   B. 16–18   C. 7–10   D. 18–20

19. A Moslem passenger will not have _____.

    A. pork   B. beef   C. mutton   D. seafood

20. Which one of the following term means "三角面包"？

    A. Baguette.   B. Bun.   C. Croissant.   D. Rye rolls.

21. When serving special passengers, flight attendants should _____.

A. separate the passenger properly to avoid contact with him/her

B. loosen the passenger's seat belt, open the ventilator and airsickness bag for them

C. arrange for priority boarding, help passengers carry their luggage and assist them to take their seats

  D. contact ground staff in advance before landing and arrange them to be the first to deplane

22. The capital of the Netherlands is _____ and the national flower is _____.

  A. Copenhagen; the lotus   B. Helsinki; the lilac

  C. Amsterdam; tulips   D. Brussels; lavender

23. Frankfurt International Airport (FRA) is located in _____.

  A. France   B. Germany   C. Netherlands   D. Italy

24. Which airport is located in America?

  A. HAN.   B. ATL.   C. MAD.   D. SIN.

25. The headquarters of the International Air Transport Association is located in _____.

  A. Berlin, Germany   B. Beijing, China

  C. Washington, D.C.   D. Montreal, Canada

26. What is the two-letter code of Shanghai Airlines _____ ?

  A. MF.   B. KN.   C. FM.   D. CZ.

27. What type of aircraft is known as the "Giant of the Air"?

  A. B707.   B. B737.   C. C919.   D. A380.

28. When the cabin is filled with smoke during evacuation, the cabin crew must direct passengers to _____.

  A. run to the cabin door

  B. remain seated

  C. bend over, stay low and cover the mouth and nose to the exits

  D. move freely

29. Which city is located at the "crossroads" between Asia and Oceania, the Pacific Ocean and the Indian Ocean?

  A. Singapore.   B. Beijing.   C. Hong Kong.   D. Seoul.

30. Which of the following cities is known as "Golden City"?

  A. Sun City.   B. Johannesburg.   C. Pretoria.   D. Cape Town.

31. Which of the following descriptions of France is wrong?

  A. It is the largest agricultural producer in the European Union and a major exporter of agricultural products in the world.

  B. It's well known all over the world for the wines, fashion, gourmet and perfume.

  C. Its capital is the largest city on the European continent and one of the most prosperous cities in the world.

D. It has tourist attractions such as the Peace Arch, Cologne Cathedra, Wurzburg Residence, etc.

32. The "superjumbo" refers to _____.

    A. A380　　　　　B. B747　　　　　C. B707　　　　　D. C919

33. First aid kit means "_____".

    A. 急救箱　　　　B. 医用药箱　　　　C. 救生包　　　　D. 工具箱

34. Survival kit means "_____".

    A. 药箱　　　　　B. 信号筒　　　　　C. 救生包　　　　D. 食品包

35. Which symbol is indicated for Oxygen Mask?

    A. 　　　B. 　　　C. 　　　D.

36. May I suggest that you _____ the shoes in the reusable bag?

    A. to keep　　　B. kept　　　C. keeping　　　D. keep

37. I will set up a baby bassinet for you _____ the airplane reaches the cruising altitude.

    A. at　　　B. before　　　C. after　　　D. since

38. Please be the _____ one to disembark, the ground staff will arrange a wheel chair for you after landing.

    A. first　　　B. last　　　C. second　　　D. third

39. You can change your baby's diaper in the lavatory. There is _____ in it. Let me help you.

    A. a blackboard　　　　　　　　B. a baby nursery board

    C. a basin　　　　　　　　　　　D. a dustbin

40. _____! You are the lucky one to get the network connecting successfully. Now you can surf the net as you like. Please enjoy it!

    A. What a pity　　　B. Congratulations　　　C. Welcome　　　D. Kidding

41. Who are not allowed to use the onboard first aid kit?

    A. Flight attendants.　　　　　　B. Certified doctors.

    C. Specially trained personnel.　　D. Patients themselves.

42. Which of the following is the location of chest compressions（胸外按压）for adults?

    A. The upper sternum.

    B. Middle sternum.

    C. The midpoint of the line between the two nipples.

    D. The lower sternum.

43. What are the treatments for otitis media（中耳炎）on board?

A. Initiate a swallowing motion during the descent of the aircraft.

B. Do nasal pinching and puffing motion when ear discomfort occurs.

C. Do nasal puffing and swallowing at the same time.

D. All of the above.

44. In the event of a serious injury or illness on board, the person who requests to open and use the emergency medical kit must _____.

    A. state that he or she is a doctor

    B. state that he or she is a nurse

    C. state that he or she is a professionally trained nursing staff

    D. show valid documents proving his or her identity as a doctor

45. How long is our effective time of consciousness if the cockpit is depressurized and the oxygen supply is completely cut off at the height of 8,000 ～ 12,000m?

    A. 5 ～ 10 seconds.   B. 5 ～ 30 seconds.

    C. 30 seconds ～ 1 minute.   D. 30 seconds ～ 3 minutes.

46. When a suspected infectious patient is found on board, the cabin crew should _____.

    A. promptly take isolation measures, separately collect the items the patient has touched and promptly broadcast for medical assistance

    B. give the patient anti-bacterial and anti-inflammatory medication

    C. tell other passengers not to touch the patient

    D. keep quiet and keep warm

47. There are no restrictions on the transport of passengers at pregnancy of _____.

    A. 32 ～ 36 weeks   B. more than 36 weeks

    C. less than 32 weeks   D. less than 33 weeks

48. When passengers get on and off the plane, the cabin lighting should be adjusted _____.

    A. to the brightest   B. to medium bright

    C. to medium dark   D. to the darkest

49. Which one of the following statements is correct?

    A. Black tea needs to be served with both lemon and milk.

    B. When offering iced drinks, add ice afterwards.

    C. Alcoholic beverages can be served in unlimited quantities on board.

    D. When the halal meal is out, vegetarian food can be used instead.

50. PORT（波特酒）belongs to _____.

A. distilled alcoholic drinks B. fermented alcoholic drinks

C. infused alcoholic drinks D. None of the above

II. True or False (*1'×50=50'*)

1. The symbol ? means Baggage Claim.   ( )

2. The international code for the British pound is GAP.   ( )

3. Duty-free goods on board include tobacco, alcohol, perfume and cosmetics, and general categories.   ( )

4. Cabin service procedures can begin 10 minutes after aircraft departure. ( )

5. The conversion formula between Celsius and Fahrenheit is $°C × 9/5 + 32 = °F$. ( )

6. First aid kit means "救生包".   ( )

7. Sponge refers to "海锚".   ( )

8. The meaning of "shoulder harness" is "肩带".   ( )

9. The expression for "中转柜台" is transfer counter.   ( )

10. "Shot Glass" refers to "鸡尾酒杯".   ( )

11. "Hors d'oeuvre" means "开胃菜".   ( )

12. Tonic water means "干姜水".   ( )

13. Asparagus means "萝卜".   ( )

14. Broccoli means "西兰花".   ( )

15. Light meal means "简餐".   ( )

16. The expression for "请问您预订了一份儿童餐对吗？" is "Have you ordered a vegetarian meal?".   ( )

17. E-cigarettes are not prohibited on board.   ( )

18. The main symptom of ear distress is nausea and vomiting.   ( )

19. Passengers should recline their seatbacks during take-off.   ( )

20. Incheon International Airport is located in Japan.   ( )

21. When the oven in the galley catches fire, we can use the H_2O type extinguisher. ( )

22. Safety instruction cards are located in the magazine rack.   ( )

23. Overhead lockers must be securely closed and latched during aircraft movement. ( )

24. If a passenger has special meal requirement, he can book the meal within 24 hours. ( )

25. Jewish people are more likely to choose Muslim Meal.   ( )

26. A departing domestic passenger does not have to fill out an embarkation card. ( )

27. Portable power banks can be placed in the checked baggage.   ( )

28. If a flight is delayed due to unfavorable weather conditions, airline is not obliged to compensate the delayed passengers. ( )

29. Soft drinks refer to alcoholic beverages. ( )

30. Parents should put on the oxygen masks for their children first, then put one their own masks in case of decompression in the cabin. ( )

31. 15A is an aisle seat. ( )

32. China Eastern Airlines is a member of Star Alliance. ( )

33. Infants needn't life vests during ditching. ( )

34. In water evacuation, you only need to take off your high-heeled shoes. ( )

35. Lufthansa is an airline of Germany. ( )

36. Bloody Mary is a kind of cocktail. ( )

37. Taj Mahal is in Thailand. ( )

38. Coatroom is in the galley on board. ( )

39. Halon Fire Extinguisher can only be used for electrical five. ( )

40. Floating Cushion is used in emergency ditching. ( )

41. New York is the largest city of USA, and also its capital. ( )

42. Mooring line is located on the forepart of the life raft. ( )

43. Shanghai Airlines and Air China are both members of Star Alliance. ( )

44. The normal checked-in baggage allowance for Y class is 20 lb. ( )

45. Compress Bandages are usually stored in survival kits. ( )

46. Cabin doors can be armed or disarmed manually or automatically. ( )

47. The landing forms can only be filled out after the passengers get off the plane. ( )

48. Amsterdam is the capital of Denmark. ( )

49. Passengers can put their luggage in the galley. ( )

50. The full name of IATA is the International Air Transport Association. ( )

三、**Written Test 3**

I. Choice (1′×50=50′)

1. Which one of the following is NOT a soft drink?

    A. Coke cola.   B. Juice.   C. Seven-up.   D. Beer.

2. Which of the following instructions regarding exit seats is incorrect?

    A. Cabin crew should show the Emergency Exit Seat Instructions Cards to passengers seated at the exit seats.

B. Before the doors are closed, the obligations of the passengers seated at the emergency exit seats as facilitators must be confirmed.

C. Passenger who does not want to assume the obligations associated with an exit seat shall be immediately relocated to a non-exit seat.

D. Passengers may be seated in an exit seat as long as they are over 15 years of age.

3. In the event of a moderate turbulence in flight, _____.

A. cabin service will be suspended immediately

B. crew members should put away the meal trolley and drinks

C. crew members sit in duty positions and fasten seat belts

D. All of the above

4. If a passenger wants to have a fully toasted steak, he will say, "Cook it _____."

A. rare　　　　B. medium　　　　C. well-done　　　　D. full

5. Which meal serves first in western dinner?

A. Appetizer.　　B. Soup.　　　　C. Salad.　　　　D. Main course.

6. The Western European country known as the "Kingdom of Bullfighting" is _____.

A. India　　　　B. Spain　　　　C. Italy　　　　D. Monaco

7. Which airline two-letter code refers to China Southern Airlines?

A. CA.　　　　B. MU.　　　　C. CZ.　　　　D. CX.

8. The three-character code of Guangzhou Baiyun Airport is _____; the three-character code of Hong Kong Chek Lap Kok International Airport is _____.

A. CAN; HGK　　B. CAN; HKG　　C. MAC; HKG　　D. TPE; HGK

9. Which of the following belongs to narrow body aircraft?

A. A380.　　　　B. A330.　　　　B. B747.　　　　D. B757.

10. On May 14th, 2018, an aircraft of _____ suffered an emergency situation at high altitude when the windscreen came off and the cockpit lost pressure, and finally landed safely after calm handling by the crew.

A. Air China　　　　　　　B. Shandong Airlines

C. Sichuan Airlines　　　　D. Hainan Airlines

11. In the event of cabin decompression, the oxygen masks should be worn in the following order _____.

A. crew member – adult – minor　　B. crew member – minor – adult

C. minor – adult – crew member　　D. adult – crew member – minor

12. If a passenger _____ himself as a doctor, the cabin attendants should ask to see his certificate or proof.

    A. tells   B. identifies   C. informs   D. notifies

13. In land evacuation, passengers should choose _____ direction to get away from the aircraft; in water evacuation passengers should choose _____ direction.

    A. upwind; upwind   B. upwind; downwind

    C. downwind; downwind   D. downwind; upwind

14. Flammable solids belong to _____ of DGR.

    A. Class 3   B. Class 4   C. Class 5   D. Class 6

15. The Halon fire extinguishing bottle emits _____.

    A. an inert gas   B. carbon dioxide   C. dry powder   D. fog

16. Which of the following countries is in the Western Hemisphere?

    A. Japan.   B. Russia.   C. Spain.   D. Canada.

17. The largest air show in the world is _____.

    A. Farnborough Airshow   B. Zhuhai Airshow

    C. Singapore Airshow   D. Paris Airshow

18. _____ is the International Civil Aviation Day.

    A. September 7th   B. October 7th   C. November 7th   D. December 7th

19. _____ is the largest international airport in Japan and the main international gateway to Japan.

    A. Narita Airport   B. Haneda Airport

    C. Osaka Kansai International Airport   D. Sendai Airport

20. Canopy means "_____".

    A. 海锚   B. 天棚   C. 海绵   D. 生存指南

21. Sea anchor means "_____".

    A. 海锚   B. 海绵   C. 海水手电   D. 海水电池

22. H_2O type extinguishers can be used for _____.

    A. any type of fire   B. electrical fire

    C. paper, wood, cloth and fabric on fire   D. grease items on fire

23. Halon extinguisher is applicable to _____.

    A. any type of fire   B. electrical fire

    C. paper, wood, cloth and fabric items on fire   D. grease items on fire

24. A tailwind can be of great _____ as it increases the ground speed and results in a reduction in fuel consumption.

    A. administration   B. agent   C. admission   D. advantage

25. A cabin attendant must be trained to _____ her own assigned duties and to provide whatever assistance the other cabin attendants require.

    A. prepare   B. perform   C. provide   D. possess

26. In an emergency evacuation, when one of the exits is blocked, you should _____.

    A. continue to try to open the exit

    B. seek the help of passengers

    C. wait for the right moment

    D. immediately direct passengers to evacuate through other exits

27. During forced landing, the high-heeled shoes and spiked-shoes should be put _____.

    A. in the seat pocket   B. under the seat

    C. in the luggage   D. in the bathroom

28. Stretcher passengers should be arranged in _____ of the cabin.

    A. the first row   B. the middle   C. the last row   D. any position

29. If the type of fire cannot be determined, you should use _____ to extinguish the fire.

    A. water fire extinguishing bottle   B. Halon fire extinguishing bottle

    C. tea or coffee   D. the nearest fire extinguishing bottle

30. The time difference between Beijing and Paris in winter is 7 hours and the plane is expected to land at 0:50 a.m. Beijing time on Thursday, then Paris time is _____.

    A. Thursday 5:50 p.m.   B. Wednesday 5:50 p.m.

    C. Wednesday 5:50 a.m.   D. Thursday 7:50 p.m.

31. There are emergency and survival equipment on board _____ an emergency incident should happen.

    A. so that   B. in order that   C. in case that   D. as though

32. If the flight departs Beijing at 11:30 a.m. Beijing time on Thursday, the flight time is 10 hours 20 minutes and the time difference is known to be −6 hours, what is the local time when arriving?

    A. Thursday 15:50.   B. Thursday 3:50 a.m.

    C. Thursday 21:50.   D. None of the above is correct.

33. A passenger buys two cartons of cigarettes and a bottle of whisky. One carton of cigarette

is US$ 22 and the whisky is US$121. The exchange rate is 1US$ = 0.6 £. The passenger should pay _____.

      A. £99   B. £85.80   C. £275   D. £238

34. The first convention made by ICAO that specifically provided for anti-hijacking is _____.

      A. the Hague Convention   B. the Tokyo Convention

      C. the Montreal Convention   D. the Warsaw Convention

35. The corporate logo of China Southern Airlines is _____.

      A. Kapok   B. Blue Sky Egret   C. Swallow   D. Phoenix

36. Which symbol means a flashlight?

A.   B.   C.   D.

37. The sharp or loose objects include _____.

      A. jewelry and glasses   B. hair clips and spike-heeled shoes

      C. pens and pencils   D. all of the above

38. PSU (Passenger Service Unit) contains all these items except _____.

      A. NO SMOKING sign   B. FASTEN SEAT BELT sign

      C. reading light and air vent   D. overhead bin

39. Passengers should be _____ to the Customs control and declare accurately all the baggage they carry to the Customs for inspection.

      A. got   B. subject   C. taken   D. objective

40. Which one is a loud speaker used in emergency evacuation when the interphone is inoperative?

      A. Megaphone.   B. Release tool.   C. Baton.   D. Protective gloves.

41. Which one of the following words means "加长安全带"?

      A. Extension.   B. Protection.   C. Manual.   D. Survival.

42. Which item is NOT included in Demo Kit?

      A. Instruction card.   B. Oxygen mask.   C. Life jacket.   D. Megaphone.

43. _____ is a model airplane or a part of mode airplane in a real size for the training of cabin crew.

      A. Mock-up   B. Fuselage   C. Lounge   D. Panel

44. The toilet on the airplane is also called _____.

空乘实用英语教程

| A. lavatory | B. galley | C. cockpit | D. closet |

45. The Kitchen on the airplane is also called _____.

| A. lavatory | B. galley | C. cockpit | D. closet |

46. The cabin crew's seat on the airplane is called _____.

| A. retractable seat | B. panel seat | C. jump seat | D. deck seat |

47. If the London time is 16:00, then the Beijing time is _____.

| A. 24:00 | B. 8:00 | C. 12:00 | D. 4:00 |

48. _____ will be rolled for giving out meals and beverages in the aisles.

| A. Drawers | B. Ovens | C. Carts | D. Trays |

49. The executive body of IATA is located in _____.

| A. Geneva | B. Montreal | C. London | D. Waysaw |

50. If a passenger wants to vomit, he can use the _____.

| A. first aid kit | B. paper cup | C. tray table | D. airsickness bag |

II. True or False (1′×50=50′)

1. The symbol ⬩ means departure.   (   )

2. The international code for the Swiss franc is CHF.   (   )

3. The international common code for the Swedish krona is SK.   (   )

4. The international code for the Japanese yen is JPY.   (   )

5. The flight attendant should refrigerate white wine after boarding the aircraft, as the optimal serving temperature for white wine is 8–12℃.   (   )

6. Burn ointment means "烫伤膏".   (   )

7. Canopy refers to "海绵".   (   )

8. "Correct lenses" refers to "隐形眼镜".   (   )

9. Contraband means "违禁物品".   (   )

10. Over wing window exit means "翼上窗体出口".   (   )

11. Air Traffic Control (ATC) means "航空管制".   (   )

12. "Goblet" refers to "高脚水杯".   (   )

13. Cabbage means "卷心菜".   (   )

14. Fresh brewed coffee means "现煮咖啡".   (   )

15. Cereal means "香菜".   (   )

16. Cucumber means "豌豆".   (   )

17. Obese passenger means "肥胖旅客".   (   )

18. The main symptom of airsickness is coma. ( )

19. In case of emergency evacuation, the elderly and children should be seated at the emergency exits to facilitate evacuation. ( )

20. Takasaki International Airport is located at Xiamen. ( )

21. The oxygen mask can also be used as PBE in emergency. ( )

22. Cabin attendants usually use PSU system to make announcements. ( )

23. Before take off, cabin attendants need to tell passengers to remove sharp and pointed goods. ( )

24. When doing the bracing position, passengers in bulkhead seats should cross the arms on the seat back in front. ( )

25. The number of the cabin attendants for each flight is often the same. ( )

26. DBML is designed for those with kidney or liver problems who need to manage it. ( )

27. If there is a medium turbulence, we need to evacuate. ( )

28. If you want to put out the fire caused by flammable liquid, you can use H_2O type extinguisher. ( )

29. To ease the ear distress, passengers can eat chewing gum. ( )

30. Bar service is complimentary for all passengers. ( )

31. Moslem meal is a kind of vegetarian meals. ( )

32. People who have digestive problems could take HFML. ( )

33. Passenger seats can be reclined during take off and landing. ( )

34. A teenager at the age of 13 can hold a children ticket. ( )

35. A mother can hold her infant on her laps and then fasten the seatbelt around two of them together. ( )

36. You can inflate your life vest in the cabin in order to save time. ( )

37. Delta Airlines is an American airline. ( )

38. Passengers can exchange their seats freely before take-off. ( )

39. Gin is a non-alcoholic drink on board. ( )

40. Haneda Airport is in Japan. ( )

41. If the cabin baggage is too big to put into the overhead compartment, it can be placed in the aisle. ( )

42. During forced landing, you should remove sharp objects and put them in the seat pocket in front of you. ( )

43. Crew manifest means the name list of aircrew. （ ）

44. Passenger's air vent system is a part of PSU. （ ）

45. Low Calorie Meal is a kind of medical meals. （ ）

46. If a passenger is suffering from airsickness, you will prepare tranquilizer. （ ）

47. Boarding Ladder is only located on the back of the life raft. （ ）

48. Anybody can take the Exit Seat as long as he or she would like to. （ ）

49. Tea and coffee are hot drinks and they are complimentary for all passengers. （ ）

50. Economy class passengers can enjoy bar service on a complimentary basis. （ ）

第三节　口语测试题库

1. Translate the Words and Phrases (Chinese-English or English-Chinese)（词汇短语翻译）

（1）航前准备会 pre-flight briefing　　（2）航后讲评会 post-flight meeting

（3）驾驶舱 flight deck/cockpit　　（4）机长 captain

（5）副机长 copilot　　（6）头等舱 first class

（7）公务舱 business class　　（8）经济舱 economy class

（9）主任乘务长 chief purser　　（10）乘务员 cabin attendant/flight attendant

（11）安全员 security guard　　（12）地勤人员 ground staff

（13）常旅客 frequent flyers　　（14）国际乘客 international passenger

（15）国内乘客 domestic passenger　　（16）值机柜台 check-in counter

（17）登机牌 boarding pass/card　　（18）指定座位 assigned seat

（19）靠过道座位 aisle seat　　（20）靠窗座位 window seat

（21）空闲座位 vacant seat

（22）手提行李 hand baggage/cabin baggage/carry-on baggage

（23）托运行李 checked baggage　　（24）易碎物品 fragile items

（25）座椅靠背 seatback　　（26）座椅扶手 armrest

（27）座椅口袋 seat pocket　　（28）小桌板 tray table

（29）脚踏板 footrest　　（30）乘务员座椅 jump seat

（31）遮光板 window shade/sun shade/window blind

（32）通风口 ventilator/ air outlet/air flow　　（33）呼唤铃 call button

（34）阅读灯 reading light　　（35）娱乐系统 entertainment system

（36）头顶上方行李架 overhead locker/compartment/bin/rack

（37）手提电脑 laptop　　　　　　（38）手机 mobile phone/ cell phone

（39）移动电源 portable power bank

（40）关闭（手机或电子设备）power off/ turn off（phone or electronic devices）

（41）飞行模式 airplane mode/flight mode

（42）干扰导航设备 interfere with navigation system

（43）配载平衡 weight and balance　　（44）巡航高度 cruising altitude

（45）安全带指示灯 seatbelt sign　　　（46）婴儿安全带 infant seatbelt

（47）加长安全带 extension seatbelt　　（48）烟雾探测器 smoke detector

（49）机上洗手间 lavatory　　　　　（50）安全演示 safety demonstration

（51）救生衣 life vest　　　　　　　（52）氧气面罩 oxygen mask

（53）氧气瓶 oxygen cylinder　　　　（54）手电筒 flash light

（55）灭火瓶 fire extinguisher　　　　（56）紧急出口 emergency exit

（57）预计起飞时间 estimated departure time（58）空中交通管制 air traffic control

（59）通行许可 take-off clearance　　　（60）能见度低 low visibility/poor visibility

（61）晴空湍流 clear air turbulence　　（62）备降机场 alternate airport

（63）不利的天气情况 bad/unfavorable weather conditions

（64）机械故障 mechanical trouble/problem/failure

（65）航班被延误 / 取消 the flight has been delayed/canceled

（66）食宿 accommodation　　　　　（67）改签 endorsement

（68）机上厨房 galley　　　　　　　（69）咖啡机 coffee maker

（70）烤箱 oven　　　　　　　　　（71）托盘 food tray

（72）湿纸巾 wet tissue　　　　　　（73）餐车 trolley/cart

（74）菜单 menu　　　　　　　　　（75）加冰 on the rocks

（76）免费的 complimentary/free　　　（77）含酒精饮料 alcoholic beverage

（78）葡萄酒 wine　　　　　　　　（79）香槟 champagne

（80）啤酒 beer　　　　　　　　　（81）不含酒精饮料 non-alcoholic beverage

（82）红茶 black tea　　　　　　　（83）绿茶 green tea

（84）柠檬茶 lemon tea　　　　　　（85）矿泉水 mineral water

（86）气泡水 sparkling water　　　　（87）苏打水 soda water

（88）热水 hot water　　　　　　　（89）温水 warm water

（90）冰水 ice water　　　　　　　（91）黑咖啡 black coffee

（92）速溶咖啡 instant coffee

（93）三合一咖啡 mixed coffee

（94）低因咖啡 decaffeinated coffee

（95）酸奶 yogurt

（96）苹果汁 apple juice

（97）橙汁 orange juice

（98）雪碧 sprite

（99）可乐 coke

（100）主菜 entrée / main course

（101）开胃菜 appetizer

（102）羊肉 mutton

（103）牛肉 beef

（104）猪肉 pork

（105）鸡肉 chicken

（106）虾 prawn

（107）虾仁 shrimp

（108）海鲜 seafood

（109）米饭 rice

（110）面条 noodle

（111）粥 congee

（112）煎蛋卷 omelet

（113）牛排 steak

（114）汉堡 hamburger

（115）三明治 sandwich

（116）意面 pasta

（117）黄油 butter

（118）点心 snack

（119）甜点 dessert

（120）巧克力 chocolate

（121）坚果 nut

（122）饼干 biscuit

（123）特殊餐 special meal

（124）儿童餐 child meal

（125）婴儿餐 baby meal

（126）素食餐 vegetarian meal

（127）穆斯林餐 Muslim meal

（128）犹太餐 Kosher meal

（129）印度餐 Hindu meal

（130）溃疡餐 bland meal

（131）无人陪伴儿童 unaccompanied minor

（132）老年旅客 senior passenger

（133）轮椅旅客 wheelchair passenger

（134）孕妇 pregnant woman

（135）肥胖旅客 obese passenger

（136）糖尿病旅客 diabetic passenger

（137）免税品 duty-free items

（138）信用卡 credit card

（139）汇率 exchange rate

（140）急救药箱 first aid kit

（141）体温计 thermometer

（142）医用酒精 medical alcohol

（143）绷带 bandage

（144）药膏 ointment

（145）冰敷 ice compress

（146）症状 symptom

（147）晕机 airsickness

（148）眩晕的 dizzy

（149）恶心的 nauseous

（150）呕吐 vomit

（151）头疼 headache

（152）消化不良 indigestion

（153）腹泻 diarrhea

（154）压耳 ear distress

（155）耳朵疼 earache

（156）嗓子疼 sore throat （157）流鼻血 nose bleeding

（158）流涕 runny nose （159）鼻塞 stuffy nose

（160）窒息 choke （161）昏厥 faint

（162）中风 stroke （163）休克 shock

（164）分娩 childbirth/delivery （165）烫伤 scald

（166）骨折 fracture （167）扭伤脚踝 sprained ankles

（168）心脏病 heart attack （169）心搏停止 cardiac arrest

（170）对药物过敏 be allergic to medication （171）紧急情况 emergency situation

（172）客舱释压 cabin depressurization （173）紧急迫降 emergency landing

（174）水上迫降 ditching

（175）采取防冲撞姿势 assume the bracing positions

（176）撤离 evacuation （177）滑梯 slide

（178）原住地 country of origin （179）前往国 destination country

（180）签证签发地 place of visa issuance （181）边检人员 immigration officer

（182）海关、边检、检疫 Customs, Immigration and Quarantine

（183）入境卡 disembarkation card/landing card/ entry card

（184）护照号码 passport number

（185）海关申报单 Customs declaration form

（186）应纳税物品 taxable items/dutiable items

（187）随身物品 personal effects/ personal belongings

（188）转机乘客 transfer passenger

（189）经停乘客 transit passenger

（190）中转航班 connecting flight

（191）中转柜台 transfer counter （192）转机手续 transfer formality

（193）问讯处 information desk （194）自动售票机 ticket dispenser

（195）当地时间 the local time （196）到达厅 arrival hall/ arrival lobby

（197）航站楼 terminal building （198）下机 disembarkation

（199）行李认领处 Baggage Claim Area （200）机场摆渡车 airport shuttle bus

2. Sentence Translation（Chinese-English or English-Chinese）（句子英汉互译）

（1）Good afternoon, Miss Robinson. I'm the chief purser of this flight, Ivy.

下午好，鲁宾逊小姐。我是本次航班的主任乘务长艾薇。

（2）If there is anything you need during this trip, please don't hesitate to call me.

如果旅途中您有任何需要，请随时告诉我！

（3）18K. Walk straight ahead. The stewardess there will show you where your seat is.

18K，请一直向后走，那边的乘务员会指给您看的。

（4）Sir, please take this aisle. Your seat is in the third row from the last.

先生，请走这条过道，你的座位在倒数第三排。

（5）We are not responsible for any valuables or important items.

我们不负责保管任何贵重物品。

（6）I am sorry, that's an emergency exit. It's not safe to put luggage there.

很抱歉，这里是紧急出口，不能放行李。

（7）Please take your seat according to your seat number.

请对号入座。

（8）Excuse me, sir. I'm afraid you are in the wrong seat. Would you please show me your boarding pass?

对不起，先生，您可能坐错了座位，请出示一下您的登机牌。

（9）You should be seated in the assigned seat, in order to ensure proper weight and balance for the aircraft when it takes off.

为了飞机起飞时的配载平衡，您应坐在指定的位置。

（10）Excuse me, miss. Could you please make room for other passengers to pass?

劳驾女士，可否麻烦您让出一些空间让其他旅客通过？

（11）You don't mind if I put down the shade, do you?

我把遮阳板放下您不会介意吧？

（12）You shouldn't walk about in the cabin while taking off or landing.

在飞机起飞或降落时，您不应该在机舱内走动。

（13）I'm afraid you'll have to put your bag under the seat in front of you.

恐怕您要将行李放在您前排的座椅下面。

（14）Our flight has to be cancelled because of the unfavorable weather condition.

因为天气恶劣，我们的航班不得不取消。

（15）We will serve dinner after take-off. For main dishes today we have beef steak, seafood and chicken, which one would you prefer?

起飞后我们将供应晚餐，今天的主菜有牛排、海鲜和鸡肉，您喜欢哪一种？

（16）I'm sorry, we are out of the seafood dishes, but we still have beef steak and chicken. They are both delicious.

对不起，海鲜已经订完了，我们还有牛排和鸡肉，味道都很不错。

（17）Here is the menu for today. Please order the main dish as you like.

这是今天的餐谱，请选择您喜欢的主菜。

（18）Here we have some drinks for you, such as orange juice, water, coffee and champagne. Which one would you prefer?

我们为您准备了饮品，有橙汁、水、咖啡和香槟，您想喝点什么？

（19）Excuse me, sir. Would you please put your seatback upright so that the lady behind you may be more comfortable to have her meal?

对不起，先生，可以劳烦您将座椅收直以便后面的女士用餐吗？

（20）How would you like your whiskey? On the rock, as a chaser or straight up?

请问您的威士忌需要加冰、追水还是直饮？

（21）Could you please tell me where the lavatory is?

您能告诉我洗手间在哪里吗？

（22）There are toilets in the front and rear of the cabin.

客舱的前面和后面都有洗手间。

（23）This one is occupied. Please wait a moment, or you can go to the one on the left.

这个洗手间有人用，请稍等，或者您可以去到左边那个。

（24）Excuse me, this is a non-smoking flight. Please refrain from smoking during the whole flight.

对不起，本次航班是禁烟航班，请不要吸烟。

（25）We have in-flight magazines and some local newspaper. Which one would you prefer?

我们有机上杂志和地方报纸，请问您要哪种？

（26）If you want to read the newspaper, you can turn on the reading light.

如果你想读报，可以打开阅读灯。

（27）This is the passenger service unit which includes a call button, a reading light, an air flow system and a set of emergency oxygen masks.

这是乘客空中服务组件。它包括呼唤铃、阅读灯、空气流通系统和氧气面罩。

（28）For movies, we have a wide selection for you, and many of them are new releases.

电影方面，您有很多选择，不少都是最新上映的电影。

（29）What's your opinion about our in-flight entertainment system?

您对我们的机上娱乐系统有什么看法吗？

（30）Please turn to Channel 2 and adjust the volume by pressing the plus or minus sign.

请调到频道 2，按增加或减少键调整音量。

（31）You may adjust your seat back by pressing the button on the armrest.

您可以通过座椅扶手的按钮来调节座椅靠背。

（32）I will give you the airsickness bag and a cup of warm water as well. If you need any help, please do not hesitate to call me.

我会为您提供清洁袋和温水。如果您需要任何帮助，请随时告诉我。

（33）If there is anything we can do for you, please press your call button. We are happy to serve you.

如果您还有什么需要，请按此呼唤铃，我很愿意为您提供服务。

（34）Don't worry. Take it easy. Because of a change in air pressure, you can swallow or chew to relieve the earache.

请不要担心。请放松。因为压力变化，您可以通过吞咽和咀嚼来缓解耳痛。

（35）We seem to have a slight technical problem with the cabin temperature at the moment but we are sorting it out.

我们的客舱温度似乎出了点小问题，但是我们正在解决。

（36）Due to the air turbulence, our cabin service will be suspended for this moment.

由于气流颠簸，我们的客舱服务将会暂停一会儿。

（37）Excuse me, madam. Please hold your baby outside the belt. It will be safer and more comfortable for him that way.

对不起，女士。请您将婴儿抱在安全带外边，那样对婴儿更安全，婴儿也会感到更舒服。

（38）After take off, I'll set up a baby bassinet for you. By the way, would you care for the disposable diapers as well?

起飞后我帮您放个婴儿摇篮，另外您需要一次性尿片吗？

（39）Excuse me, madam, now the plane is descending and we will be landing soon. May I take the baby bassinet away?

对不起，太太，现在飞机正在下降，很快就要落地了，我可以拿掉婴儿摇篮吗？

（40）We have arranged the wheelchair for you. For your convenience, please remain in your seat until all the other passengers have left.

我们已经为您准备好了轮椅，为了您的方便起见，待会降落后请您待在座位上，等候其他乘客先下机。

（41）We'll be landing in 30 minutes and the drink service has concluded. May I get you a bottle of mineral water?

我们还有 30 分钟就要下降了，我们已经结束酒类供应。如您不介意，我为您准备一瓶矿泉水好吗？

（42）How about today's cabin service or catering? We appreciate your suggestions.

您觉得今天的客舱服务或者餐食怎么样？我们非常感谢您的宝贵意见。

（43）Today is our National Day. We have prepared some gifts for you. We hope you like them.

今天是国庆节。我们为您准备了礼品，希望您能喜欢。

（44）We will ask our captain to inform the ground staff to look for it. Well, if we find your camera, we will bring it to you in time. Please write down your name, address and telephone number on this paper.

我们会请机长通知地面部门帮您寻找。这样吧，我们如果找到了，我们会及时带给您，请您在这张纸上写下您的姓名、地址和电话号码。

（45）We are encountering some turbulence. Please return to your seats and fasten your seat belts.

我们遇到了颠簸，请回到您的座位坐好，系好安全带。

（46）The turbulence is very serious because there is a thunderstorm en route.

飞机颠簸得很厉害，因为航路上有雷雨。

（47）Turbulence is not like a thunderstorm. Flying around a thunderstorm would delay our flight.

颠簸不像绕雷雨，如果是绕雷雨飞行时间就会晚一些。

（48）You may leave your hand baggage onboard, since we have to stay overnight in Guangzhou.

你可以将手提物品留在飞机上，因为我们将在广州过夜。

（49）Would you please stow your tray table? Oh, let me show you. Just put it upright and turn this knob tightly. Now, it is stowed properly.

请您将小桌板收好。我来做给您看，把它放直，转动这个旋钮，现在好了。

（50）Excuse me, sir. Please remain seated until the plane comes to a complete stop.

对不起，先生，在飞机完全停稳前，请您不要离开座位。

（51）When the boarding bridge is ready, you can disembark.

等登机桥靠好后，您就能下飞机了。

（52）You may go to the transfer counter at the terminal building to check your reservation.

您可以去候机楼的中转柜台办理中转手续。

（53）Just a moment. Let me clean it first. There is an electrical outlet in the lavatory.

请让我先打扫一下厕所好吗？厕所内有电源插座。

（54）According to the regulation of CAAC, the departure time on your ticket refers to the time for closing cabin doors but not for taking off. There is usually a 15-minute interval between door closing and taking off.

根据民航局的规定，您机票上的离港时间是指关机舱门的时间，而不是起飞时间，两者之间大约相隔 15 分钟。

（55）Sir, you are not allowed to go to the cockpit under any circumstances. It's against the aviation regulations.

先生，您在任何情况下都不能进入驾驶舱。那样是违反航空规定的。

（56）We apologize for the delay in taking off. If we have any further information, we'll let you know.

我们对推迟起飞深表歉意。如果有进一步的消息，我们会立即通知您的。

（57）We are waiting for a few passengers to complete boarding formalities.

我们正在等待几位乘客办理登机手续。

（58）Owing to the heavy air traffic, we'll wait until a take off clearance is given.

由于空中航路拥挤，我们要等待通行许可才能起飞。

（59）We have just been informed that this flight has been cancelled due to mechanical problem.

我们刚接到通知，由于机械故障本次航班已经取消。

（60）I'm sorry to tell you that the flight has been delayed due to bad weather.

很抱歉，我要告诉您，本次航班由于天气恶劣延误了。

（61）The lavatory is occupied now. Please wait a moment.

洗手间有人，请您稍等。

（62）According to the latest weather report, the outside temperature is 20 degrees Centigrade.

根据最新的天气消息，舱外温度为 20℃。

（63）Please remain seated until the plane comes to a complete stop.

在飞机完全停稳前，请不要离开您的座位。

（64）Could you give us some advice on improving in-flight service?

您能就提高机上服务质量给我们提些建议吗？

（65）I hope you have a nice trip in Beijing.

希望您在北京玩得开心。

（66）Excuse me, sir. Could you please step aside and allow other passengers to go through?

对不起，先生。您能往边上站一点让其他旅客过去吗？

（67）Would you mind me putting your baggage somewhere else?

您不介意我帮您把行李放到别的地方吧？

（68）Excuse me, sir. May I remind you that passengers are not allowed to remove emergency equipment by themselves? Please put back the life vest.

对不起，先生。我提醒您，旅客们不允许私自移动紧急设备。请将救生衣放回原处。

（69）You feel pain in your ears because of a change in air pressure. You can relieve earache by chewing gum or candy.

您感到耳朵痛是由于气压改变的缘故。嚼块口香糖或糖果就会好些。

（70）We'll have to stay here overnight. Please take your belongings and prepare disembarkation.

我们将在这里过夜，请拿好随身物品准备下飞机。

（71）Don't worry. We'll provide free accommodation for every passenger.

请不要担心，我们将为每位乘客提供免费住宿。

（72）Vegetables, fruits and meat are restricted by customs regulation.

根据海关的规定，蔬菜、水果和肉品是不能携带入境的。

（73）Please write down your name, address, telephone number and everything you know about your handbag. We'll try to locate it for you. If we have any information about it, we'll contact you.

请留下您的姓名、地址、电话号码和有关您手提包的详细情况。我们会尽力帮您寻找的。如果有消息，我们会马上通知您的。

（74）You have to claim your checked luggage in the terminal.

您的托运行李必须到候机楼认领。

（75）You may leave your baggage on the plane but take all valuables and important documents with you. The plane will stop here for one hour and ten minutes.

您可以将行李留在飞机上，但贵重物品和重要文件必须随身携带。飞机将在此停留一小时十分钟。

（76）Inflate the life vest by pulling down the red tab while you leave the airplane.

一离开飞机立即拉下红色充气阀。

（77）Well, please leave your name, address, telephone number and the description of your handbag. I mean the size, color, material and brand.

请留下您的姓名、地址、联系电话和对包的描述，如大小、颜色、材质、品牌。

（78）If you need any assistance, please contact our ground staff after you disembark.

下机后，我们的地勤人员会协助您解决相关事宜。

（79）Thank you for flying with us and we hope to have the pleasure of being with you again.

感谢您乘坐我们的航班，希望能有幸再次和您见面。

（80）Thank you for taking China Eastern Airlines. Looking forward to seeing you soon.

感谢您搭乘中国东方航空班机，期待不久后再次与您相见。

3. Announcement-Making（广播词编播）

在口语测试中，要求根据以下情景编写广播词，以下为具体要求。

（1）The flight CA1521 is from Beijing to Shanghai. The Aircraft type is Airbus 330. Please make a boarding announcement informing the flight information and the stowage of baggage.

（2）It's Mid-Autumn Day. You are the chief purser of today's flight. Please make a welcome announcement and make your holiday greetings as well as introducing the flight information.

（3）The flight is delayed because of air traffic control. Please make a delay announcement to the passengers.

（4）The plane is going to take off. Please make an announcement about electronic devices restriction.

（5）The plane is taxiing for departure. Please make an announcement about safety check.

（6）It's fifteen minutes after take-off. Please make an announcement introducing the routes and in-flight service.

（7）The plane encounters moderate turbulence. Please make an announcement.

（8）Make an announcement about depressurization.

（9）There is a sick passenger on board. It's urgent to find a doctor. Please make an announcement to call for a doctor.

（10）The plane has just landed at the destination airport—Vancouver International Airport. Make a landing announcement including the local time, the ground temperature and necessary instructions.

4. Situational Questions（情景问答）

情景问答类题目如下。

（1）What should the cabin attendants do at the pre-flight briefing?

（2）What do the cabin attendants do in the cabin before passengers get on board?

（3）Try to list the objects in a cabin. (at least five objects)

（4）What information is on a boarding pass?

（5）Would you say something about the weather conditions at your base city?

（6）How would you greet passengers when they board the plane?

（7）How does a cabin attendant make a self-introduction to passengers?

（8）A passenger's seat number is 6A. How can you help to find his seat?

（9）When passengers are boarding, one of them is blocking the way in the cabin. What do you say to him?

（10）Will passengers be able to change seats freely before take-off?

（11）What would you say if one passenger takes the seat of somebody else?

（12）If a passenger says, "The seat pitch here is too narrow. Can you change my seat?" What would you say?

（13）A passenger wants to change his seat to sit with his friends/family, what would you do?

（14）How would you answer if a passenger asks "Can I upgrade to first class?"

（15）A passenger's bag is too big to go in the overhead compartment or under the seat. How do you help him?

（16）When a passenger wants to put baggage in the galley, what would you say?

（17）A passenger doesn't know where to put his coat. How do you help him?

（18）Please explain the correct way for the passenger to fasten his seat belt with the baby.

（19）A passenger with a baby wants to have a cot, but there are no cots on the plane. What would you say?

（20）How can you help a passenger to adjust his seatback?

（21）What would you say if a passenger's baggage is too large for the overhead compartment?

（22）How would you explain to passengers the delay of the flight due to mechanical failure?

（23）The plane is going to take off. But a passenger wants to go to the lavatory. What

192

空乘实用英语教程

would you say to him?

（24）A passenger is smoking in the cabin. How do you stop him?

（25）A passenger is using his mobile phone prior to take-off. How do you stop him?

（26）Why couldn't lithium power banks be used on board?

（27）What safety issues should cabin attendants remind passengers to do just before the plane takes off?

（28）If a passenger asks, "Can I leave this set of china cups in your custody?". What would you do?

（29）What is the presentation of service supplies for business class?

（30）How do the cabin attendants tell the passengers what drinks are available?

（31）A passenger wants a bottle of Johnnie Walker that has run out of stock on board. What would you say to the passenger?

（32）Could you list at least 10 kinds of beverages on the airplane?

（33）How do you explain when the drink accidentally spills on a passenger?

（34）A passenger said that he was sleeping and didn't have meal. What will you say to him?

（35）Generally, what is the main dish on board?

（36）A passenger wants some more chicken, but actually there is no more chicken left in the galley. What would you say?

（37）When passengers are offered meals on board, besides the main dish, what else can they be served?

（38）If a cabin attendant wants to pass the tray to the passenger by the window, who is out of her reach, what should she do?

（39）A passenger has ordered a vegetarian meal. He asks, "What will I have for my vegetarian meal today?" What do you say?

（40）A mother asks a cabin attendant, "My baby is not used to the food on the plane. Do you have anything else for him?" What would you say?

（41）If it is a short haul flight, what can passengers be served?

（42）When a passenger isn't satisfied with the food served on the menu, what would you say?

（43）A passenger wants to eat vegetarian food, but there are no spare ones on the plane, how will you explain to the passenger?

（44）How would you serve the first-row passengers during the meal service?

（45）A passenger wants to read something. What do you say?

（46）How do you introduce the in-flight entertainment to passengers?

（47）When passengers don't know how to use the headsets, how do you instruct them?

（48）How do you instruct a passenger to adjust the air flow?

（49）What do you often provide for children on board?

（50）On an international flight from New York to Beijing, how do you tell passengers to adjust their watches?

（51）A passenger wants to use the lavatory during the turbulence, what would you say?

（52）How will you ask passengers for advice about the flight experience?

（53）When a passenger would like to buy a necklace but it has been sold out. How would you explain to the passenger?

（54）How would you recommend duty-free items to passengers?

（55）When a passenger plans to buy something typically Chinese such as cloisonné（景泰蓝）, which you don't carry on board, what do you say to him?

（56）How will you help a passenger who is airsick?

（57）How can you help a passenger who has a sore ear when the plane goes down?

（58）When a passenger asks, "How many days should I reconfirm my open ticket before I return?", what do you say?

（59）The plane will return to the alternate airport due to bad weather conditions and passengers will stay overnight there. What would you say to passengers before landing?

（60）How will you explain flight cancellations to passengers?

（61）What kinds of bad weather conditions can affect flight schedule? (List 3 examples)

（62）When does a plane divert to an alternate airport? Please give four situations.

（63）A passenger asks, "Where is the Baggage Claim Area?" What do you say?

（64）When the plane has just landed, a passenger unfastens his seat belt. What do you say to stop him?

（65）The lavatory was on fire. After extinguishing it, what do you say to passengers on board?

（66）How would you tell the passengers to use the oxygen mask?

（67）How would you teach a passenger to help his infant put on the life vest?

（68）Could you list some serious emergencies on board?

（69）How do you communicate with a passenger who lost his item?

（70）If a passenger wants to sleep, how would you suggest him?

（71）What should cabin attendants do with noisy children?

（72）What does unruly and disruptive behavior on board refer to?

（73）What kinds of accidents require medical attention? List three of them.

（74）What is the standard response to medical problems on board?

（75）Could you list some types of complaints on board?

（76）What are the procedures when dealing with complaints?

（77）How will you explain to passengers that fruits are not allowed to enter the country?

（78）When a passenger wonders why he needs to fill out a Customs form, how do you explain?

（79）How will you explain to passengers that there are no more entry cards on the plane?

（80）A passenger says, "It's my first time to come to this airport. Can you suggest how I can get downtown?" What do you say to him?

本章参考答案

附 录

附录 1　客舱常用语句

一、起飞前

1. 欢迎登机

（1）Good morning/afternoon/evening, welcome aboard!

早上好 / 下午好 / 晚上好，欢迎登机！

（2）Welcome aboard Air China/China Eastern Airlines/China Southern Airlines.

欢迎乘坐中国国际航空公司班机 / 中国东方航空班机 / 中国南方航空班机。

（3）My name is ×××, the purser of this flight.

我是本次航班的乘务长 ×××。

（4）Can I help you? / What can I do for you?

请问您需要帮忙吗？

（5）May/Can I see your boarding card/boarding pass? I want to confirm your seat number.

我可以看一下您的登机牌吗？我想确认一下您的座位号。

（6）Please take this aisle to your seat.

您的座位在这边通道。

（7）It's a window/middle/aisle seat.

您的座位是靠窗 / 中间 / 过道位置。

（8）Your seat number is indicated/shown/displayed on the edge of the overhead bin/locker/compartment/rack.

您的座椅号码位于行李架边缘。

（9）Excuse me sir/madam, could you please step aside for the passengers behind to go through?

打扰一下先生 / 女士，麻烦您侧身让后面的旅客过一下。

（10）I am afraid you've taken a wrong seat here.

恐怕您坐错位置了。

（11）Excuse me sir/madam, that lady would like to sit with her husband. Would you mind changing your seat with her?

打扰一下先生/女士，那位女士想和她的先生坐在一起，您介意和她换个座位吗？

（12）In order to ensure weight balance when the plane takes off, you should be seated in the assigned seat for this moment.

为了飞机起飞时的配载平衡，您现在应坐在指定的位置。

（13）I'll see if there is any vacant seat for you after boarding.

旅客登机完毕后，我帮您看看有没有空座位。

（14）62K is available. You could go and sit there after take-off.

62K 座位没有旅客，起飞后您可以去坐。

（15）You can upgrade your class, but you need to pay the extra.

您可以升舱，但需要支付升舱费用。（国际航线旅客表示想要升舱的特殊需求时）

（16）Unfortunately, upgrade service is not available because first class is fully booked today.

非常遗憾，头等舱已满，无法为您办理升舱服务。

（17）How may I address you?

我该怎么称呼您？

（18）Mr./Ms. ×××, would you like to put on the slippers? It will make you feel more comfortable.

××× 先生/女士，您需要换一下拖鞋吗，这样会舒服些。

（19）Mr. / Ms. ×××, May I help you hang up your coat in the closet?

××× 先生/女士，我帮您把衣服挂在衣帽间，好吗？

（20）Would you mind taking out your passport, the valuables and the fragile items from your luggage?

请您取出行李中的护照、贵重及易碎物品。（帮客人保管行李时的提示）

（21）Excuse me, sir, I do apologize that there is no space in the overhead locker above your seat. May I suggest you stowing it under the seat in front of you?

实在抱歉，先生，您座椅上方的行李架满了。我建议您放在您前面座椅下方好吗？

（22）Excuse me, sir. I'm afraid that your baggage is too big for the cabin. May I help you check it in?

打扰一下，先生。恐怕您的行李太大了，没法放在客舱。可以帮您托运吗？

（23）Excuse me. Is this your baggage? Here is the emergency exit. Please put your baggage on the overhead locker for the sake of safety.

您好，这是您的行李吗？这里是紧急出口，安全起见请把您的行李放在行李架上。

（24）Would you mind putting your baggage somewhere else?

您介意把您的行李放到别的地方吗？

（25）Just a moment, I'll check if there is any space for your baggage.

请稍等，我看看是否还有地方能放下您的行李。

（26）Sir, do you need any newspaper?

先生，您需要报纸吗？

（27）Sorry, sir. The newspapers have been already served out.

对不起，先生。报纸已经发完了。

（28）We've prepared some in-flight magazines instead. Is that okay？

我准备了一些机上杂志，您看可以吗？

2. 安全检查

（1）Excuse me, sir/madam, the seat you are taking today is the emergency exit seat of this aircraft. Please do not touch the operating handle in normal situation. Here is the emergency exit safety instruction card, could you please read it carefully. If you have any questions, please let us know. Thank you!

打扰一下，先生／女士，您乘坐的是本架飞机的应急出口座位，正常情况下请勿触动舱门，相关规定请您阅读出口座位须知卡。如有疑问，请及时和我们联系，谢谢！

（2）This is the emergency exit seat. Please read the safety instruction/information card/ pamphlet/ leaflet carefully.

这是紧急出口座位，请仔细阅读安全须知卡。

（3）Please return to your seat and retract the seat back to the upright position/put your seat-back upright, stow your tray table and open the sunshade/window shade.

请回到座位，调直座椅靠背，收好小桌板，打开遮阳板。

（4）Excuse me, sir/madam, our plane is taxiing now. Please switch off your portable electronic devices. And switch your cellphones to airplane/flight mode.

打扰一下，先生／女士，我们的飞机已经开始滑行，请将您的电子设备关闭，手机调制到飞行模式。

（5）Portable electronic devices will interfere with the airplane communication and navigation system. Please switch them off right now.

便携式电子设备会干扰飞机通信和导航系统。请您现在关闭。

（6）Thank you for your cooperation.

谢谢您的配合。

（7）I'm sorry to bother you.

很抱歉打扰到您。

（8）As we are taking off shortly, lavatories have been suspended. Could you please remain seated until we get to the cruising level?

飞机马上就要起飞了，洗手间已经停止使用。请您在飞机平稳飞行之后再使用好吗？

（9）Ladies and gentlemen. The plane is going to take off immediately/ as soon as possible. Please return to your seats and fasten your seat belts.

女士们，先生们。飞机马上就要起飞了，请您回到座位做好，系好安全带。

（10）Excuse me, sir/madam, the plane is still taxiing. For your safety, could you please remain seated with your seat-belt fastened?

打扰一下，先生 / 女士，飞机正在滑行，为了您的安全，请您在座位上坐好并系好安全带。

二、起飞后

1. 派发和娱乐服务

（1）Sorry, all blankets have been distributed now.

对不起，毛毯已经发完了。

（2）I can turn up our cabin temperature a little bit, and it will be warmer soon.

我可以把客舱温度适当调高一点，一会儿客舱温度就会升上来。

（3）How much hot water would you like？

您需要多少热水？

（4）The mini TV set is stored in your armrest. Would you like me to help you take it out?

您的微型电视储藏在您的座椅扶手里。需要我帮您拿出来吗？

（5）I'm terribly sorry about the condition of your personal TV. Please allow me a moment to see if we can have it reset for you.

我非常抱歉您的个人娱乐系统出现问题。请您稍等，我马上为您重启系统。

（6）This is our portable multimedia device for you. It offers movies, games, music and a lot of other interesting programs.

这是我们专门为您准备的多媒体播放器，里面有电影、游戏、歌曲等很多有趣的程序。

（7）Here is the earphone jack.

这里是耳机插孔。

（8）Maybe the earphone doesn't work. Let me get you another one.

这个耳机可能坏了，马上帮您换一个。

2. 餐饮服务

（1）Excuse me, sir? Would you like something to drink？

打扰了先生，您需要喝点什么饮品吗？

（2）Mr. / Ms. _____, we have prepared orange juice, mineral water, ginger ale, tonic water and champagne for you. Which one would you like?

_____先生 / 女士，我们为您准备了橙汁、矿泉水、干姜水、汤力水和香槟酒，请问您喜欢哪一种？

（3）Excuse me, Mr. /Ms. _____, we have prepared Oolong Tea, Long Jing Tea, Black Tea, Chrysanthemum Tea, Jasmine Tea and Green Tea for you. Which one would you prefer?

打扰一下，_____先生 / 女士，我们为您准备了乌龙茶、龙井茶、红茶、菊花茶、茉莉花茶、绿茶，请问您喜欢哪一种？

（4）For Chinese tea, we have Dragon Well green tea, Tieh-Kwan-Yin Oolong tea and Pu'er tea.

中国茶我们为您准备了龙井、铁观音和普洱。

（5）Would you care for some fresh brewed coffee?

请问您需要现煮的咖啡吗？

（6）Which kind of whiskey do you prefer? Scotch or Bourbon?

您喜欢哪种威士忌？苏格兰还是波本？

（7）How would you like your whiskey? On the rock, as a chaser or straight up?

请问您的威士忌需要加冰、加水还是直饮？

（8）I'm sorry, sir. We don't serve that on board. Would you like to try other drinks? Red wine, white wine and beer are available on board.

不好意思，先生。飞机上没有配备您需要的种类。要不要试试其他的？我们有红酒、白酒和啤酒。

（9）I am afraid the wine is not available. May I offer you beer instead?

实在抱歉，葡萄酒没有了，给您啤酒好吗？

（10）We didn't disturb you when you were having a rest. Would you like something to drink? We have prepared mineral water, juice, tea and coffee. Which one would you like?

刚才您在休息，我们没有打扰您，请问您需要喝点饮料吗？我们有矿泉水、果汁还有热茶和咖啡，您比较喜欢哪种？

（11）Certainly, a glass of apple juice. I'll be right back with your drink. Would you like any ice in your juice? Please enjoy your drink.

好的，一杯苹果汁，我马上给您送过来。请问您的果汁需要加冰吗？请您慢用。

（12）Here's your drink, madam. Enjoy it.

这是您的饮品，女士。希望您能喜欢。

（13）Mind the cup, miss, it's very hot.

请您拿好水杯，女士，小心烫。

（14）Would you like some bread? We have soft roll, hard roll, rye roll, garlic slices and sesame bread.

请问您需要来点面包吗？我们为您准备了软包、硬包、黑麦面包、蒜蓉面包和芝麻面包。

（15）We will serve you with a wide selection of cheese.

我们为您准备了品种丰富的芝士。

（16）For hard cheese we have both British Cheddar and Dutch Edam.

如果您喜欢偏硬的口感，我们有英国车达和荷兰红波。

（17）For soft cheese we have French Camembert which is creamy and for crumbly cheese we have Danish blue. Which one would you like?

法国金文笔芝士口味柔软，具有奶香味，而丹麦蓝芝士则显得较为松碎。您喜欢哪一种？

（18）Sir, we have chicken with rice and beef with noodles. Which would you like?

先生，今天的餐食有鸡肉饭和牛肉面。您想要哪一个？

（19）We have prepared fried rice with seafood and fried noodles with chicken. The fried noodles are really delicious. Would you like to try it?

我们为您准备了海鲜炒饭和鸡肉炒面。炒面味道非常不错，您愿意试一试吗？

（20）Well, let me check for you. I will bring it over if there is an extra.

好的，我去帮您看一下，如果有，我马上帮您拿过来。（旅客想再要一份餐食的时候）

（21）Let me see if we have extra ones in other galleys. Give me a few minutes.

让我看看别的厨房是否还有一些。请稍等。

（22）I'm sorry, madam. We don't have beef with noodles now. Is chicken with rice ok? It also tastes great.

很抱歉，女士。牛肉面已经发完了，鸡肉饭可以吗？味道也很不错。

（23）Thank you for your understanding. You will have priority to make a choice for the next meal.

感谢您的理解，下一餐我们一定请您优先选择。

（24）Excuse me, Mr. /Ms. _____ , we also have prepared pickled vegetables and chili sauce, would you like some of them?

打扰一下，_____先生／女士，我们还准备了榨菜和辣酱，您需要品尝一下吗？

（25）Excuse me, Mr. / Ms. _____ , these are the menu and the wine list for this flight. Would you mind taking a look at it? We'll take your order later.

打扰一下，_____先生／女士，这是今天的餐谱和酒单，请您浏览，稍候我们将为您订餐。

（26）Excuse me, Mr. /Ms. _____ , we provide two meals for you on this flight. When would you like to take them? How about 12 o'clock for the lunch service?

打扰一下，_____先生／女士，今天为您准备了两顿正餐，请问您需要什么时候用餐？您看午餐在12点左右提供可以吗？

（27）If you don't need the main course, how about some fruit?

如果您不太想吃主菜，愿意尝点儿水果吗？（客人不用主菜时）

（28）Excuse me，Mr. /Ms. _____ , may I set the table for you?

打扰一下，_____先生／女士，我可以为您铺餐巾吗？

（29）Here is your pumpkin cream soup and tuna with crushed truffle potato.

这是您的奶油南瓜汤和金枪鱼配松露土豆泥（西式冷荤）。

（30）Here is your duck soup and pan-fried abalone and scallops with truffle jam.

这是您的红枣银耳香梨炖老鸭汤和煎鲜鲍鱼带子佐松露酱。

（31）For Chinese style, we have pan-fried duck breast with rice and stir-fried prawn and abalone with UDON noodles in a hot bean sauce.

中式主菜有煎蜜糖鸭胸饭和鲍鱼虾仁乌冬面配干烧汁。

（32）For western style, we have pan-fried AUS beef steak with pumpkin duchesse in a red wine sauce and pan-fried lobster with crushed truffle potato in a lobster sauce.

西式主菜有红酒汁煎澳大利亚牛眼肉配南瓜土豆花和煎龙虾配黑菌土豆泥。

（33）We have Chinese style and western style breakfast. For Chinese breakfast, we have congee with exquisite Chinese dim sum. While for western breakfast, we have cereal with fresh milk and sausage with an omelet.

　　我们有中西式早餐。中式早餐是中式粥配中式精美小点，西式早餐则包含麦片配牛奶还有蛋饼卷配香肠。

（34）We have two choices of salad dressing. Thousand island dressing and an oil and vinegar dressing.

　　我们有两种色拉浇汁，千岛汁和法醋汁。

（35）For red wine, we have a French Mouton Cadet Bordeaux, 2008 vintage; Australian Penfolds Koonunga Hill Shiraz Cabernet, 2014 vintage; and Girard Napa Old Vine Zinfandel from Napa valley, USA, 2013 vintage.

　　关于机上葡萄酒，向您推荐我们今年的三款年度酒，分别有 2008 年法国的木桐嘉棣，2014 年澳大利亚的奔富酒庄蔻兰山设拉子赤霞珠，2013 年美国的纳帕仙芬黛干红。

（36）This wine is supple, well-textured and well-balanced. It is a perfect partner for the seafood.

　　这款酒柔顺细腻，单宁均匀有致，是最适合搭配海鲜的。

（37）I would suggest French red wine to go with the steak, which is Mouton Cadet from Bordeaux.

　　我建议您牛排配法国红酒，这是产自法国波尔多地区的木桶嘉棣。

（38）This is a good wine. It's well-balanced and the finish is clean and long.

　　这是一款很好的红酒，它很平衡，余味既干净绵长。

（39）For dessert, which one would you prefer, coconut cake or ice cream?

　　甜品有两个选择，椰子蛋糕和冰淇淋。请问您喜欢哪个？

（40）Sure. I will take away your tray in a minute.

　　没问题，我马上为您收走空餐盘。

（41）Have you made the reservation?

　　请问您有预定特殊餐吗？

（42）Please don't worry, we will try to meet your need. However, please reserve the special meal next time when you book a ticket and confirm it 24 hours before departure.

　　您别担心，我们会尽力满足您的要求。但请您在下次订票时预订，并于乘机前 24 小时再次确认餐食。

（43）Sorry, sir. This flight does not have special food that you need. But we have some vegetarian food. Is that okay?

　　对不起，先生。航班上没有您需要的特殊餐，但是我们有素食。您看可以吗？

（44）I can prepare some bread, salad and fruit for you. How's that?

我为您准备一些面包、沙拉和水果，您看如何？

（45）Excuse me, sir. Could you please turn your head inward to avoid being hit by our food trolley?

先生，请您在休息时把头朝里，以防餐车经过时碰到您。

（46）We'll be landing in 30 minutes and the drink service has concluded/is finished. May I get you a bottle of water?

抱歉，先生，我们还有三十分钟就下降了，我们已经结束酒类供应。若您不介意，我为您准备一瓶矿泉水吧。

（47）The food allergen information could be provided on this flight. If you want to check, please contact us.

我们可以提供食物过敏源信息，如果您需要，请联系乘务员。

3. 免税品服务

（1）Do you want to buy any duty-free goods?

请问您需要购买免税品吗？

（2）Sorry, sir. The Item No.12 has been sold out.

对不起，先生。12 号商品已经卖光了。

（3）May I recommend some duty-free items for you?

我可以向您推荐几款适合您的免税商品吗？

（4）The color of this lip sticks quite fit for elegant ladies like you.

这款口红的颜色非常适合像您一样的优雅的女士。

（5）You can fill out the order form if you want to order the duty-free items.

您可以通过填写免税品预订单预订所需商品。

（6）Would you like to pay by cash or credit card?

请问您是用现金还是用信用卡支付？

（7）This credit card has expired. Would you please pay in other ways or by another card?

这张信用卡已经过期了，请您选择其他的付款方式或者换另外一张信用卡好吗？

（8）We don't accept Union Pay Cards or traveler's check.

我们不接受银联或者支票。

（9）I'm sorry. All the items sold on board are fix-priced.

很抱歉，所有的商品都是固定价格。

（10）I am afraid only some of the duty-free items have discount during sales promotion.

真不好意思，我们只有在促销活动期间部分免税商品可以打折。

（11）Here are your change and perfume. Hope you like it.

这是您的找零和您购买的香水。希望您能喜欢。

（12）Can I have a look at your passport? I need your passport number.

我可以看下您的护照吗？我需要您的护照号码。

（13）Here is your change, please keep it.

这是找给您的钱，请您收好。

（14）Here's your receipt.

这是您的收据。

4. 海关、边防、检疫

（1）This is the entry card/landing card/disembarkation card/arrival card for you. If you have any questions, please press the call button above your head.

这是您的入境卡。如果有问题，请按呼头顶上方的呼唤铃。

（2）Please fill out the form before arrival/landing and give/submit it to the immigration officers.

请您在飞机落地前填好，落地后交给移民局官员。

（3）Local resident doesn't need to fill out immigration card.

本地公民不需要填写入境卡。

（4）Please use capital letters to complete the entry card and customs declaration form.

请您用英文大写字母填写入境卡和申报单。

（5）Only one written declaration per family is required.

每个家庭只需填写一份海关申报单。

（6）The excess part should be declared.

超出的部分需要申报。

（7）Australia does not allow entry of meat.

肉类不可以带进澳大利亚。

（8）According to the quarantine requirements of the local government, fresh fruits are not allowed to be brought into the country.

根据当地检疫规定，乘客不能携带新鲜水果入境。

（9）You are required to submit these forms to the officers when going through the immigration, customs and quarantine.

当您办理入境、海关和检疫等手续时需要出示这些表格。

（10）Sorry, we've run out of the declaration forms. You can get one from the Customs once you get off.

对不起，我们没有多余的申报单了，您可以在地面海关柜台领取。

5. 服务沟通

（1）According to weather forecast/report, the weather temperature today is 28 degrees Celsius/ Centigrade, 82 Fahrenheit.

根据天气预报，今天的温度是 28℃，82 ℉。

（2）The flight distance is 10 thousand kilometers. And the estimated flying time is 7 hours. The estimated arrival time is a quarter past eight p.m.

本次航班的飞行距离是 1 万千米，预计飞行时间 7 小时。预计到达时间是晚上 8 点 15 分。

（3）Mr. /Ms. ×××, my name is ×××. I'm working in this part of the cabin. Please let me know if there is anything I can do for you.

×××先生 / 女士，我叫×××。本次航班在这个区域服务。如您有任何需要请随时联系我。（自我介绍时）

（4）Currently, our Boeing 777-300ER aircrafts are mainly used for those directly long-haul flights to the North America, and for domestic destinations for business purposes.

目前，我们的波音 777-300ER 飞机主要用于直飞北美远程和国内商务航线。

（5）Currently, we are now flying over ×××. (the Pacific Ocean/a tributary of Yellow River/a tributary of Yangtze River/a tributary of Lantsang River)

目前，我们正在×××上空。（太平洋 / 黄河的一条支流 / 长江的一条支流 / 澜沧江的一条支流）

（6）Beijing, as the capital city of the PRC, also is the Four Great Ancient Capitals of China. It has been the political center of the country for much of the past eight centuries.

北京作为中华人民共和国的首都，同样也是中国著名的四朝古都，已经成为我国的政治中心超过八个世纪之久。

（7）I would be happy to recommend a restaurant in the central area, Madam. If you would like to try local food, I'd suggest Quanjude Roast Duck Restaurant. It is popular and famous for its roast duck.

女士我非常乐意给您推荐一家市中心的餐厅。如果您想品尝当地美食，我给您推荐"全聚德"烤鸭店，烤鸭非常有名。（特色推荐沟通时）

（8）Shanghai is one of the largest cities in China and it is also the business and financial center of our country.

上海是中国最大的城市之一，也是中国的经贸中心。

（9）Shanghai is also a famous historical and cultural city. You may have a tour of the Yu Garden, the Bund, People's Square, Lujiazui Area, Nanjing Road, etc. All of them have their own particularities and charms.

上海也是一座历史文化名城，你可以去游览豫园、外滩、人民广场、陆家嘴、南京路等地，它们均各有特色。

（10）Shanghai has a very long rainy period, called the plum rain season, which is in June and July of summer.

在初夏的六七月，上海会经历一段很长的雨季，被称为梅雨季节。

（11）It's the hottest season in Shanghai, we call it "dog days of the summer".

现在正是上海最热的时期，被称为"三伏天"。

（12）How do you feel like today's cabin service or catering? We really appreciate your advice.

您觉得今天的客舱服务和餐食怎么样？我们非常感谢您的宝贵意见。

二、落地前

（1）The expected arrival time is 10 p.m..

预计到达时间是晚上 10 点。

（2）The ground temperature is 9℃. You'd better put on your coat when disembarking.

地面温度是9℃。下机时，最好穿上外套。

（3）Please put your baggage in a proper place.

请您把行李放好。

（4）We may experience some turbulence when the plane is flying in clouds while landing.

下降期间飞机在穿越云层时会有些颠簸。

（5）It'll be fine when we are out of the cloud.

等我们穿过云层就好了。

（6）Please fasten your seat belt.

请您系好安全带。

（7）When the plane is taking off or landing, all passenger electronic devices must be turned off.

在起飞和下降时，所有的电子设备需要关闭。

（8）For your safety, please return to your seat as soon as possible.

为了您的安全，请您尽快回到座位上。

（9）You can use the toilet when the plane comes to a complete stop.

等飞机完全停稳后您可以使用洗手间。

（10）You may claim your checked baggage in the Arrival Hall with your luggage tag.

您可以凭行李牌在进港厅领取您的托运行李。

（11）Did you order a wheelchair service before?

您之前有预约过轮椅服务吗？

（12）The ground staff will bring the wheelchair and wait for you.

地面工作人员会准备好轮椅等候您。

三、落地后

（1）The plane will still be taxiing for some time.

飞机还需要滑行一段时间。

（2）Please keep seated and fasten your seat belt.

请您先坐好系好安全带。

（3）You can pick your baggage when the plane comes to a complete stop.

您可以等飞机完全停稳后再拿行李。

（4）You can get your checked baggage at the baggage claim area.

请您在行李提取处领取您的托运行李。

（5）You may also ask our ground staff for assistance.

您可以询问地面服务人员，他们会协助您的。

（6）We are at domestic arrival hall.

我们停在国内到达厅。

（7）All passenger baggage must be subject to Customs inspection.

旅客所有的行李都要带下飞机接受海关检查。

（8）We hope to see you onboard again.

希望能再次遇见您。

（9）Wish you a pleasant day.

祝您度过愉快的一天。

（10）Please watch your step.

请您留心脚下。

四、特殊情况

1. 航班延误解释

（1）We apologize for the delay and inconvenience.

对于航班的延误和不便我们深表歉意。

（2）Since there is still one passenger not on board yet, please wait for a moment.

由于我们的航班上还缺少一位旅客，请稍等一会儿。

（3）We will inform you as soon as we get the exact take off time.

一有准确的起飞时间我们会尽快通知您。

（4）We are expecting the takeoff clearance from the Air Traffic Control.

我们在等待航空管制起飞的命令。

（5）We have to wait for 30 minutes due to the unfavorable weather conditions on our route. We'll provide you with further information. We'll apply for the take-off clearance as soon as the weather is getting better.

由于航路天气不好，我们还须等待 30 分钟才能起飞，我们乘务组会随时将最新的信息告诉您。当接到天气转好的信息时，我们会尽快申请排队，争取能够尽快起飞。

（6）We have to wait for a few minutes due to a minor technical problem. Would you care for something to drink?

我们的飞机有些小故障，正在维修排除，还需要等待一会儿。您需要喝些饮料吗？

（7）We have to change to another aircraft because of the technical problem. Please disembark with all your belongings. We sincerely apologize for the inconvenience.

由于机械故障无法排除，我们需要换乘另外一架飞机，请您下机时带好随身物品。对此带来的不便我们深表歉意。

（8）The airport has been closed due to the bad weather. For safety reasons, we are informed that the flight has been canceled. If you need any assistance, please contact our ground staff after disembarkation. We apologize for the inconvenience and thank you for your understanding.

机场由于天气不好已经关闭。出于安全考虑，我们被通知本次航班取消。我们的地勤人员会协助您解决航班取消后的相关事宜。由此带来的不便，我们深表歉意，感谢您对我们工作的理解。

（9）While waiting, we'll keep you constantly updated of the latest information.

在等待期间我们会及时将有关信息通知您。

（10）We feel awfully sorry for the delay. And we will arrange the further accommodation.

Thank you for your patience.

对于飞机延误我们深感抱歉。我们会尽快安排后续住宿事宜。感谢您耐心等待。

2. 特殊旅客服务

（1）For the baby's safety, I'll fix the bassinet after take-off.

为了孩子的安全，等飞机起飞后我会帮您把婴儿摇篮安置好。（旅客地面期间需要安置婴儿摇篮时的沟通解释）

（2）You can go to the lavatory if you want to change the diapers for the baby.

您可以去卫生间给婴儿换尿布。（对带婴儿旅客的温馨提示）

（3）May I bring you a pillow? It will make you feel more comfortable.

我给您拿个枕头吧！这样会舒服一些。（对怀孕旅客的细微服务）

（4）One ground staff will take responsible for only one unaccompanied minors during the whole journey before boarding. Flight attendants will take good care of all the unaccompanied minors.

每名无人陪伴儿童都会由一名地勤人员全程负责，直至登机。乘务员会认真照顾每位无人陪伴的儿童。（回答旅客关于"无人陪伴儿童服务"的问询）

（5）I'll keep your traveling documents and ticket, and give them to the ground staff when you disembark.

我先帮你保管旅行证件和机票，下机时我会将这些证件交接给地服人员。（与无人陪伴小旅客的沟通）

（6）You may stand up and walk around in the cabin when the flight is in a relatively stable condition.

如果飞机飞行状态相对平稳，您可以站起来在机舱走动走动。（国际长航线与老年旅客的温馨沟通）

（7）We will help you to keep your crutch for the whole flight.

我们会在整个飞行航程中替您保管拐杖。（对于携带拐杖登机旅客的提示）

（8）Should I know your seat number? May I assist you with your hand luggage?

我可以知道您的座位号吗？我帮您拿行李好吗？（登机时见到行动不便的旅客时）

（9）Our flight attendants will help you if you would like to go to the lavatory.

如果您需要去卫生间的话，我们的乘务员可以帮助您。（关于机上轮椅旅客的温馨提示）

3. 机上紧急医疗救护

（1）Do you need medical attention?

您需要医疗帮助吗？

（2）Where do you feel pain?

您感觉哪里不舒服吗?

（3）You don't need to worry about it. You are just a little bit tired.

您不用担心。您只不过是有点儿劳累过度。

（4）Please explain your symptom to me slowly and clearly so that I can help you.

请您仔细清楚地描述一下您的症状以便我帮助您。

（5）Do you feel headache, nausea or vomiting? Judging from your symptoms, I think you might be suffering airsick.

您觉得头痛、恶心或想吐吗? 从症状来看，您可能是晕机。

（6）When the plane is taking off or landing, air pressure changes accordingly. That's why you feel the pain in your ears.

当飞机起飞和下降时，气压会发生变化，所以您耳朵才会疼。

（7）You may do some swallowing to make yourself feel better.

您可以做吞咽动作来缓解疼痛。

（8）Your blood pressure is relatively high. Do you have your prescribed medicine with you?

您的血压很高，您有自带的常用药吗?

（9）Have you got any medication with you along?

您有随身携带药物吗?

（10）Sorry, we don't have the medicine you need.

对不起，我们没有您需要的药。

（11）How long have you had it?

您这样多久了?

（12）How are you feeling now? Are you feeling all right?

您现在感觉怎么样? 是否有所好转?

（13）Please don't worry. I will make an announcement to see if there are any medical personnel onboard.

别着急，我马上为您广播寻找医务人员。

（14）May I have your attention please! Is there a doctor on board? A passenger is having a heart attack and needs your help immediately.

请问，飞机上有医生吗? 有一位旅客突发心脏病，需要您的帮助。

（15）He feels like everything around him is spinning. He feels bloated and uncomfortable after meal. He has bouts of abdominal pain and the pain is mainly in the lower (upper) right part of the abdomen. When he bends over or lies down, the abdominal pain gets worse.

（与外籍医生描述生病旅客症状）他感到周围的东西在打转。他餐后肚子觉得胀胀的，很不舒服。他感觉一阵腹痛，痛点是在肚子下（上）半部分。他弯腰或躺下时，腹痛更厉害。

（16）We can contact the airport ambulance service if it's needed.

如果您需要，我们可以帮助您联系机场救护车。

（17）First aid treatment has been given but he is still in unconsciousness.

（国际航班外站落地后与地面医护人员的沟通）他接受了机上急救，但还是没有恢复意识。

4. 旅客物品丢失

（1）Where did you put it, do you remember?

您记得把它放在哪里了吗？

（2）Please tell us your phone number, address and a description of your briefcase.

请告诉我们您的电话号码、地址并描述一下您公文包的模样。

（3）We'll ask our ground staff to help you.

我们会让地面人员帮助您。

（4）Here's the number for Lost & Found at the airport. Please contact them to get your briefcase back.

这是失物招领处的电话，请联系他们取回您的公文包。

5. 服务致歉

（1）I'm sorry about the delay with your special meal, sir/madam. May I confirm which special meal you've ordered and I'll check the galley for you straight away.

（旅客提出预定了特殊餐食时）先生/女士，我非常抱歉您的特餐未能及时送来。我可以和您确认一下特餐的种类吗？我马上回厨房为您查询特餐情况。

（2）Sir/madam, I am sorry about the confusion with your drink. I'll serve you (a glass of white wine) straight away.

（错发旅客饮料时）先生/女士，我很抱歉给您送错饮料了。我现在马上给您送（一杯白葡萄酒）来。

（3）I'm sorry to hear that you are not enjoying your meal. We are also serving fruit, cheese and cake. Would you care to try it?

（旅客对餐食不满时）我非常抱歉您对餐食不满意。我们还为您准备了水果、起司和蛋糕，您愿意品尝一下吗？

（4）Sir/madam, I'm really sorry about this. I fully appreciate how important the special meal is for you. I will do my best to arrange a vegetarian meal for you.

（旅客特餐预订未满足时）先生／女士，我非常抱歉，我完全懂得这个特殊餐食对您有多么重要。我会尽我所能给您准备一份素食替代。

（5）Mr./Ms. ×××, I can understand that you are feeling disappointed with the facilities on this flight. Please do accept my apology. I will check to see if we can reset your personal TV or alternatively I can check if we have another seat available.

（两舱旅客因娱乐系统无法使用而感到不满时）××× 先生／女士，我非常理解您不能正常使用设备的失望。请您接受我的道歉。我马上去为您重启系统或者为您调换其他空座。

（6）I'm sorry about the problems with the headset. I'll replace it for you straight away.

（经济舱旅客耳机不能使用时）我非常抱歉您的耳机不能使用。我马上为您更换一个。

（7）I'm sorry about the problems with the television. I'll ask my colleague to reset it for you straight away. It will take about 5-10 minutes.

（经济舱旅客娱乐系统死机时）我很抱歉您的电视出现了故障。我马上让我的同事为您重启。系统重启大概需要 5 ～ 10 分钟的时间。

（8）I'm sorry you are not able to rest. Would you like me to check for a seat in another part of the cabin? Alternatively, I can offer you some earplugs or headphones to help lower the noise.

（旅客抱怨邻座婴儿很吵时）我很抱歉打扰了您的休息。您愿意我为您换个座位吗？或者我为您送耳塞或者耳机过来，以便降低吵闹声。

（9）I apologize for the condition of the blanket. I will bring you another one straight away.

（旅客毛毯有异味时）我非常抱歉毛毯的清洁问题。我马上给您更换另一条干净的毛毯。

一、机上用品

airsickness bag/ disposal bag 呕吐袋 / 清洁袋

blanket 毛毯

coat hanger 衣架

axe 斧头

escape rope 紧急用绳

evacuation slide 撤离滑梯

extinguisher 灭火器

eye shade 眼罩

first aid kit 急救药箱

garbage bag/litter bag 垃圾袋

flashlight 手电筒

headset 耳机

life raft 救生筏

life vest/ jacket 救生衣

megaphone 扩音器

magazine/newspaper 杂志 / 报纸

oxygen mask 氧气面罩

passenger comment 旅客意见簿

portable oxygen bottle 手提氧气瓶

pillow 枕头

smoke hood 防烟面罩

socks 袜套

souvenir 纪念品

towel 毛巾

wet tissue 湿纸巾

二、行李

baggage check 行李提取单

baggage check-in counter 行李过磅处

baggage/ luggage 旅客行李

briefcase 公事包

carry-on baggage 随身行李 / 手提行李

checked baggage 交运行李

excess baggage 超重行李

handbag 手提包

free allowance for luggage 免费行李额度

interline baggage 转机行李

overweight 超重

suitcase 衣箱

traveling bag 旅行袋

trunk 大箱子

unaccompanied shipment 非随身载运行李 / 无人陪伴的行李载运

三、酒水及饮料

beer 啤酒

black coffee 清咖啡

black tea 红茶

brandy 白兰地

champagne 香槟

Chinese spirits 中国白酒

chrysanthemum tea 菊花茶

cocktail 鸡尾酒

draught beer 生啤

gin and tonic 杜松子酒

green tea 绿茶

lemonade 柠檬茶

martini 马丁尼酒

milk 牛奶

rice wine 米酒

Seven-up 七喜

Sprite 雪碧

tomato juice 番茄汁

vodka 伏特加酒

white coffee 奶咖啡

yellow spirits 黄酒

Coca cola 可口可乐

concentrate 浓缩水

fruit juice 果汁

ginger ale 姜汁茶

jasmine tea 茉莉花茶

liquor 烈性酒

mineral water 矿泉水

Pepsi cola 百事可乐

scented tea 花茶

soda 苏打水

tonic 奎宁水 / 开胃水

vermouth 味美思酒 / 苦艾酒

whisky 威士忌酒

wine 葡萄酒

yogurt 酸奶

四、调味品

anchovy paste 鱼酱

butter 黄油

chili sauce 辣酱

cream 奶油

caviar 鱼子酱

condensed milk 炼乳

Camembert cheese 金门比奶酪

French cheese 法汁

garlic and coriander dressing 蒜蓉香菜汁

ketchup 番茄酱

milk powder 奶粉

oyster sauce 蚝油

salt 盐

sugar 糖

shrimp sauce 虾酱

sweet bean paste 甜面酱

aniseed 大茴香子

cube sugar 方糖

curry powder 咖喱粉

cheese 奶酪

cabbage seed oil 菜油

Cheddar cheese 车达奶酪

Edam cheese 红波奶酪

gourmet powder 味精

jam 果酱

mustard 芥末

mousse/paste 奶油冻

pepper 胡椒

soy sauce 酱油

spices 香料

sesame 芝麻

salad dressing 沙拉汁

thousand island dressing 千岛汁

vinegar 醋

五、烹饪

baked 烤制

braised 炖的

bitter 苦的

cuisine 烹饪法

crisp 脆的

Chinese food 中餐

delicious/ tasty 美味的

devilled 加辣调味烧烤的

fragrant 香的

fat 肥的

fresh 新鲜的

grilled 烧烤的

hot 热的

heavy 不易消化的

Hindu food 印度餐

insipid 无味的

iced 冰镇的

juicy 多汁的

light 清淡的

lean 瘦的

medium 不老不嫩的

mashed 泥状的

mellow 芳醇的

moslem food 清真饭

nourishing 有营养的

raw 生的

rich /oily/ greasy 油腻的

rinsed 涮的

smoked 烟熏的

simmered 煨的

stewed and braised 文火焖的

steamed 蒸的

starchy 糊状的

sweet 甜的

sour 酸的

salted 腌制的

roast 烤

boil 煮

stew 炖

stir fry 炒

fry 煎

heat 加热

tasteless 淡味的

toasted 烤的

tough 老的

tender 嫩的

with soy sauce 红烧

well-done 全熟的

Western food 西餐

六、海关

Customs formalities 海关手续

Customs declaration form 海关申报单

contraband 违禁物品

duty-free articles 免税物品

dutiable articles 应上税物品

exit formalities 出境手续

entry visa 入境签证

foreign currency registration certificate 外币登记表

identity card 身份证

travel permit 旅行证

entry formalities 入境手续

exit visa 出境签证

form 表格

health certificate 健康证书

transit card 过境签证

vaccination certificate 预防接种证书

七、疾病与药物

angina pectoris 心绞痛

anesthetic 麻醉剂

airsick tablet 晕机药

bandage 绷带

belladonna 颠茄 / 莨菪

disinfectant 消毒剂

diarrhea 腹泻

eye drops 眼药水

fracture 骨折

for external use 外用药

have a runny nose 流鼻涕

heart attack 心脏病发作

insanity 精神病

laxative 泻药

mercurochrome 红药水

malaria 痢疾

nose drops 滴鼻子药水

pill 丸剂

pneumonia 肺炎

smallpox 天花

shiver 寒战

swelling 膨胀

tablet 片剂

to be not feeling very well 感到身体不舒服

appendicitis 阑尾炎

aspirin 阿司匹林

alcohol 酒精

bump 绷带

capsule 胶囊

diabetes 糖尿病

epilepsy 癫痫病

first aid 急救

for oral administration 内服药

gentian violet 紫药水

headache 头痛

hepatitis 肝炎

indigestion 消化不良

liquid solution 水剂

myocardial infarction 心肌梗死

mixture 合剂

ointment 药膏

powder 粉剂

painkiller 止痛片

stomachache 胃痛

scald 烫伤

sleeping pill 安眠药

tranquilizer 镇静剂

to be air sick 晕机

217

to suffer form a slight indisposition 身体不适

to have a fever 发烧

to feel sick/ to feel nausea 恶心

to vomit/ to throw up 呕吐

to bring down the fever 使退烧

to have a cold 感冒 / 伤风

to have a stuffed-up nose 鼻塞

to have lung trouble 肺病

to have heart trouble 心脏病

to have kidney trouble 肾病

to have convulsions/ cramps 抽筋

to be down with influenza 得流感

to be short of breath 气短

to suffer from shock 休克

to feel sore all over 全身酸痛

to sprain one's ankle 扭了脚踝

to feel dizzy 头晕

to have a bad cough 咳得厉害

to faint/ to lose consciousness/ to pass out 晕倒

to take one's blood pressure 量血压

to fain/ to recover consciousness/ to come to 苏醒

to examine one's chest 听心肺

to take one's temperature 量体温

to feel one's pulse 诊脉

to take medicine 服药

to dress a wound 包扎伤口

to relive a cough 止咳

tincture of iodine 碘酒

八、机上设备

BRT 明亮位置

DIM 昏暗位置

extend 放下（起落架）

fasten seat belt sign 系好安全带指示灯

front auto air stair 前门自备梯

light 灯光

lift 提

music 音乐

no smoking sign 禁烟灯

NIGHT 夜间使用位置

on 开启

normal 正常

occupied（洗手间）有人

off 关闭

open 打开

push 推

ready 准备灯

retract 收回

start 启动键

stop 停止键

standby 备用 / 待用

turn 旋转

vacant（洗手间）无人

volume 音量

work light 工作灯

九、水果及糖果

apple 苹果

banana 香蕉

chewing gum 口香糖

cherry 樱桃

coconut 椰子

cashew 腰果

chestnut 栗子

chocolate 巧克力

fruit jelly 水果软糖

grape 葡萄

haw 山楂

kiwi 猕猴桃

lotus seed 莲子

lichee 荔枝

lemon 柠檬

loquat 枇杷

mango 杧果

orange 橙子

olive 橄榄

pear 梨

peach 桃子

pineapple 菠萝

peanut 花生

preserved fruit 蜜饯

preserved orange peel 九制陈皮

raisin 葡萄干

strawberry 草莓

tangerine 橘子

toffee 太妃糖

watermelon 西瓜

walnut 核桃

十、机场主要设施

aerodrome/airport 飞机场

alternate airport 备用机场

apron 停机坪

automatic door 自动出入门

arrival lounge 到港大厅

air bridge 廊桥

airport fire services 机场消防队

baggage claim area 行李提取处

animal and plant quarantine 动物与植物检疫

airport tax sales 机场税购买柜台

baggage trolley 行李手推车

boarding gate 登记口

Customs 海关

check-in counter 办理登记手续柜台

Customs inspection counter 海关检查柜台

coffee shop 咖啡屋

carousel 旋转行李传输带

catering department 配餐供应部门

connection counter 联运柜台

control tower 管制塔台

duty-free shop 免税商品

departure lounge 出港大厅

dispatch office 签派室

emigration control 出境检查

elevator/ lift 电梯

entrance 入境

exit 出口

emergency service 急救站

exchange and tax payment 兑换与付税

flight information board 航班显示牌

freight building/ cargo center 货运大厦 / 货运中心

fuel farm 油库

hangar 机库

hotel and limousine service 旅馆与机场交通服务处

information desk/ inquiries 问讯处

lavatory/toilet 盥洗室

maintenance area 维修区

moving walkway/ automatic walkway 自动步道

public address 广播室

passenger route 旅客通道

quarantine 检疫

seeing-off deck 送客区

snack bar 快餐部

security center 保安中心

taxiway 滑行道

transit lounge 过站大厅

telephone, telegram and fax room 电话 / 电报 / 传真间

transfer correspondence 中转柜台

imports shop 进口商品点

immigration control 入境检查

localizer 信标台

limousine stand 航班车站

medical center 医疗中心

parking bay 停机位

police office 机场公安局

passport control 护照检查柜台

runway 跑道

special waiting room 特别休息室

stand-by ticket counter 候补旅客售票处

security check station 安检站

terminal building 机场大厦 / 候机楼

Taxi stand 出租汽车站

weather office 气象站

VIP room 贵宾室

十一、肉蛋类

bacon 咸肉

beef steak 牛排

chicken 鸡肉

curry beef 咖喱牛肉

game 野味

ham 火腿

lamb chop 羊排

omelet 煎蛋卷

poached egg 水煮荷包蛋

roast duck 烤鸭

stewed beef 红烩牛肉

spare ribs 排骨

vegetable omelet 素菜鸡蛋卷

bacon and eggs 咸肉蛋

bird's nest 燕窝

consommé with chicken chips 清汤鸡块

fillet steak 肉片

ham and eggs 火腿蛋

hard-boiled egg 煮鸡蛋

minced meat 肉末

preserved egg 松花蛋

roast beef 烤牛肉

scrambled egg 咸蛋

sausage 香肠

turkey 火鸡

yolk 蛋黄

十二、乘客与飞机工作人员

arriving passenger 进港旅客

airhostess 乘务员

aircraft maintenance personnel 机务维修人员

air traffic controller 航空管制员

connecting passenger 转机旅客

cabin crew 乘务机组

captain 机长

copilot 副驾驶

cabin attendant 空乘

catering service 食品供应人员

cabin service manager/ chief purser 主任乘务长

cargo personnel 货运人员

departing passenger 出港旅客

domestic passenger 国内旅客

flight crew 飞机机组

flight engineer 飞机机械师

ground attendant 地面服务员

navigator 领航员

handicapped/ incapacitated passenger 残疾旅客

international passenger 国际旅客

pursur 乘务长

pilot 飞行员

repatriate 遣返旅客

stand-by passenger 候补旅客

stowaway 偷渡旅客

transit passenger 过境旅客

ticket reservation personnel 客票销售人员

security guard 安全员

unaccompanied minor/child 无人陪伴儿童

stewardess 女乘务员

十三、飞机与飞机部件

airfoil/ wing 机翼

aileron 副翼

aisle seat 靠过道座位

attendant seat 乘务员座位

armrest 座椅扶手

ashtray 烟灰缸

aisle 过道

attendant panel 乘务员面板

air vent/ air ventilator 通风装置

bassinet/ cot 摇篮

baby change table 换尿布板

business class 公务舱

bulkhead 隔板 / 舱壁

beverage container 饮料箱

charter plane 包机

cockpit 驾驶舱

cushion 靠垫

carpet 地毯

closet 储藏室

curtain 帘子

ceiling 天花板

call system 呼叫系统

call button 呼唤铃

channel selector 频道选择器

cargo plane 货机

deck 地板

dripper 汲取器

engine 发动机

emergency exit 紧急出口

electric oven 电烤箱

fuselage 机身

first class 头等舱

film projector 放像机

fresh water container 净水箱

handle 舱门开启器

headset socket 耳机插孔

interphone 舱内电话

loud speaker 扬声器

non-smoking section 非吸烟区

nose wheel 前轮

passenger plane 客机

plug-in meal tray 插座式小桌板

pressure gage 压力表

rudder 方向舵

seat number 座位号

seat pocket 座椅口袋

smoking section 吸烟区

supplies container 供应品箱

stretcher 单价

trident 三叉戟

tap 水龙头

volume control 音量控制

window seat 靠窗座位

waste water container 污水箱

wheelchair 轮椅

elevator 升降舵

economy class 经济舱

entry door 登机门

fin 垂直尾翼

flap 襟翼

footrest 脚踏板

fold-away meal table 折叠式小桌板

galley 厨房

hot cup 烧水杯

helicopter/ chopper 直升机

jet plane 喷气式飞机

landing gear 起落架

narrow-bodied jet 窄体客机

overhead compartment 头顶上的行李箱

propeller plane 螺旋桨飞机

passenger service unit 旅客服务装置

reading light 阅读灯

refrigerator 冰箱

seat cover 座椅套

sunshade/window shade 遮光板

serving cart 餐饮手推车

screen 屏幕

transport plane 运输机

toilet flush handle 冲厕把手

trolley 手推车

wide-bodied jet 宽体客体

wash basin 洗手池

water boiler 烧水器

water meter 水表

十四、海鲜

abalone 鲍鱼

clam 蛤肉

carp 鲤鱼

crab 螃蟹

jellyfish 海蜇

oyster 牡蛎 / 蚝

sardine 沙丁鱼

shark fin 鱼翅

tuna 金枪鱼

white bait 银鱼

cuttlefish 墨鱼

eel 鳗鱼

lobster 龙虾

prawn 对虾

salmon 三文鱼

sea cucumber 海参

trout 鳟鱼

yellow croaker 黄花鱼

十五、主食 / 甜品 / 汤

apple pie 苹果派

BBQ pork bun 叉烧包

cooked rice 米饭

croissant 牛角包

chocolate cake 巧克力蛋糕

Danish pastry 丹麦圈

fried rice 炒饭

hot dog 热狗

honey 蜂蜜

macaroni 通心粉

noodles with chicken shreds 鸡丝汤面

porridge 粥

pie 馅饼

steamed rolls 画卷

soft roll 软面包

Swiss gateau 瑞士蛋糕

Udon noodles 乌冬面

wafer 威化面包

biscuit 饼干

butter ball 黄油球

congee 稀饭

cracker 克力架

cookie 曲奇饼干

fried rice noodle 炒米饭

garlic bread 葱茸面包

hamburger 汉堡

hard roll 法尖

noodles 面条

oat meal 麦片粥

pancake 煎饼

rye bread 黑面包

scallion pancake 三明治

spaghetti 意大利面

toast 烤面包

white sesame seed roll 全麦包

十六、餐具与厨房用品

bottle opener 开瓶器

beer mug 啤酒瓶

bowl 碗

corkscrew 拔瓶塞的螺丝锥

carver 切肉用的大刀

chopsticks 筷子

cutlery/dinner set 餐具

fruit knife 水果刀

glass 玻璃杯

napkin/ serviette 餐巾

saltcellar 盐瓶

saucer 点心盆

table cloth 桌布

tea spoon 茶勺

tea set 茶具

thermos bottle 暖水瓶

tin opener 开罐头刀

cruet 调味瓶

cup 水杯

dessert plate 菜盆

fork 叉子

kettle 烧水壶

pepper pot 胡椒瓶

soup plate 汤盆

straw 吸管

table spoon 汤勺

tray 托盘

tumbler 大玻璃瓶

tooth-pick 牙签

water jug 水壶

十七、机票、航班和航线

charter flight 包机

cancel the reservation 取消预定

confirmed ticket 定期机票

domestic route 国内航线

free ticket 免票

flight number 航班号

get the ticket refunded 退票

international flight 国际航班

international route 国际航线

morning flight 早班航班

night flight 夜行航班

non-scheduled flight 不定期机票

one forth-fare ticket 不定期机票

overseas flight 国外航班

regional flight 地区航班

return ticket 回程机票

trunk line 交通干线

cargo flight 货机

connecting flight 衔接航班

domestic flight 国内航班

extra flight 加班航线

full-fare ticket 全票

feeder line 交通支线

half-fare ticket 半票

incoming flight 进港航班

local line 地方航线

maiden flight 首航

non-stop flight 直达航班

one way ticket 单程机票

one tenth-fare ticket 十分之一机票

regular flight 正常航班

round ticket 双程航班

scheduled flight 定期航线

十八、时间

ahead of schedule 比预定时间早

behind schedule 比预定时间晚

connecting time 转机时间

estimated time of arrival 预计达到时间

estimated time of departure 预计起飞时间

local time 当地时间

Greenwich mean time (GMT) 格林尼治标准时间

time difference 时间差别

on schedule 准时

time zones 时区

十九、蔬菜

asparagus 芦笋

beans 豆子

baby corn 小玉米

broad beans 蚕豆

bean sprout 绿豆芽

bean curd 豆腐

cabbage 卷心菜

carrot 胡萝卜

cauliflower 菜花

celery 芹菜

cucumber 黄瓜

eggplant 茄子

French beans 扁豆

fungus 木耳

garlic 大蒜

ginger 姜

lettuce 莴苣，生菜

leek 青葱

mushroom 蘑菇

mixed vegetables 什锦菜

onion 洋葱

peas 豌豆

pumpkin 南瓜

ranch potato 炸土豆饺

radicchio 红生菜

parsley 欧芹

pepper 辣椒

potato 土豆

radish 小萝卜

salted potato dice 炒土豆丁

spinach 菠菜

string beans 四季豆

tomato 西红柿

二十、机场车辆

commissary truck 补给车

drinking-water truck 饮水供应车

emergency service vehicle 紧急救援车

fork lift truck 装卸货叉车

fuel tanker 燃料车

ground powder unit 地面动力装置

passenger bus 乘客班车

passenger step/ ramp 客梯车

rubbish truck 垃圾车

tug 拖车

shuttle 摆渡车

二十一、天气

blowing sand 扬沙

breeze 微风

climate 气候

cloud base 云底

cloud top 云顶

clear air turbulence 晴空颠簸 / 湍流

cloud 云

ceiling 云幕

cold front 冷锋

dew point 露点

degree Centigrade 摄氏度

drizzle 毛毛雨

fog 雾

frost 霜

front 锋面

gust 阵风

hurricane 飓风

hail 冰雹

head wind 顶风

high pressure 高压

mist 薄雾

monsoon 雨季

pour 大雨

rain 雨

rainbow 彩虹

stationary front 静止锋面

shower 阵雨

snow 雪

storm 风暴

tropical storm 热带风暴

terminal forecast 航站预报

thunder 雷

tail wind 顺风

tornado 龙卷风

typhoon 台风

wind 风

warm front 暖锋面

空乘实用英语教程

附录 3　国外航空公司安全演示广播词范例

Safety Demonstration (Delta)

Welcome aboard and thanks for flying with Delta. Our first priority on every flight is safety. So before we depart, I'll be giving you a brife safety presentation.

OK, be sure all carry-on items are securely stowed in the overhead bin and place smaller items under the seat in front of you. And ensure all aisles, exits and bulkhead areas are clear. And ensure your mobile phones and electronic devices are turned off. If you are seated in an emergency exit, please review the responsibilities for emergency exit seating on the back of your safety information card which is in your seat pocket.

—Are you willing and able to assist with the operation of the exit if necessary?

—Yes. / No.

If you are unable to perform these functions, please let us know and we'd be happy to find you another seat.

As we leave the gate, make sure your seat belt is fastened. To fasten, insert the metal tip into the buckle and adjust the strap so it's low and tight across your lap. To release the belt, just lift the top of the buckle. Please remain seated with your seat belt securely fastened anytime the seat belt sign is on, and even if the sign is off, please keep your seat belt fastened in case we experience unexpected rough air.

For everyone's safety, federal regulations require all passengers to comply with the posted placards and lighted information signs located throughout the cabin in addition to any crew member instructions. Smoking is not allowed on any Delta flight and federal law prohibits tampering with disabling or destroying a restroom's smoke detector.

There are ten exits on this plane, six doors, three on each side, and four window exits over the wings. Each door has a detachable slide that can be used as a raft. And additional raft is located in a sealing compartment at the back of the plane. All exits are clearly marked with an exit sign. However, if there is a loss of power, and cabin visibility is reduced, lights will luminate the aisles to guide you to an exit. Please take a moment to find the exits closest to you and remember they might be behind you.

It's unlikely but if cabin pressure changes, the panels above your seat will open revealing oxygen masks. If this happens, reach up and pull a mask toward you until the tube is fully extended. Place the mask over your nose and mouth, slip the elastic strap over your head and adjust the mask if necessary. Breathe normally and note that oxygen is flowing so don't worry if the bag doesn't inflate. Be sure to adjust your own mask before helping others.

A water evacuation is also unlikely but just in case. Life vests are located under your seats in the economy cabin. If you are seated in the first class or business class cabin, life vests are either between your seats, under your seat or in the compartment under your armrest. To use, remove the vest from its container by pulling on the tab and then opening the pouch. Slip the vest over your head. If your vest has one strap, wrap it around your waist and attach it to the buckle in front. If your vest has two straps, fasten the straps to the front of the vest and then adjust them loosely around your waist. As you leave the plane, inflate the vest by pulling down on the red tabs at the bottom of the vest or manually inflate it by blowing into the tubes at shoulder level. You can activate the light by pulling down on the tab in front, but if your vest doesn't have a tab, the lights will activate automatically in the water. If necessary, we will distribute infant life vests or other floatation devices for children who weigh 35 pounds or less. Also, most seat cushions can be used for floatation.

Now, before we take off, be sure your seat is upright, your aisle armrests are lowered, your tray table is put away, and all carry-on items are properly stowed. If this plane features Wi-Fi, internet access will be available while we're above 10,000 feet.

Once airborne we'll let you know when you can use approved electronic devices, but know that some items may not be used in flight at any time. You'll find a list of approved electronic devices in the in-flight information section of sky magazine.

As we come through the cabin for our final safety check, please let us know if you have any questions. And finally, now it'll be a good time for everyone to review the safety information card which is in your seat pocket.

On behalf of everyone of Delta Airlines, we want to thank you for paying attention to our safety presentation. Sit back, relax and enjoy the flight.

Safety Demonstration (Qantas)

Welcome aboard. Before we take off, we are going to give you an important safety briefing. So, keep a sharp eye on the cabin crew or the screen in front of you and together we'll make sure that your journey is a safe one.

Every aircraft is different, so it's important to pay attention even if you've flown with us before.

Today you're flying on a Qantas Airbus A380.

Before we take-off, make sure all your cabin baggage are stowed in the overhead locker or under the seat in front of you. All electronic devices must be completely powered off for take-off and landing. Before you do so, ensure you disable cellular, bluetooth and Wi-Fi capability by switching to flight mode and then turning off.

Fasten your seatbelt by inserting the clasp into the buckle and tighten by pulling the strap. If you are seated in First also ensure that your sash-belt is in place for take-off and landing. Undo your seatbelt by pressing the button. You must have your seatbelt done up, low and tight including infants and children, during take-off, landing and whenever the seatbelt sign is on. While seated at other times, we require that you keep your seatbelt fastened.

And in the unlikely event of an emergency, it's important that you are familiar with the brace position, appropriate to your seat. If you can reach the seat in front of you, brace by folding your arms on the back of the seat in front, and rest your forehead on your arms. If you can't reach the seat in front of you, put your head on your knees or lean as far forward as you can and hold onto your legs. Keep your feet firmly on the floor to prevent them from moving forward. If you are seated in First, your brace position is to sit upright, place your hands on your knees, and bring your chin towards your chest.

Take a moment now to check where the nearest exits are on this aircraft as the cabin crew point them out. Be aware that your nearest exit may be behind you. A good way of remembering your nearest exit is to count the number of rows between you and that exit. Our cabin crew are pointing out the lights that show a path to the exit.

This aircraft is fitted with escape slides and life rafts, which the crew will operate in an emergency. If we do have to evacuate, you must leave all items carried onto the aircraft behind. A loss of oxygen at altitude may lead to a loss of consciousness. If emergency oxygen is required, a mask will drop from above you. Pull down on it firmly to activate the flow of oxygen. Put it on quickly and tighten the strap. Oxygen will flow without the bag inflating. Once you're breathing normally, it's OK to help others.

Make sure you're familiar with the location and use of your life jacket. In Economy, yours is under your seat. If you're in Premium Economy, or First, it's inside your leg rest. If you're in Business, it's next to your leg rest.

Your crew member is now demonstrating how to put your life jacket on. Remove the life jacket from the pouch by pulling the tab. Slip the jacket over your head, pass the strap around your waist, clip the waist-strap together at the front, then tighten. Your life jacket comes with a red tag and a mouthpiece for inflation, and a whistle and a light for attracting attention. And remember only inflate your life jacket as you leave the aircraft. Take a moment now to look where your life jacket is located. If you're unsure, please ask the cabin crew.

Smoking is a fire hazard and is not permitted anywhere on this aircraft. This includes the toilets which are fitted with smoke detectors. In preparation for take-off, ensure your seat is upright and your tray table is stowed. And just in case you've missed any of this, simply refer to our safety card located in your seat pocket.

Remember, the cabin crew are here to look after you, so follow their instructions at all times. Now settle back and enjoy your Qantas flight.

Please read the Health and Safety information in the Onboard Information section of Qantas *The Australian Way* magazine. This section will help to make your flight more comfortable. It also details important information on Deep Vein Thrombosis or DVT, precautions you can take and recommended exercises.

Safety Demonstration (Air Canada)

Welcome aboard Air Canada. For your safety and comfort, we ask that you pay attention to this short video.

Please place baggage in the overhead bin and heavier items under the seat in front of you. In preparation for take-off, make sure you're comfortably seated, with your seat-back upright, and tray table stowed. For your safety, you must wear your seat belt when the seat belt light has been turned on, and we suggest wearing it even when the sign is turned off. Fasten your seat belt by adjusting it around your hips. To release it, lift the upper portion or press on the release button.

Air quality is important to us. That's why we always ensure that you enjoy a non-smoking environment. At this time, your portable electronic devices must be set to airplane mode until an announcement is made upon arrival. The illustrated card in your seat pocket or magazine rack explains the many safety features of this aircraft. Please review it sometime before take-off.

If there is a need to evacuate the aircraft, leave your personal belongings behind and follow the seat-mounted lighting in the aisle to the nearest emergency exit. There are four exits located on each side of the aircraft. All of these are indicted by a green exit sign. Please locate the one nearest you.

If the cabin pressure changes, an oxygen mask or a red tab will drop from the panel above you. Remain seated. Pull the mask or the tab to bring the mask towards you. Use the support strap to hold the mask over your mouth and nose. Breathe normally to start the flow of oxygen. Always secure your own mask before assisting another person.

If there is an emergency landing on water, reach under the seat or beside your leg rest, remove the elastic band if required. Pull out the life vest from the pouch. Slip it on, fasten the waist clip and tighten the belt. Pulling the tab will inflate the life vest. You can also inflate it by blowing into the tube. The life vest should only be inflated as you leave the aircraft.

If you need any assistance, or have any concerns, please let one of us know. Thank you for choosing to fly with Air Canada.

Item	British English	American English	Meaning
1	baggage	luggage	n. 行李
2	life jacket	life vest	n. 救生衣
3	sweets	candy	n. 糖果
4	crisps	chips; potato chips	n. 薯片
5	napkin	diaper	n. 尿布
6	wardrobe	closet	n. 衣帽间
7	fizzy drink	soda	n. 苏打水
8	film	movie	n. 电影
9	purse	pocketbook	n. 钱包
10	trousers	pants	n. 裤子
11	defence	defense	n. 辩护
12	licence	license	n. 执照
13	offence	offense	n. 伤害
14	programme	program	n. 节目
15	manoeuvre	maneuver	n. & v. 操纵
16	diarrhoea	diarrhea	n. 腹泻
17	aeroplane	airplane	n. 飞机
18	instalment	installment	n. 安装
19	behaviour	behavior	n. & v. 行为
20	colour	color	n. 颜色
21	favour	favor	n. 爱好
22	humour	humor	n. 幽默
23	endeavour	endeavor	n. 努力
24	metre	meter	n. 米（单位）
25	odour	odor	n. 味道
26	tonne	ton	n. 吨（单位）
27	distil	distill	v. 蒸馏
28	glycerine	glycerin	n. 甘油
29	vigour	vigor	n. 精力
30	centre	center	n. 中心
31	theatre	theater	n. 剧院
32	litre	liter	n. 升（单位）
33	artefact	artifact	n. 工艺品
34	cosy	cozy	adj. 温暖舒适的
35	gaol	jail	n. 监狱
36	doughnout	donut	n. 甜甜圈

232

空乘实用英语教程

Item	British English	American English	Meaning
37	fibre	fiber	*n.* 纤维
38	cheque	check	*n.* 支票
39	grey	gray	*adj.* 灰色的
40	jewellery	jewelry	*n.* 珠宝
41	draught beer	draft beer	*n.* 生啤
42	sceptical	skeptical	*adj.* 怀疑的
43	civilise	cililize	*v.* 教化
44	paralyse	paralyze	*v.* 偏瘫
45	analyse	analyze	*v.* 分析
46	guide dog	seeing-eye dog	导盲犬
47	anticlockwise	counterclockwise	*adj.& adv.* 逆时针的
48	car park	parking lot	*n.* 停车场
49	cinema	movie theater	*n.* 电影院
50	cash machine	ATM	*n.* 自动取款机
51	cooker	stove, range top	*n.* 锅；炊具
52	braces	suspenders	*n.* 吊带裤
53	cake tin	cake pan	*n.* 蛋糕罐
54	bank holiday	public holiday	*n.* 法定节假日
55	banknote	bill	*n.* 钞票
56	cornflour	corn starch	*n.* 玉米粉
57	candy floss	cotton candy	*n.* 棉花糖
58	CV	resume	*n.* 简历
59	cutlery	silverware, flatware	*n.* 餐具
60	dressing gown	robe	*n.* 睡袍
61	dummy	pacifier, soother	*n.* 奶嘴
62	dungarees	overalls	*n.* 连体服
63	father christmas	santa claus	*n.* 圣诞老人
64	flyover	overpass	*n.* 天桥；高架桥
65	fringe	bangs	*n.* 刘海
66	garden	yard	*n.* 花园
67	ground floor	first floor	*n.* 底楼
68	hair clip	barrette	*n.* 发夹
69	holiday	vacation	*n.* 假日
70	indicator	turn signal, blinker	*n.* 闪光警戒灯
71	lawyer	attorney	*n.* 律师
72	lift	elevator	*n.* 电梯
73	mad	crazy; insane	*adj.* 发疯的
74	merry-go-round	carousel	*n.* 转盘
75	mobile phone	cell phone	*n.* 手机
76	mum, mummy	mom, mommy	*n.* 妈妈

Item	British English	American English	Meaning
77	nought	zero	*n.* 零
78	parcel	package	*n.* 包裹
79	pants	underwear, underpants	*n.* 内衣
80	pepper	bell pepper	*n.* 辣椒
81	petrol	has, hasoline	*n.* 汽油
82	pocket money	allowance	*n.* 零花钱
83	power point	power outlet	*n.* 电源插座
84	primary school	elementary school	*n.* 小学
85	push chair	stroller	*n.* 推车
86	rubbish	trash, garbage	*n.* 垃圾
87	secondary school	middle school, high school	*n.* 中学
88	shopping trolley	shopping cart	*n.* 购物车
89	soft drink	soda	*n.* 软饮料
90	starter	appetizer	*n.* 开胃菜
91	tap	faucet	*n.* 水龙头
92	takeaway	takeout	*n.* 外卖餐馆
93	tights	pantyhose	*n.* 裤袜
94	toilet/bathroom	(public) restroom	*n.* 洗手间
95	torch	flashlight	*n.* 手电筒
96	town centre	downtown	*n.* 市中心
97	trainers	sneakers	*n.* 帆布胶底鞋
98	vest	undershirt	*n.* 汗衫
99	waistcoat	vest	*n.* 马甲
100	windscreen	windshield	*n.* 挡风玻璃

空乘实用英语教程

附录 5　机场常用标识

Emigration/Immigration 出 / 入境边防检查	Customs 海关	Parking 停车场	Car Hire 租车服务
Red Channel (Goods to Declare) 红色通道 （有申报物品通道）	Green Channel (Nothing to Declare) 绿色通道（无申报物品通道）	Waiting Hall 候机厅	First Class Lounge 头等舱候机室
VIP 贵宾候机室	Nursery 母婴室	Gate 登机口	Baggage Cart Lounge 行李手推车
Hotel Service 宾馆服务	Settle Accounts 结账	Baggage Claim 行李提取	Baggage Inquiries 行李查询
Shop 商店	Freight 货物查询	Transfer 中转联程	Information Inquiries 问询

空乘实用英语教程

附 录

附录 6 机上应急设备图标

Types	Symbols	Chinese Names	English Names
Oxygen Equipment （氧气设备）		手提式氧气瓶	portable oxygen bottle
		带有防烟面罩的手提氧气瓶	portable oxygen bottle with-smoke mask attached
		一次性氧气面罩	disposable oxygen mask
		全氧气面罩	fully face oxygen mask
Extinguisher Equipment （灭火设备）		海伦灭火器	BCF extinguisher
		二氧化碳灭火器	CO_2 extinguisher
		水灭火器	water extinguisher
		干粉灭火器	dry-chemical extinguisher
Survival Equipment （救生设备）		救生衣	life vest/life jacket
		救生船	life raft
		救生筏	life raft
		救生包	life kit/ survival kit
Medical Kits （药箱）		紧急医疗药箱	emergency medical kit
		急救药箱	first aid kit

Types	Symbols	Chinese Names	English Names
Exits（出口）		带有逃离绳的出口通道	exit path with escape strap
		带有撤离滑梯的出口通道	exit path with escape slide
		没有撤离滑梯的出口通道	exit path without escape slide
		带有撤离滑梯 / 救生船的出口通道	exit path with slide raft
	EXIT	出口指示灯	exit light
Other Equipment（其他设备）		手电筒	flash light
		紧急发报机	emergency transmitter
		麦克风	megaphone
		防烟罩	smoke hood (PBE)
		防护手套	protective gloves
		防烟镜	smoke goggles
		救生斧 / 应急斧	crash axe
		指挥棒 / 警棍	baton
		人工释放工具	release tool
		清醒剂 / 心肺复苏器	resuscitator

空乘实用英语教程

附录7 世界货币一览表

货币代码	货币名称	国家/地区/组织
CNY	人民币—Chinese Yuan	中国
HKD	港币—Hong Kong Dollar	中国香港
TWD	新台币—New Taiwan Dollar	中国台湾
MOP	澳门元—Macau Pataca	中国澳门
USD	美元—United States Dollar	美国
EUR	欧元—Euro	欧盟
GBP	英镑—British Pound	英国
AUD	澳元—Australia Dollar	澳大利亚
CAD	加元—Canadian Dollar	加拿大
JPY	日元—Japanese Yen	日本
INR	印度卢比—Indian Rupee	印度
ZAR	南非兰特—South African Rand	南非
KRW	韩元—South Korean Won	韩国
THB	泰铢—Thai Baht	泰国
NZD	新西兰元—New Zealand Dollar	新西兰
SGD	新加坡元—Singapore Dollar	新加坡
AED	阿联酋迪拉姆—United Arab Emirates Dirham	阿联酋
AFN	阿富汗尼—Afghan Afghani	阿富汗
ALL	阿尔巴尼列克—Albania Lek	阿尔巴尼亚
AMD	亚美尼亚德拉姆—Armenia Dram	亚美尼亚
ANG	荷兰盾—Dutch Guilder	荷兰
AOA	安哥拉宽扎—Angola Kwanza	安哥拉
ARS	阿根廷比索—Argentina Peso	阿根廷
AWG	阿鲁巴弗罗林—Aruba Florin	阿鲁巴
AZN	阿塞拜疆马纳特—Azerbaijan Manat	阿塞拜疆
BAM	波黑可兑换马克—Bosnia Convertible Mark	波黑
BBD	巴巴多斯元—Barbados Dollar	巴巴多斯
BDT	孟加拉国塔卡—Bangladesh Taka	孟加拉国
BGN	保加利亚列弗—Bulgaria Lev	保加利亚
BHD	巴林第纳尔—Bahrain Dinar	巴林
BIF	布隆迪法郎—Burundi Franc	布隆迪
BMD	百慕大元—Bermudian Dollar	百慕大
BND	文莱元—Brunei Dollar	文莱
BOB	玻利维亚诺—Bolivian Boliviano	玻利维亚
BRL	巴西雷亚尔—Brazilian Real	巴西
BSD	巴哈马元—Bahamian Dollar	巴哈马元

货币代码	货币名称	国家/地区/组织
BTN	不丹努扎姆—Bhutanese Ngultrum	不丹
BWP	博茨瓦纳普拉—Botswana Pula	博茨瓦纳
BYR	白俄罗斯卢布—Belarusian Ruble	白俄罗斯
BZD	伯利兹元—Belize Dollar	伯利兹
CDF	刚果法郎—Congolese Franc	刚果
CHF	瑞士法郎—Swiss Franc	瑞士
CLF	智利比索（基金）—Chilean Unidad de Fomento	智利
CLP	智利比索—Chilean Peso	
CNH	中国离岸人民币—Chinese Offshore Renminbi	中国
COP	哥伦比亚比索—Colombia Peso	哥伦比亚
CRC	哥斯达黎加科朗—Costa Rica Colon	哥斯达黎加
CUP	古巴比索—Cuban Peso	古巴
CVE	佛得角埃斯库多—Cape Verde Escudo	佛得角
CYP	塞浦路斯镑—Cyprus Pound	塞浦路斯
CZK	捷克克朗—Czech Republic Koruna	捷克
DEM	德国马克—Deutsche Mark	德国
DJF	吉布提法郎—Djiboutian Franc	吉布提
DKK	丹麦克朗—Danish Krone	丹麦
DOP	多米尼加比索—Dominican Peso	多米尼加
DZD	阿尔及利亚第纳尔—Algerian Dinar	阿尔及利亚
ECS	厄瓜多尔苏克雷—Ecuadorian Sucre	厄瓜多尔
EGP	埃及镑—Egyptian Pound	埃及
ERN	厄立特里亚纳克法—Eritrean Nakfa	厄立特里亚
ETB	埃塞俄比亚比尔—Ethiopian Birr	埃塞俄比亚
FJD	斐济元—Fiji Dollar	斐济
FRF	法国法郎—French Franc	法国
GEL	格鲁吉亚拉里—Georgian Lari	格鲁吉亚
GHS	加纳塞地—Ghanaian Cedi	加纳
GIP	直布罗陀镑—Gibraltar Pound	直布罗陀
GMD	冈比亚达拉西—Gambian Dalasi	冈比亚
GNF	几内亚法郎—Guinean Franc	几内亚
GTQ	危地马拉格查尔—Guatemalan Quetzal	危地马拉
GYD	圭亚那元—Guyanese Dollar	圭亚那
HNL	洪都拉斯伦皮拉—Honduran Lempira	洪都拉斯
HRK	克罗地亚库纳—Croatian Kuna	克罗地亚
HTG	海地古德—Haitian Gourde	海地
HUF	匈牙利福林—Hungarian Forint	匈牙利
IDR	印度尼西亚卢比—Indonesian Rupiah	印度尼西亚
IEP	爱尔兰镑—Irish Pound	爱尔兰
ILS	以色列新谢克尔—Israeli New Shekel	以色列

货币代码	货币名称	国家/地区/组织
IQD	伊拉克第纳尔—Iraqi Dinar	伊拉克
IRR	伊朗里亚尔—Iranian Rial	伊朗
ISK	冰岛克朗—Icelandic Krona	冰岛
ITL	意大利里拉—Italian Lira	意大利
JMD	牙买加元—Jamaican Dollar	牙买加
JOD	约旦第纳尔—Jordanian Dinar	约旦
KES	肯尼亚先令—Kenyan Shilling	肯尼亚
KGS	吉尔吉斯斯坦索姆—Kyrgyzstani Som	吉尔吉斯斯坦
KHR	柬埔寨瑞尔—Cambodian Riel	柬埔寨
KMF	科摩罗法郎—Comorian franc	科摩罗
KPW	朝鲜元—North Korean Won	朝鲜
KWD	科威特第纳尔—Kuwaiti Dinar	科威特
KYD	开曼群岛元—Cayman Islands Dollar	开曼群岛
KZT	哈萨克斯坦坚戈—Kazakhstani Tenge	哈萨克斯坦
LAK	老挝基普—Lao kip	老挝
LBP	黎巴嫩镑—Lebanese Pound	黎巴嫩
LKR	斯里兰卡卢比—Sri Lankan Rupee	斯里兰卡
LRD	利比里亚元—Liberian dollar	利比里
LSL	莱索托洛蒂—Lesotho Loti	莱索托
LTL	立陶宛立特—Lithuanian Litas	立陶宛
LVL	拉脱维亚拉特—Latvian Lats	拉脱维亚
LYD	利比亚第纳尔—Libyan Dinar	利比亚
MAD	摩洛哥迪拉姆—Moroccan Dirham	摩洛哥
MDL	摩尔多瓦列伊—Moldovan Leu	摩尔多瓦
MGA	马达斯加阿里亚里—Malagasy Ariary	马达加斯加
MKD	马其顿代纳尔—Macedonian Denar	马其顿
MMK	缅甸元—Myanmar Kyat	缅甸
MNT	蒙古图格里克—Mongolian Tugrik	蒙古国
MRO	毛里塔尼亚乌吉亚—Mauritania Ouguiya	毛里塔尼亚
MUR	毛里求斯卢比—Mauritian Rupee	毛里求斯
MVR	马尔代夫拉菲亚—Maldives Rufiyaa	马尔代夫
MWK	马拉维克瓦查—Malawian Kwacha	马拉维
MXN	墨西哥比索—Mexican Peso	墨西哥
MXV	墨西哥（资金）—Mexican Unidad De Inversion	
MYR	林吉特—Malaysian Ringgit	马来西亚
MZN	莫桑比克新梅蒂卡尔—New Mozambican Metical	莫桑比克
NAD	纳米比亚元—Namibian Dollar	纳米比亚
NGN	尼日利亚奈拉—Nigerian Naira	尼日利亚
NIO	尼加拉瓜新科多巴—Nicaraguan Cordoba Oro	尼加拉瓜
NOK	挪威克朗—Norwegian Krone	挪威

货币代码	货币名称	国家/地区/组织
NPR	尼泊尔卢比—Nepalese Rupee	尼泊尔
OMR	阿曼里亚尔—Omani Rial	阿曼
PAB	巴拿马巴波亚—Panamanian Balboa	巴拿马
PEN	秘鲁新索尔—Peruvian Nuevo Sol	秘鲁
PGK	巴布亚新几内亚基那—Papua New Guinea Kina	巴布亚新几内亚
PHP	菲律宾比索—Philippine Peso	菲律宾
PKR	巴基斯坦卢比—Pakistan Rupee	巴基斯坦
PLN	波兰兹罗提—Polish Zloty	波兰
PYG	巴拉圭瓜拉尼—Paraguayan Guarani	巴拉圭
QAR	卡塔尔里亚尔—Qatari Riyal	卡塔尔
RON	罗马尼亚列伊—Romanian Leu	罗马尼亚
RSD	塞尔维亚第纳尔—Serbian Dinar	塞尔维亚
RUB	俄罗斯卢布—Russian Ruble	俄罗斯
RWF	卢旺达法郎—Rwandan Franc	卢旺达
SAR	沙特里亚尔—Saudi Arabian Riyal	沙特阿拉伯
SBD	所罗门群岛元—Solomon Islands Dollar	所罗门群岛
SCR	塞舌尔卢比—Seychelles Rupee	塞舌尔
SDG	苏丹镑—Sudanese Pound	苏丹
SEK	瑞典克朗—Swedish Krona	瑞典
SHP	圣赫勒拿镑—Saint Helena Pound	圣赫勒拿（英属）
SIT	斯洛文尼亚托拉尔—Slovenian Tolar	斯洛文尼亚
SLL	塞拉利昂利昂—Sierra Leonean Leone	塞拉利昂
SOS	索马里先令—Somali Shilling	索马里
SRD	苏里南元—Suriname Dollar	苏里南元
STD	圣多美多布拉—Sao Tome Dobra	圣多美和普林西比
SVC	萨尔瓦多科朗—Salvadoran Colon	萨尔瓦多
SYP	叙利亚镑—Syrian Pound	叙利亚
SZL	斯威士兰里兰吉尼—Swazi Lilangeni	斯威士兰
TJS	塔吉克斯坦索莫尼—Tajikistan Somoni	塔吉克斯坦
TMT	土库曼斯坦马纳特—Turkmenistan Manat	土库曼斯坦
TND	突尼斯第纳尔—Tunisian Dinar	突尼斯
TOP	汤加潘加—Tongan Pa'anga	汤加
TRY	土耳其里拉—Turkish Lira	土耳其
TTD	特立尼达多巴哥元—Trinidad and Tobago Dollar	特立尼达多巴哥
TZS	坦桑尼亚先令—Tanzanian Shilling	坦桑尼亚
UAH	乌克兰格里夫纳—Ukrainian Hryvnia	乌克兰
UGX	乌干达先令—Ugandan Shilling	乌干达
UYU	乌拉圭比索—Uruguayan Peso	乌拉圭
UZS	乌兹别克斯坦苏姆—Uzbekistani Som	乌兹别克斯坦
VEF	委内瑞拉玻利瓦尔—Venezuelan Bolivar Fuerte	委内瑞拉

续表

货币代码	货　币　名　称	国家 / 地区 / 组织
VND	越南盾—Viet Nam Dong	越南
VUV	瓦努阿图瓦图—Vanuatu Vatu	瓦努阿图
WST	萨摩亚塔拉—Samoa Tala	萨摩亚
YER	也门里亚尔—Yemeni Rial	也门
ZMW	赞比亚克瓦查—Zambian Kwacha	赞比亚
ZWL	津巴布韦元—Zimbabwean Dollar	津巴布韦
XAF	中非法郎—Central African CFA Franc	中非经济共同体
XCD	东加勒比元—East Caribbean Dollar	加勒比海（英属）
XDR	IMF 特别提款权—IMF Special Drawing Rights	国际货币基金组织
XOF	西非法郎—West African CFA	非洲金融共同体

一、国内航空公司

二字代码	中文名称	英文名称	企业标识
CA	中国国际航空公司	Air China	
MU	中国东方航空公司	China Eastern Airlines	
CZ	中国南方航空公司	China Southern Airlines	
FM	上海航空公司	Shanghai Airlines	
HO	上海吉祥航空有限公司	Juneyao Airlines	
HU	海南航空公司	Hainan Airlines	
MF	厦门航空公司	Xiamen Airlines	
SC	山东航空公司	Shandong Airlines	
ZH	深圳航空公司	Shenzhen Airlines	
3U	四川航空公司	Sichuan Airlines	
9C	春秋航空公司	Spring Airlines	

二字代码	中 文 名 称	英 文 名 称	企业标识
KN	中国联合航空有限公司	China United Airlines	
CX	国泰航空公司	Cathay Pacific Airways	
KA	国泰港龙航空公司	Cathay Dragon Airlines	
CI	中华航空	China Airlines	
GE	复兴航空公司	TransAsia Airways	
NX	澳门航空公司	Air Macau	

二、国外航空公司

二字代码	中 文 名 称	英 文 名 称	企 业 标 识
AA	美国航空公司	American Airlines	
BA	英国航空公司	British Airways	
JL	日本航空公司	Japan Airlines	
AC	加拿大航空公司	Air Canada	
AF	法国航空公司	Air France	
AZ	意大利航空公司	Alitalia	

二字代码	中文名称	英文名称	企业标识
DL	美国达美航空公司	Delta Airlines	
KE	大韩航空公司	Korean Air	
LH	德国汉莎航空公司	Lufthansa	
SQ	新加坡航空公司	Singapore Airlines	
UA	美国联合航空	United Airlines	
NH	全日空航空公司	All Nippon Airways	
EK	阿联酋航空公司	Emirates	
QR	卡塔尔航空公司	Qatar Airways	
SU	俄罗斯航空公司	Aeroflot-Russian Airlines	
VS	维珍航空公司	Virgin Atlantic Airways	

246

空乘实用英语教程

参考文献

[1] Terence Gerighty. Shon Davis. English for Cabin Crew[M]. 上海：上海外语教育出版社，2014.

[2] 耿进友 . 外航空乘应聘成功指南 [M]. 北京：中国民航出版社，2018.

[3] 黄晨 . 民航面试英语教程 [M]. 北京：清华大学出版社，2019.

[4] 范建一 . 民航乘务英语实用会话 [M]. 北京：中国民航出版社，2014.

[5] 李玉梅，杨建 . 新世纪民航乘务英语（中级）口语教程 [M]. 天津：南开大学出版社，2011.

[6] 高锋 . 空乘情景英语教程 [M]. 北京：中国民航出版社，2018.

[7] 严丽，贾俊南，宫宇 . 民航空乘英语 [M]. 北京：航空工业出版社，2017.

[8] 宓肖燕，钱敦伟 . 客舱英语广播词朗读 [M]. 北京：航空工业出版社，2020.

[9] 邓丽君，邢佩玉 . 民航英语广播词训练教程 [M]. 北京：化学工业出版社，2018.

[10] 王丽蓉，胡妮 . 机上广播英语 [M]. 北京：清华大学出版社，2018.

[11] 李屹然 . 民航空乘英语实用口语教程 [M]. 北京：化学工业出版社，2019.

[12] 李勇 . 新编民航乘务员实用英语 [M]. 北京：中国民航出版社，2009.

[13] 祝蔚红 . 实用英语演讲教程 [M]. 南京：南京大学出版社，2012.

[14] 刘金来 .TED 演讲的技巧：18 分钟高效表达的秘诀 [M]. 北京：中国纺织出版社，2018.

[15] 高锋 . 航空乘务英语教程 [M]. 上海：同济大学出版社，2019.

[16] 胡壮麟 . 新世纪英汉大词典 [M]. 北京：外语教学与研究出版社，2015.

[17] 杨长进 . 空乘服务语言艺术与播音技巧 [M]. 北京：航空工业出版社，2014.